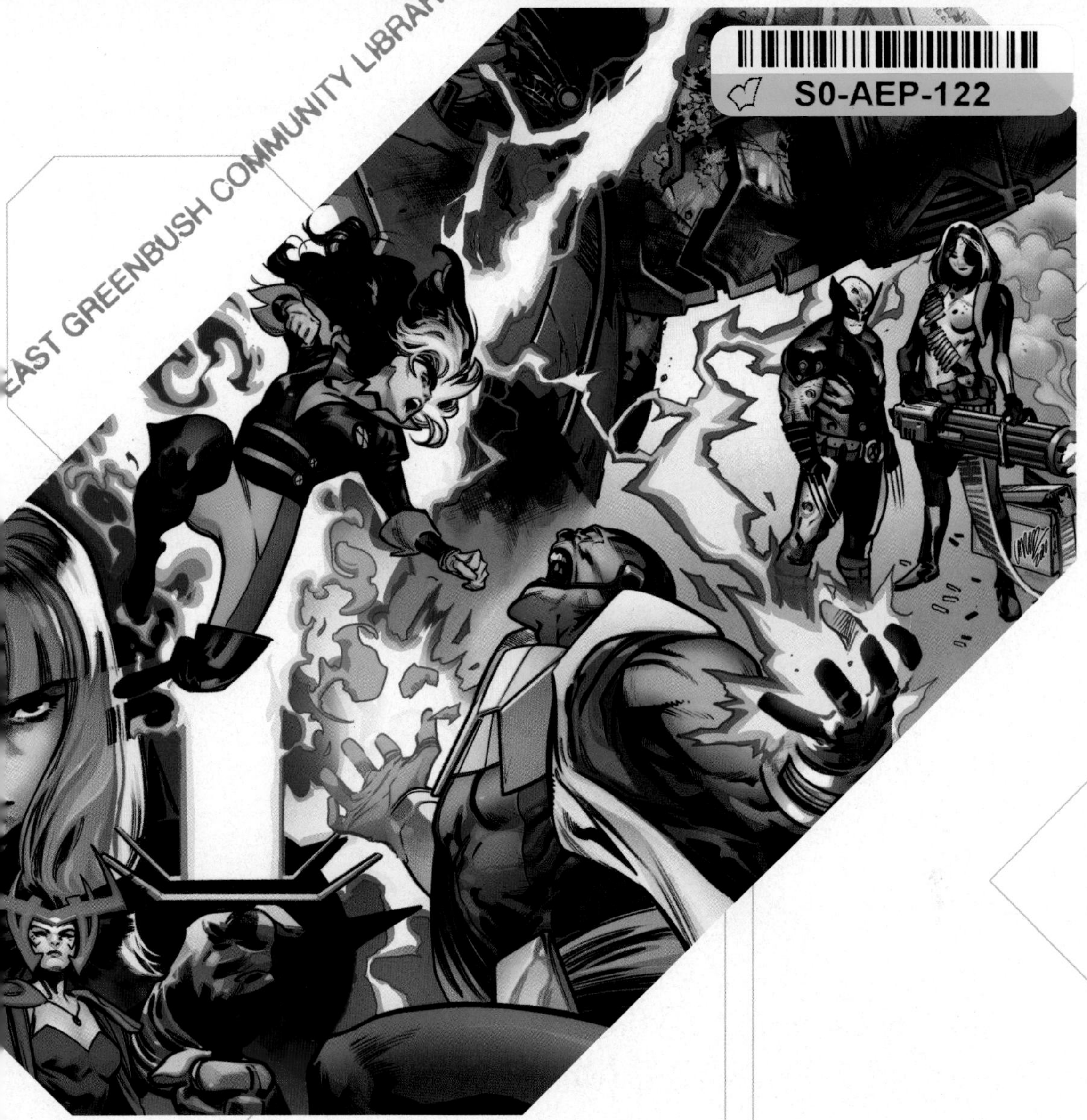

[kra_]
[koa_]

[dawn_of_x]

DAWN OF X VOL. 5. Contains material originally published in magazine form as X-MEN (2019) #5, X-FORCE (2019) #5, MARAUDERS (2019) #5, EXCALIBUR (2019) #5, FALLEN ANGELS (2019) #5 and NEW MUTANTS (2019) #5. First printing 2020. ISBN 978-1-302-92160-6. Published by MARVEL WORLDWIDE, INC., a subsidiary of MARVEL ENTERTAINMENT, LLC. OFFICE OF PUBLICATION: 1290 Avenue of the Americas, New York, NY 10104. © 2020 MARVEL No similarity between any of the names, characters, persons, and/or institutions in this magazine with those of any living or dead person or institution is intended, and any such similarity which may exist is purely coincidental. **Printed in the U.S.A.** KEVIN FEIGE, Chief Creative Officer; DAN BUCKLEY, President, Marvel Entertainment; JOHN NEE, Publisher; JOE QUESADA, EVP & Creative Director; TOM BREVOORT, SVP of Publishing; DAVID BOGART, Associate Publisher & SVP of Talent Affairs; Publishing & Partnership; DAVID GABRIEL, VP of Print & Digital Publishing; JEFF YOUNGQUIST, VP of Production & Special Projects; DAN CARR, Executive Director of Publishing Technology; ALEX MORALES, Director of Publishing Operations; DAN EDINGTON, Managing Editor; SUSAN CRESPI, Production Manager; STAN LEE, Chairman Emeritus. For information regarding advertising in Marvel Comics or on Marvel.com, please contact Vit DeBellis, Custom Solutions & Integrated Advertising Manager, at vdebellis@marvel.com. For Marvel subscription inquiries, please call 888-511-5480. **Manufactured between 2/14/2020 and 3/17/2020 by LSC COMMUNICATIONS INC., KENDALLVILLE, IN, USA.**

10 9 8 7 6 5 4 3 2 1

DAWN OF X

Volume 05

X-Men created by Stan Lee & Jack Kirby

Writers:	**Jonathan Hickman, Gerry Duggan, Tini Howard, Benjamin Percy & Bryan Hill**
Artists:	**R.B. Silva, Matteo Lolli, Lucas Werneck, Marcus To, Rod Reis, Joshua Cassara & Szymon Kudranski**
Color Artists:	**Marte Gracia, Federico Blee, Erick Arciniega, Rod Reis, Carlos Lopez, Dean White, Rachelle Rosenberg & Frank D'Armata**
Letterers:	**VC's Clayton Cowles, Cory Petit, Travis Lanham, Joe Caramagna & Joe Sabino**
Cover Art:	**Leinil Francis Yu & Sunny Gho; Russell Dauterman & Matthew Wilson; Mahmud Asrar & Matthew Wilson; Rod Reis; Dustin Weaver & Edgar Delgado; and Ashley Witter**
Head of X:	**Jonathan Hickman**
Design:	**Tom Muller**
Assistant Editors:	**Annalise Bissa & Chris Robinson**
Editor:	**Jordan D. White**
Collection Cover Art:	**Pepe Larraz & David Curiel**
Collection Editor:	**Jennifer Grünwald**
Assistant Managing Editor:	**Maia Loy**
Assistant Managing Editor:	**Lisa Montalbano**
Associate Managing Editor:	**Kateri Woody**
Editor, Special Projects:	**Mark D. Beazley**
VP Production & Special Projects:	**Jeff Youngquist**
SVP Print, Sales & Marketing:	**David Gabriel**
Editor in Chief:	**C.B. Cebulski**

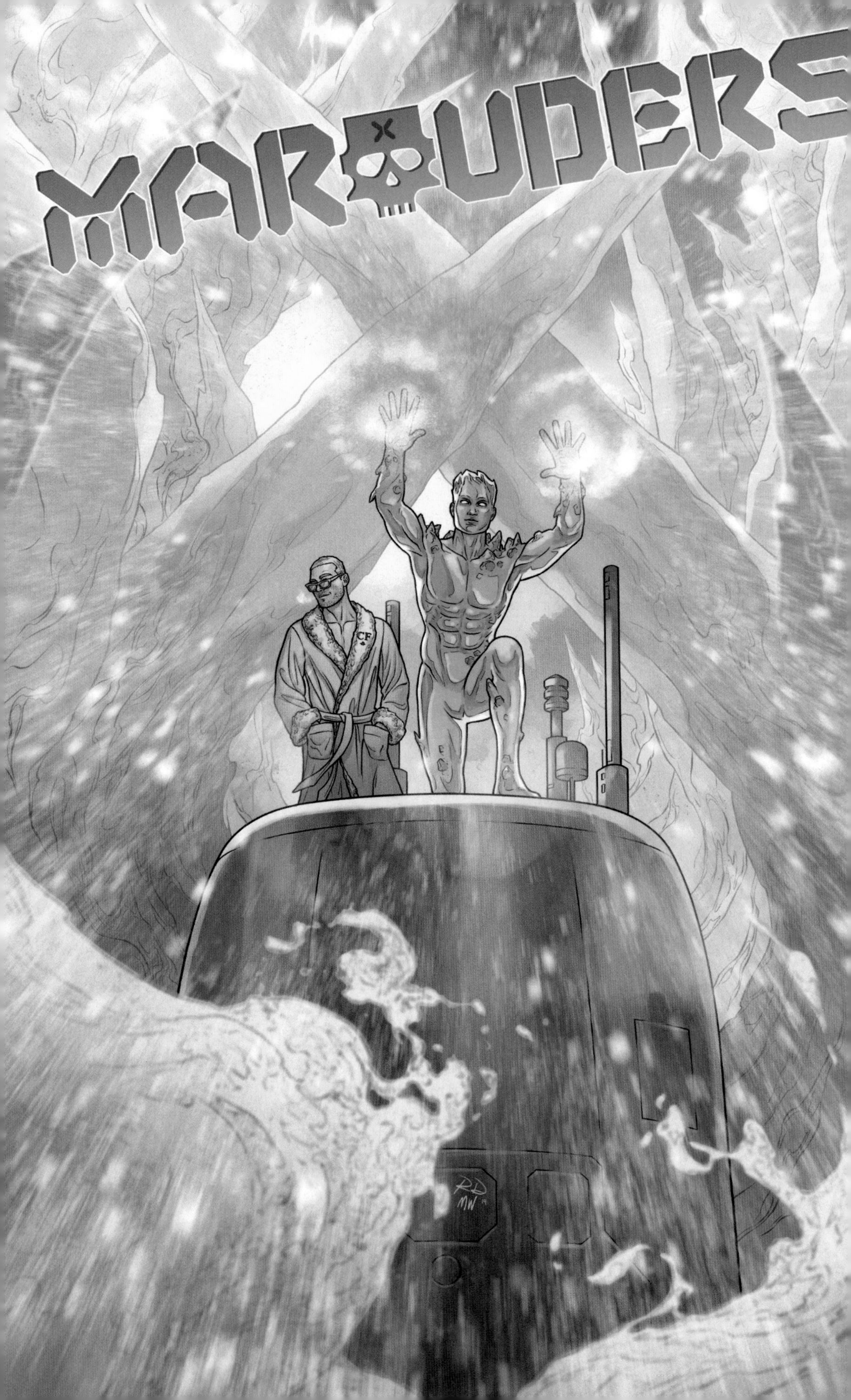
MARAUDERS

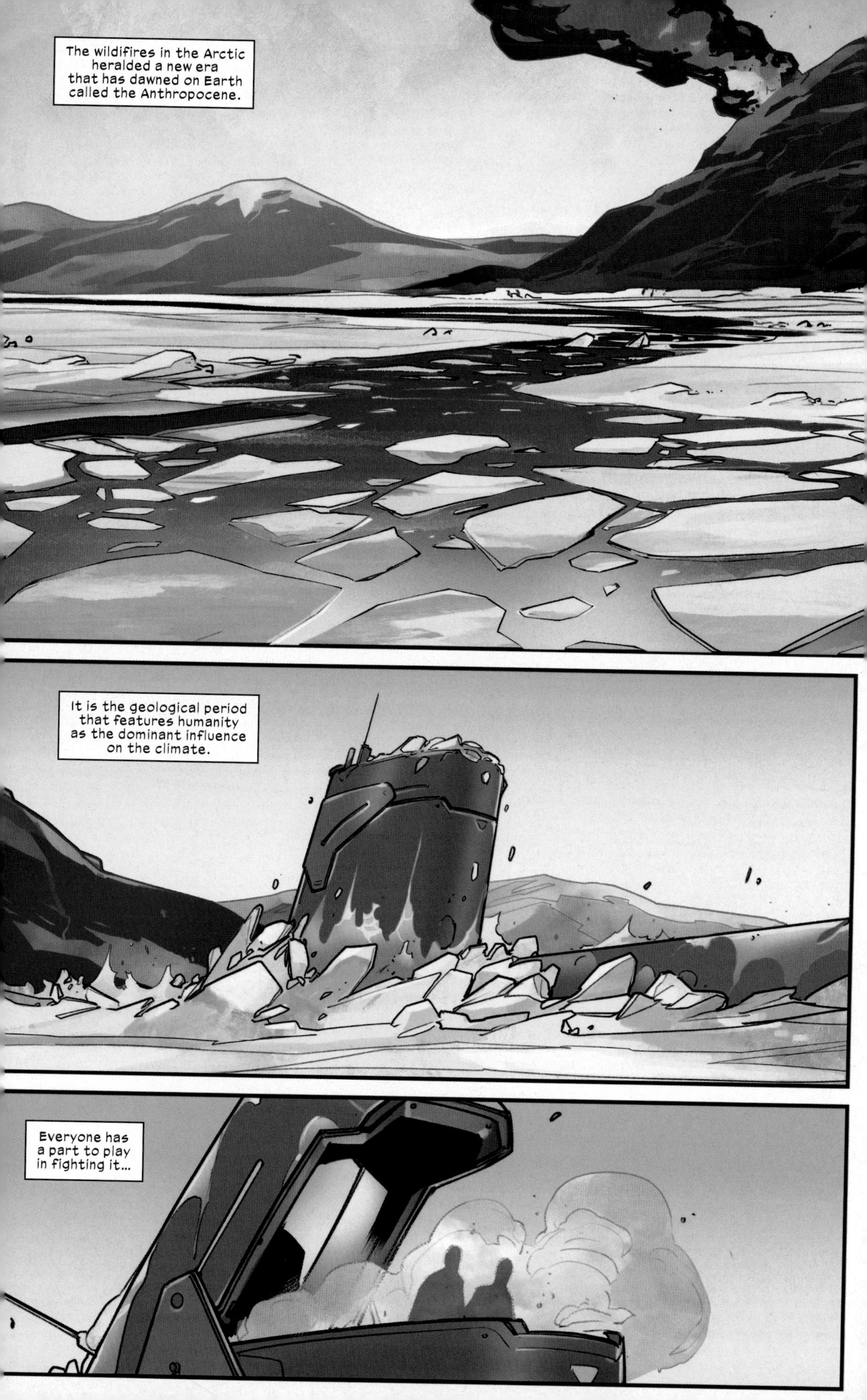
The wildifires in the Arctic heralded a new era that has dawned on Earth called the Anthropocene.
It is the geological period that features humanity as the dominant influence on the climate.
Everyone has a part to play in fighting it...

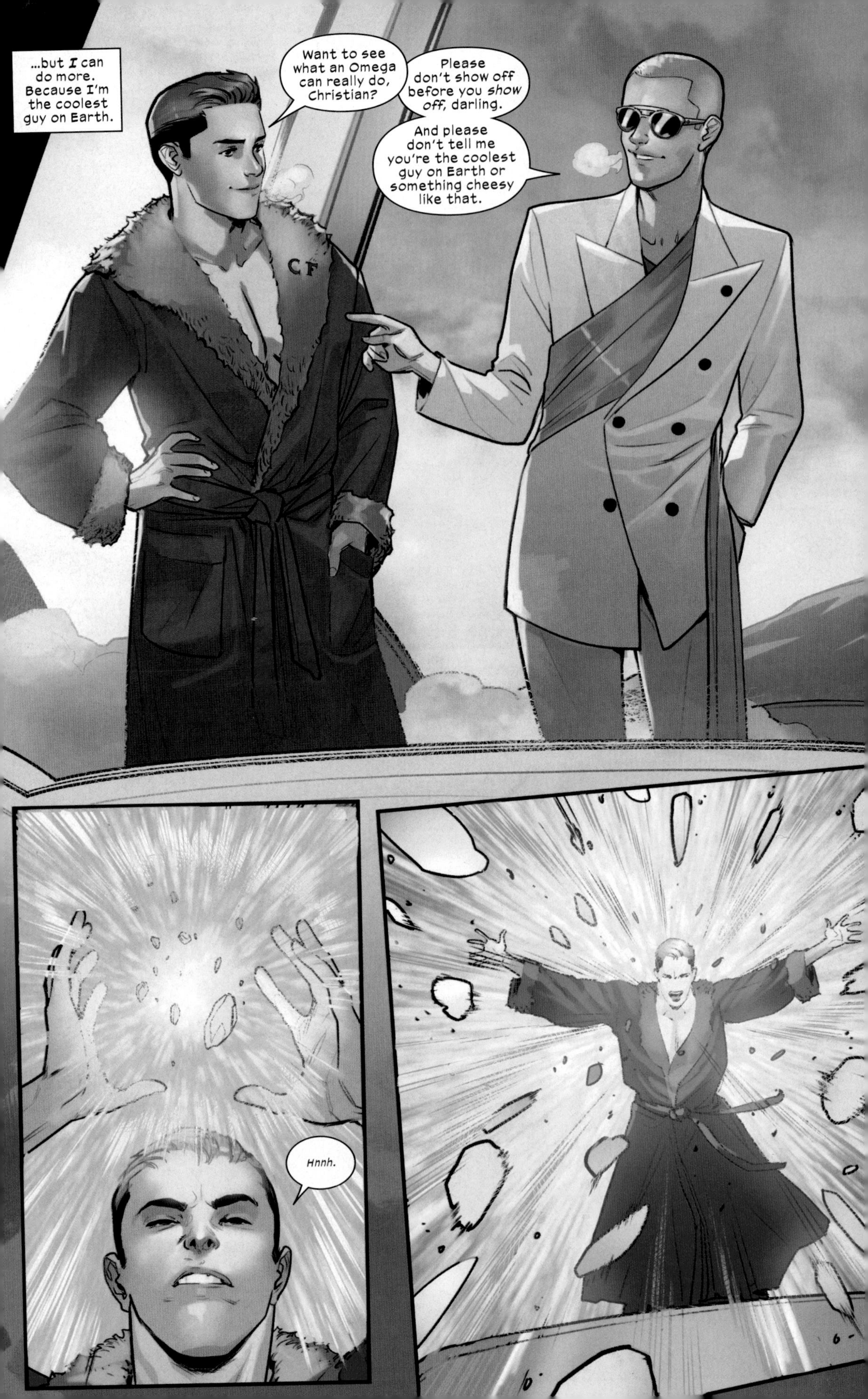
...but I can do more. Because I'm the coolest guy on Earth.
Want to see what an Omega can really do, Christian?
Please don't show off before you show off, darling.
And please don't tell me you're the coolest guy on Earth or something cheesy like that.
Hnnh.

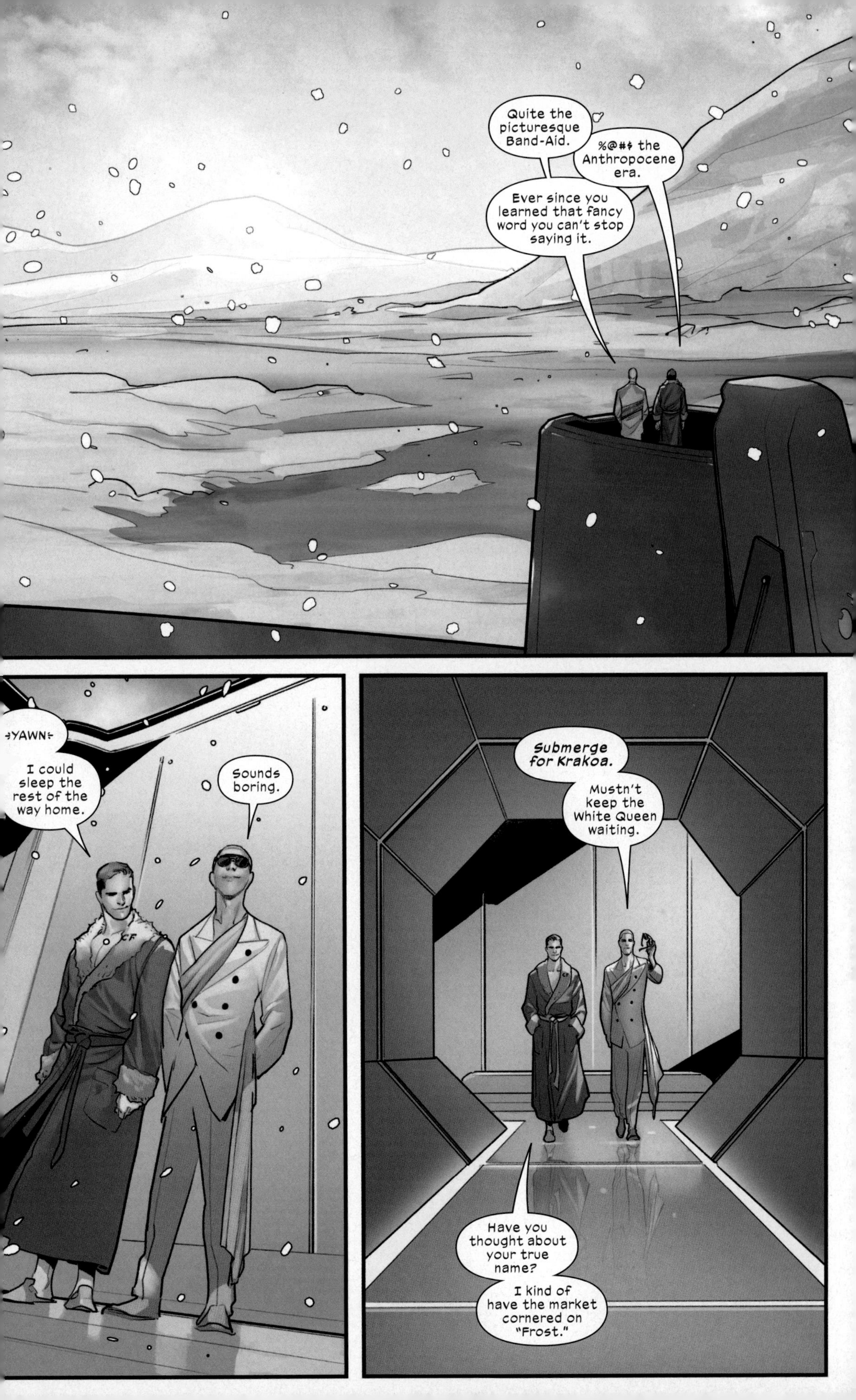
Quite the picturesque Band-Aid.
%@#$ the Anthropocene era.
Ever since you learned that fancy word you can't stop saying it.
=YAWN=
I could sleep the rest of the way home.
Sounds boring.
Submerge for Krakoa.
Mustn't keep the White Queen waiting.
Have you thought about your true name?
I kind of have the market cornered on "Frost."

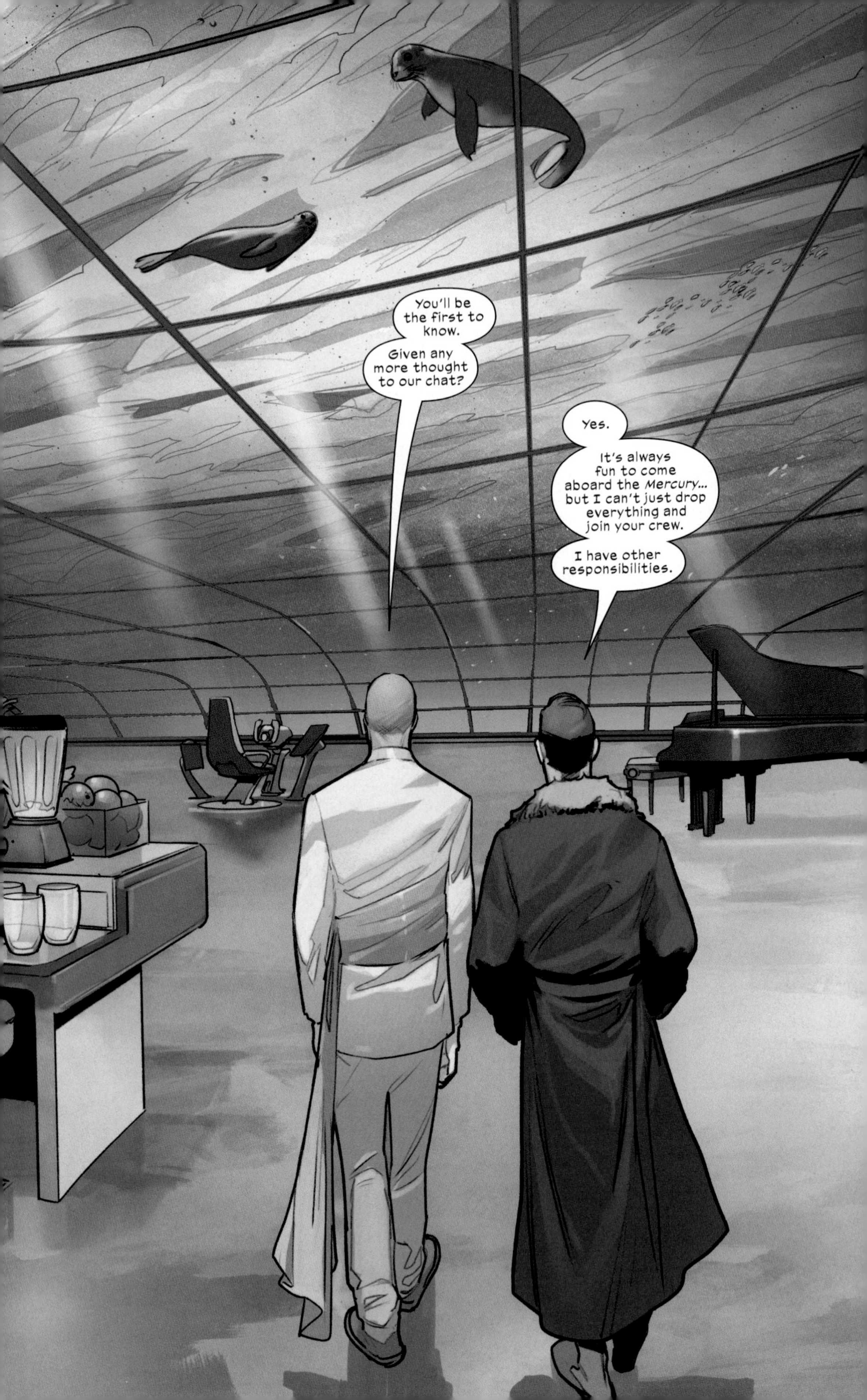
You'll be the first to know.
Given any more thought to our chat?
Yes.
It's always fun to come aboard the *Mercury*... but I can't just drop everything and join your crew.
I have other responsibilities.

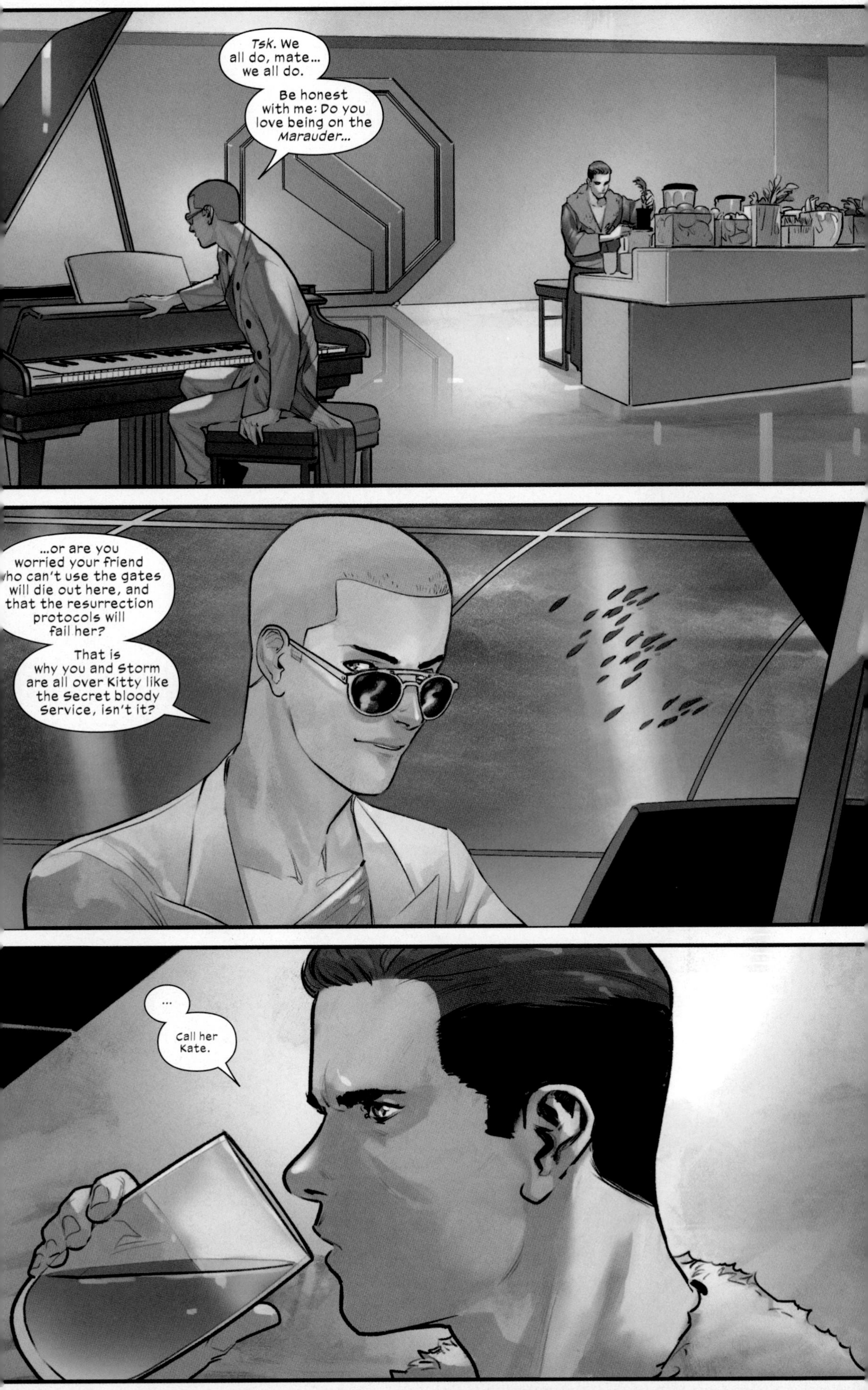

Tsk. We all do, mate... we all do.
Be honest with me: Do you love being on the *Marauder*...
...or are you worried your friend who can't use the gates will die out here, and that the resurrection protocols will fail her?
That is why you and Storm are all over Kitty like the Secret bloody Service, isn't it?
...
Call her Kate.

[00_mutant_piracy]
[00_sea_shores_X_]

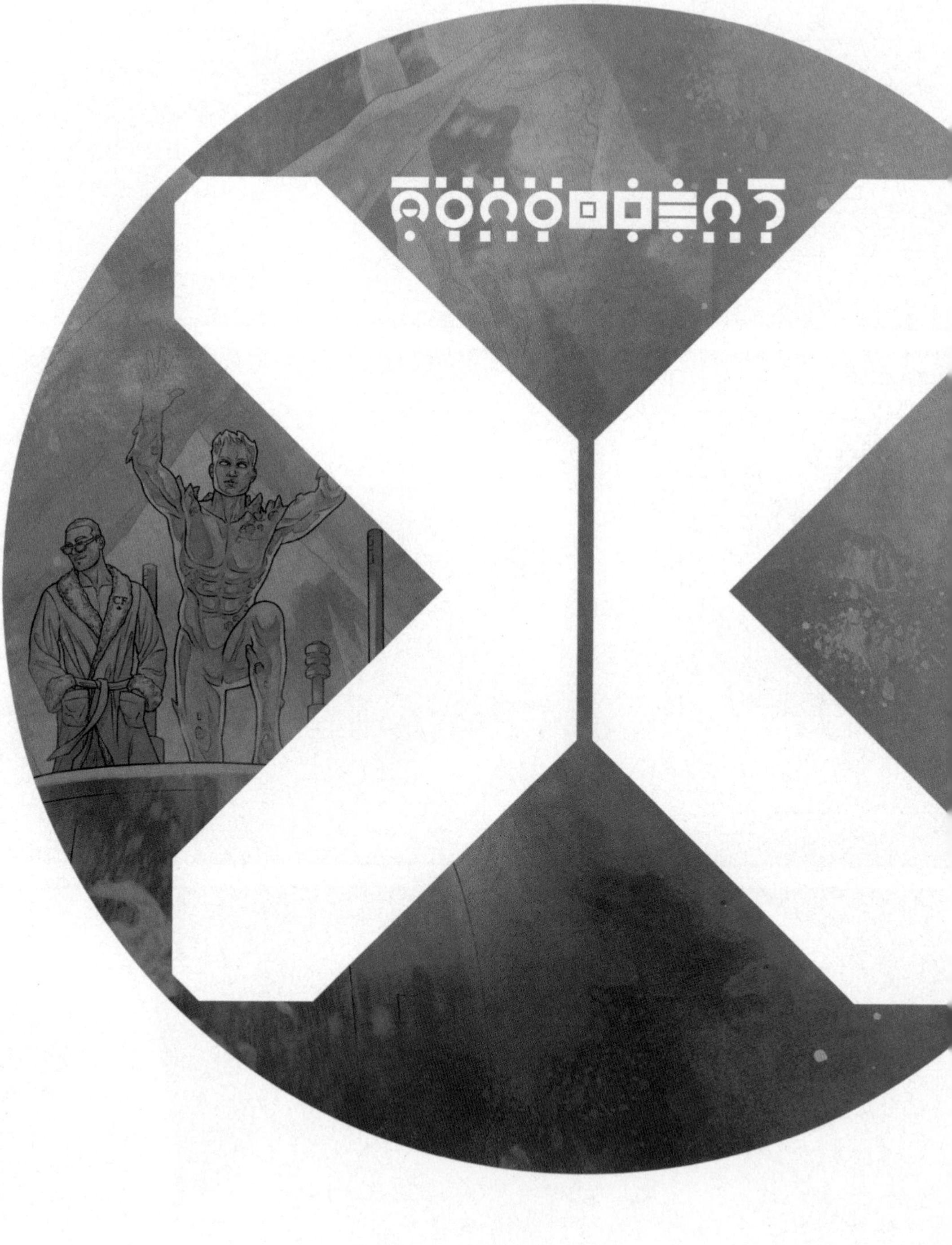

GERRY DUGGAN.....................................[WRITER]
MATTEO LOLLI & LUCAS WERNECK..................[ARTISTS]
FEDERICO BLEE............................[COLOR ARTIST]
VC's CORY PETIT.............................[LETTERER]
TOM MULLER.....................................[DESIGN]

RUSSELL DAUTERMAN & MATTHEW WILSON......[COVER ARTISTS]

TONY DANIEL & RAIN BEREDO.......[VARIANT COVER ARTISTS]

NICK RUSSELL..............................[PRODUCTION]

JONATHAN HICKMAN...........................[HEAD OF X]
CHRIS ROBINSON......................[ASSISTANT EDITOR]
JORDAN D. WHITE...............................[EDITOR]
C.B. CEBULSKI........................[EDITOR IN CHIEF]

[05] MARAUDERS

[ISSUE FIVE]..............A TIME TO SOW

[00_mutant_piracy]
[00_sea_shores_X_]

[00_00...0]
[00_00...5]

[00_boat__]
[00_____]

[00_____]

[00_____X]

[kra_[0.5]
[koa_[0.5]

[kra_[0.X]
[koa_[0.X]

WELCOME TO THE CLUB

Mutants around the world are flocking to the island-nation of Krakoa for safety, security and to be part of the first mutant society.

Captain Kate Pryde is settling into her new role as Red Queen of the Hellfire Trading Company, the organization responsible for distributing Krakoa's lifesaving pharmaceuticals to friendly nations around the world. Meanwhile, Kate and her crew smuggle mutants out of enemy nations -- a list that grows longer every day...

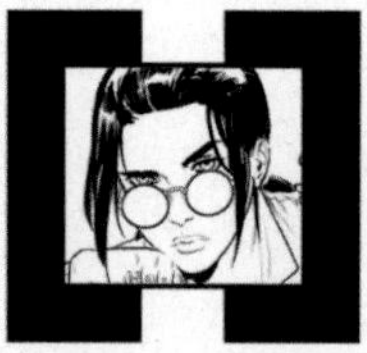

Kate Pryde

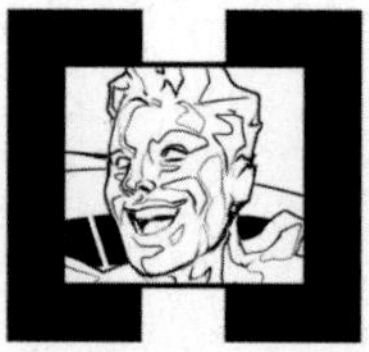

Iceman

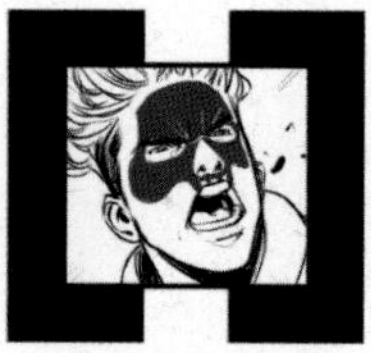

Pyro

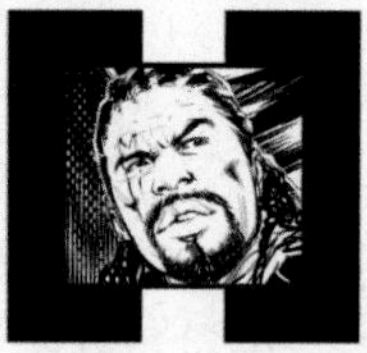

Bishop

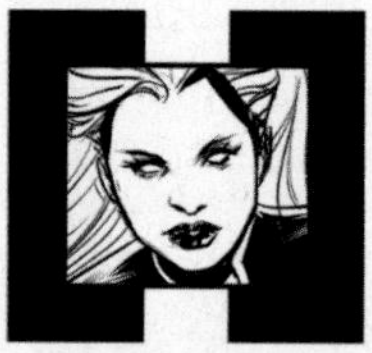

Storm

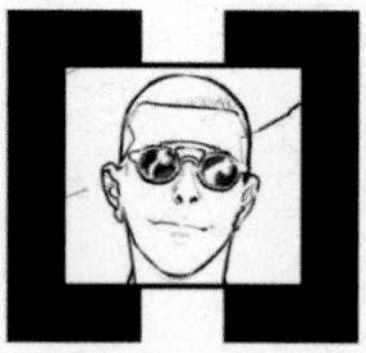

Christian Frost

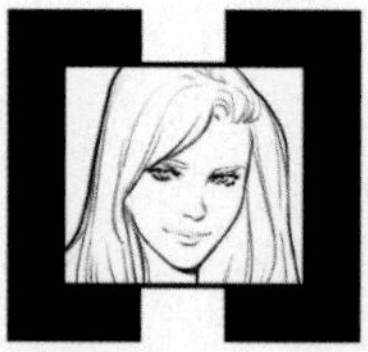

Emma Frost

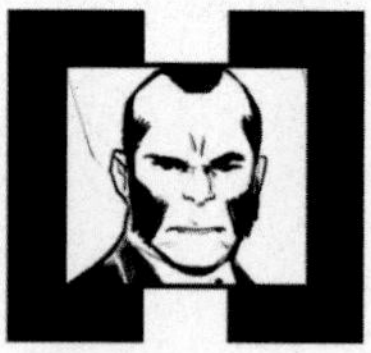

Sebastian Shaw

[kra_[0.5]...]
[koa_[0.5]...]

[A._Shore_Thing]

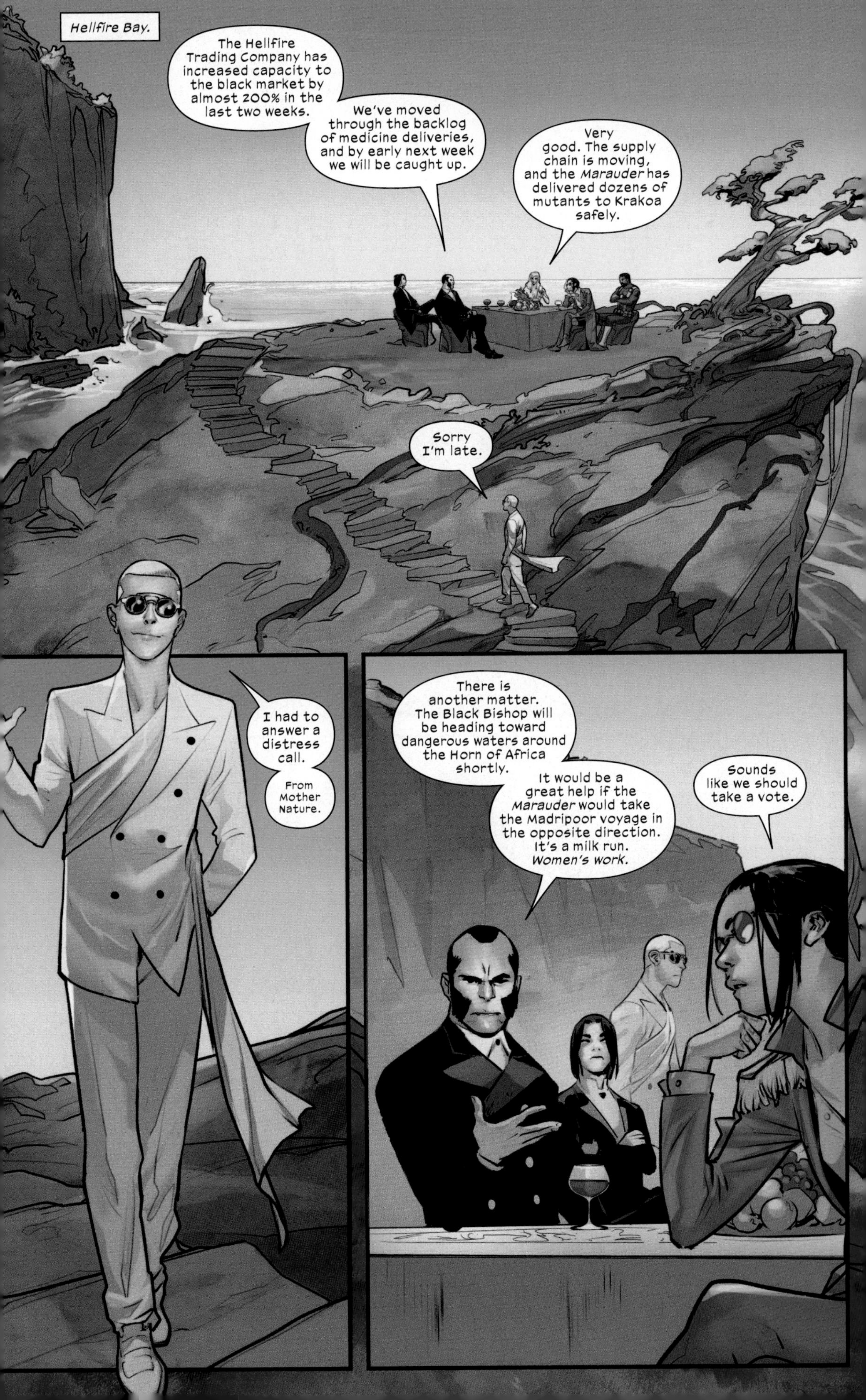
Hellfire Bay.
The Hellfire Trading Company has increased capacity to the black market by almost 200% in the last two weeks.
We've moved through the backlog of medicine deliveries, and by early next week we will be caught up.
Very good. The supply chain is moving, and the Marauder has delivered dozens of mutants to Krakoa safely.
Sorry I'm late.
I had to answer a distress call.
From Mother Nature.
There is another matter. The Black Bishop will be heading toward dangerous waters around the Horn of Africa shortly.
It would be a great help if the Marauder would take the Madripoor voyage in the opposite direction. It's a milk run. Women's work.
Sounds like we should take a vote.

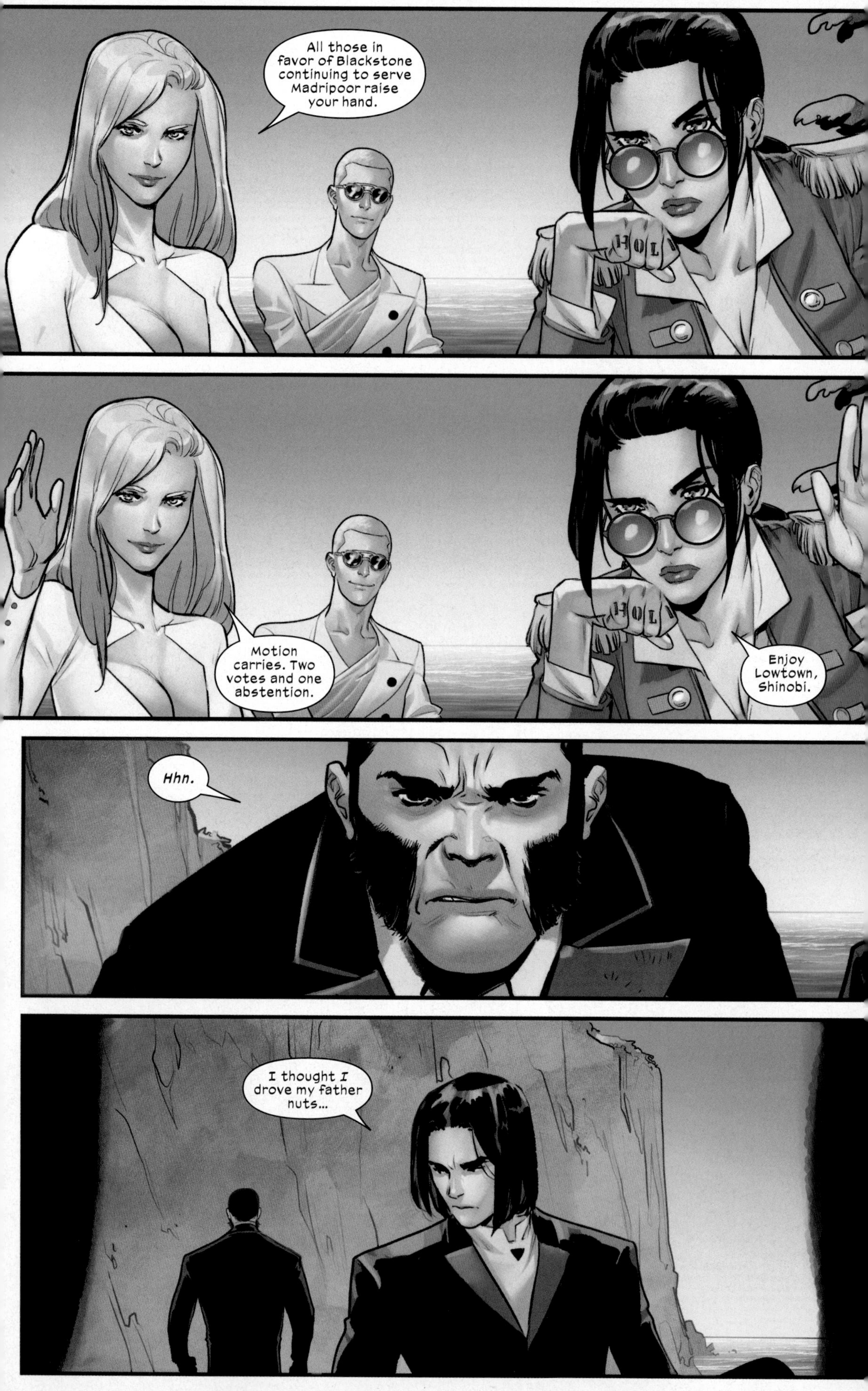
All those in favor of Blackstone continuing to serve Madripoor raise your hand.
HOLI
HOLI
Motion carries. Two votes and one abstention.
Enjoy Lowtown, Shinobi.
Hhn.
I thought I drove my father nuts...

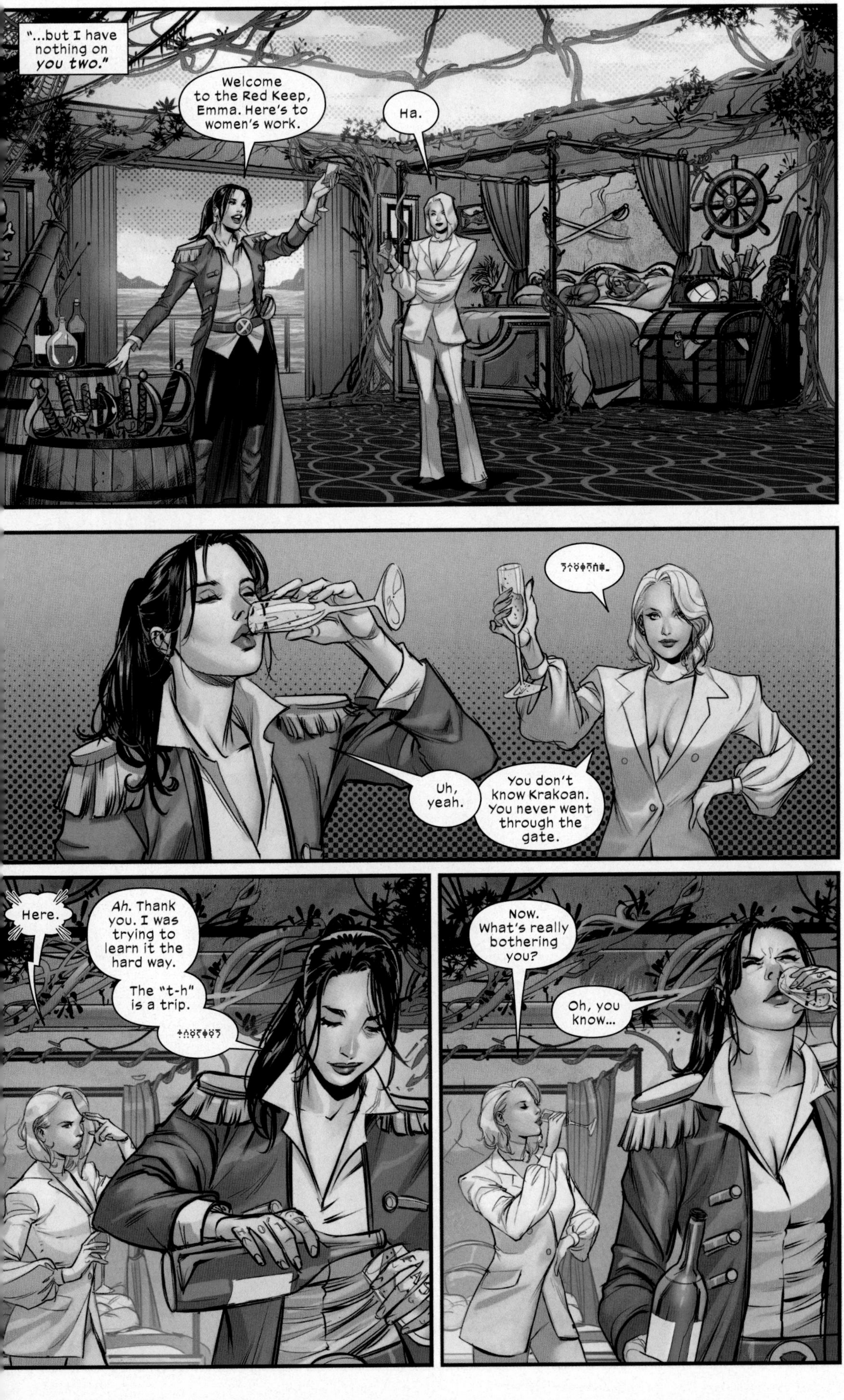
"...but I have nothing on *you two.*"
Welcome to the Red Keep, Emma. Here's to women's work.
Ha.
Uh, yeah.
You don't know Krakoan. You never went through the gate.
Here.
Ah. Thank you. I was trying to learn it the hard way.
The "t-h" is a trip.
Now. What's really bothering you?
Oh, you know...

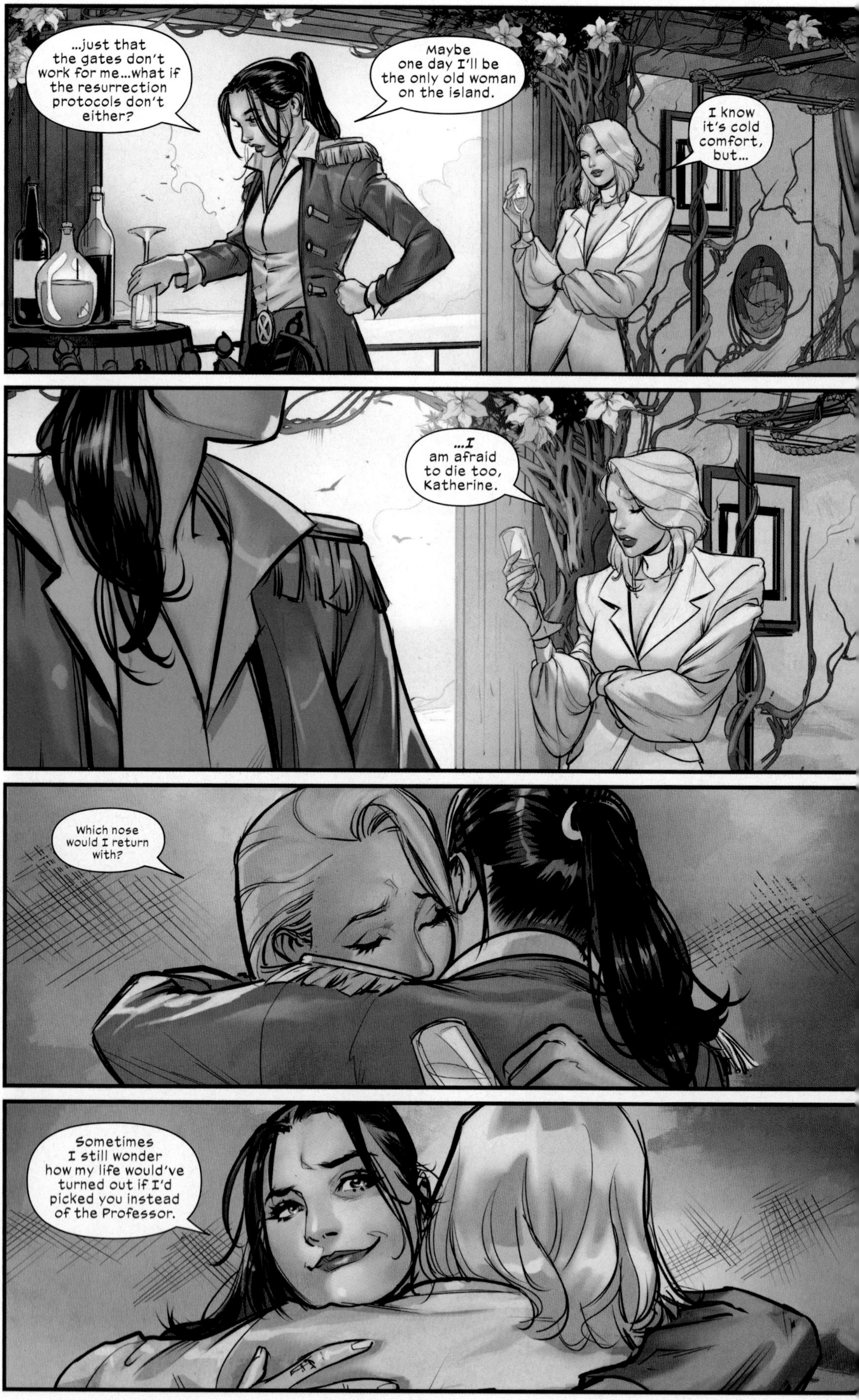
...just that the gates don't work for me...what if the resurrection protocols don't either?
Maybe one day I'll be the only old woman on the island.
I know it's cold comfort, but...
...I am afraid to die too, Katherine.
Which nose would I return with?
Sometimes I still wonder how my life would've turned out if I'd picked you instead of the Professor.

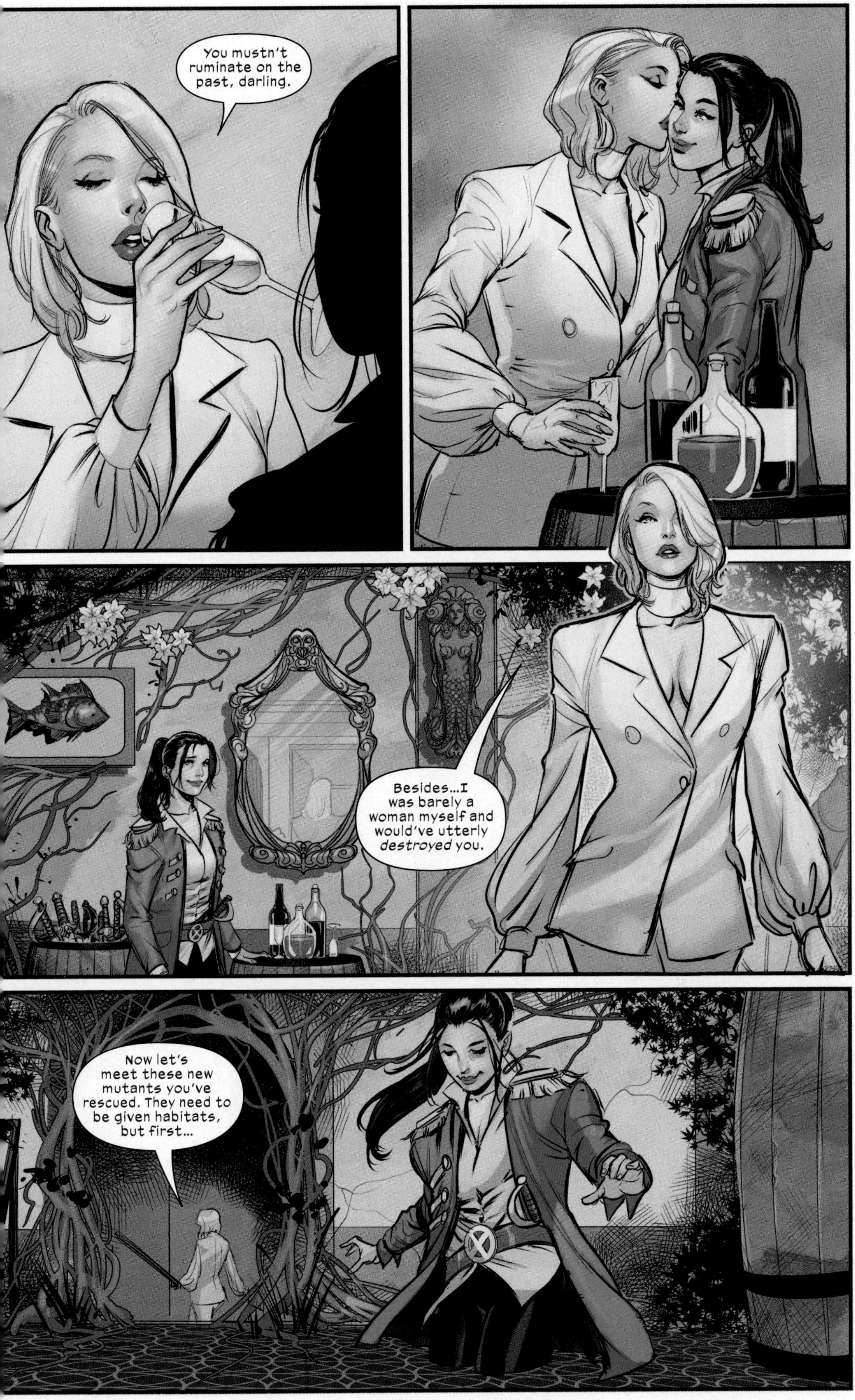
You mustn't ruminate on the past, darling.
Besides...I was barely a woman myself and would've utterly *destroyed* you.
Now let's meet these new mutants you've rescued. They need to be given habitats, but first...

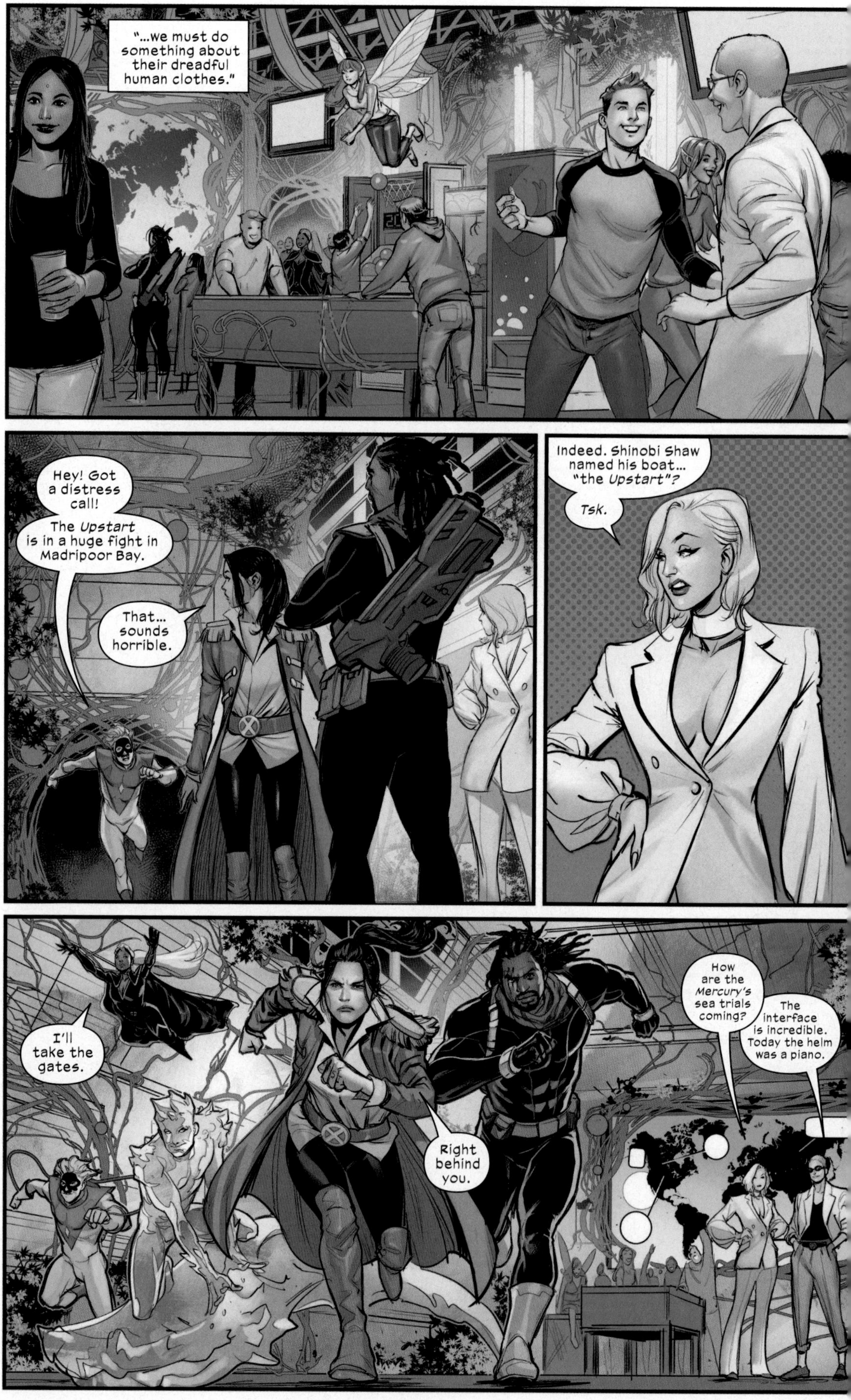
"...we must do something about their dreadful human clothes."
Hey! Got a distress call!
The Upstart is in a huge fight in Madripoor Bay.
That... sounds horrible.
Indeed. Shinobi Shaw named his boat... "the Upstart"?
Tsk.
I'll take the gates.
Right behind you.
How are the Mercury's sea trials coming?
The interface is incredible. Today the helm was a piano.

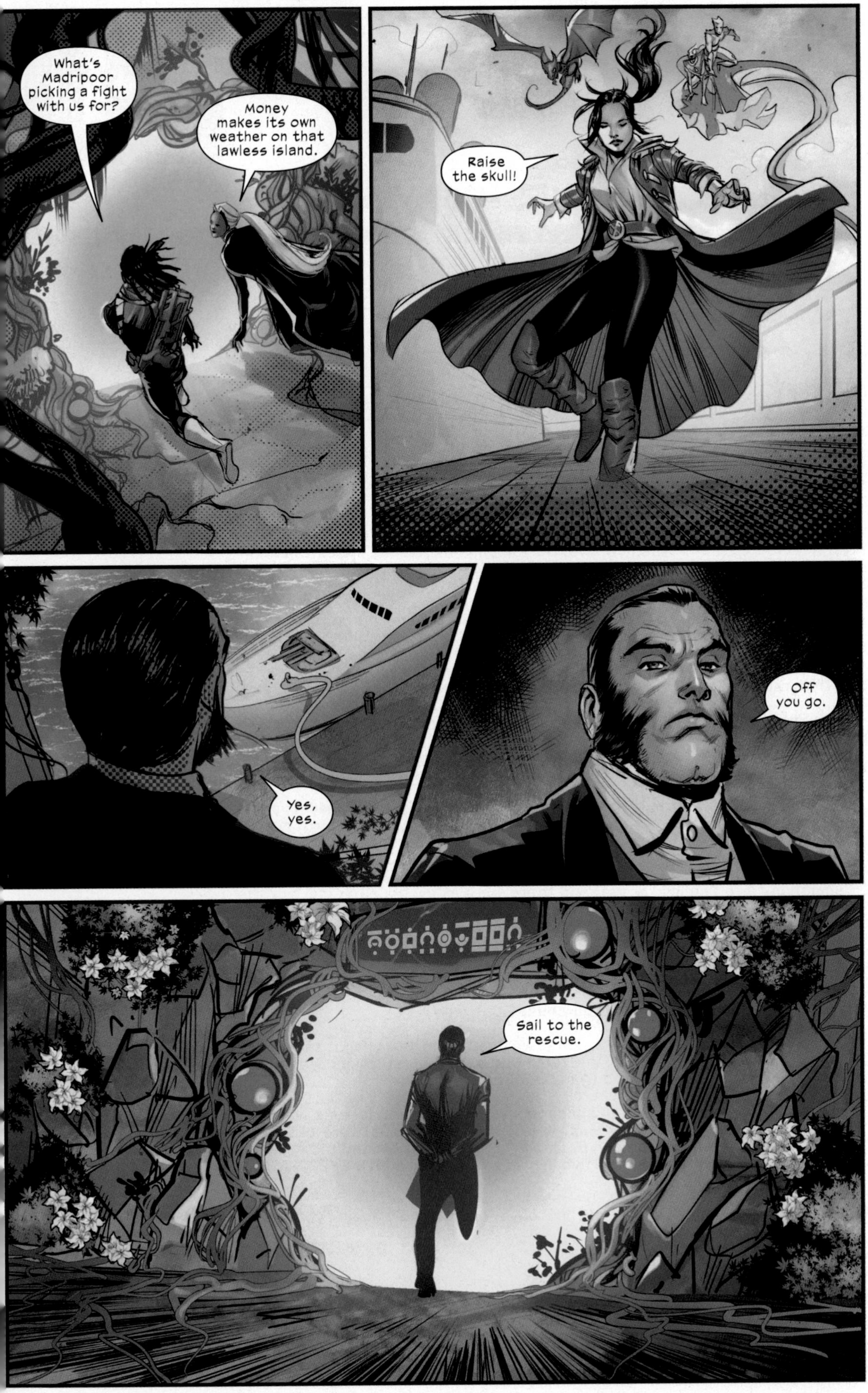
What's Madripoor picking a fight with us for?
Money makes its own weather on that lawless island.
Raise the skull!
Yes, yes.
Off you go.
Sail to the rescue.

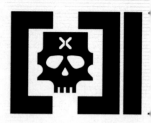

TOP SECRET EYES-ONLY ACCESS

FROM: THE X-DESK
TO: ▮▮▮▮▮▮▮▮▮
SUBJECT: RE: Krakoa

—

Another person returned from the dead this week.

This time it was my mom. My sister administered the Krakoan medicine of the mind to our mother without my knowledge. She was afraid I would say "no".

My mom has been in poor health for roughly four years and hasn't remembered me for the last two. So you can imagine my shock when she walked up to my door and knocked. I canceled her mobile service last year. She was already supposed to have died.

I'll be taking some vacation time in the coming days to spend with the family. I am not compromised by my mom's recovery, but that is probably not for me to decide. Let me know if I should clear out the desk.

There are, however, two pressing drug purchases to discuss:

Manuel Enduque made two large purchases in the last several days. He bought a large supply of Krakoan medicine from the black market, spending ten figures in heated bidding for an entire pallet of the mutant drugs that seem to have "fallen off the back of a boat."

I also have very strong reason to believe he also purchased cyanide through an associate named Kade Kilgore and a shell corp out of Madripoor called **HOMINES VERENDI**. I have no info on the corporation, but I consulted with our man at Princeton, Michael D. Gordin, who looped in Yelena Baraz from their linguistics department to translate that company into English for me, and there were a few possibilities, but the one that's most ominous and therefore likely is: ***"Man must be revered and feared."***

These subjects do not have full profiles, as they are both minors. They do not possess any inherent powers if you don't count their billions. Both subjects have held positions with the Hellfire Club in the past, and that is likely the motivation for their purchases this week.

It is my urgent recommendation that we immediately reach out to friendly Krakoans and alert them to the likelihood that a mass casualty event is being planned around their only meaningful export.

If need be, I know someone who knows someone. Let's assume we're on a clock to save some old human lives: both purchases were cash and carry. We detected the poison purchase through FINCEN and the Krakoan medicine auction was recorded via hot mic exploit by a FIVE EYES NATION to be named never.

I'm working from home the next few days. Let me know how to proceed.

▬▬▬▬▬▬▬▬

—

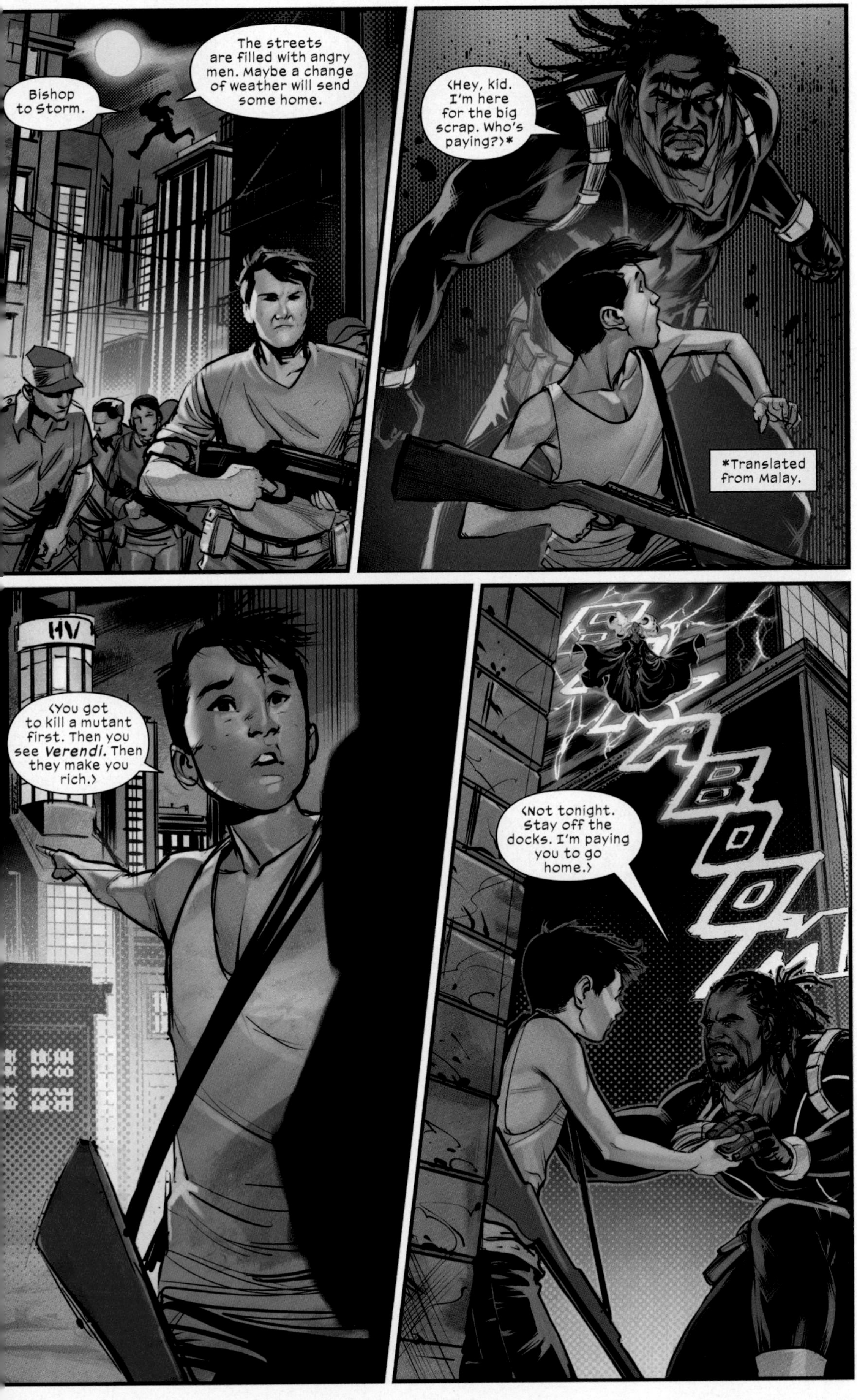

Bishop to Storm.
The streets are filled with angry men. Maybe a change of weather will send some home.
‹Hey, kid. I'm here for the big scrap. Who's paying?›*
*Translated from Malay.
HV
‹You got to kill a mutant first. Then you see *Verendi*. Then they make you rich.›
SKABOOM
‹Not tonight. Stay off the docks. I'm paying you to go home.›

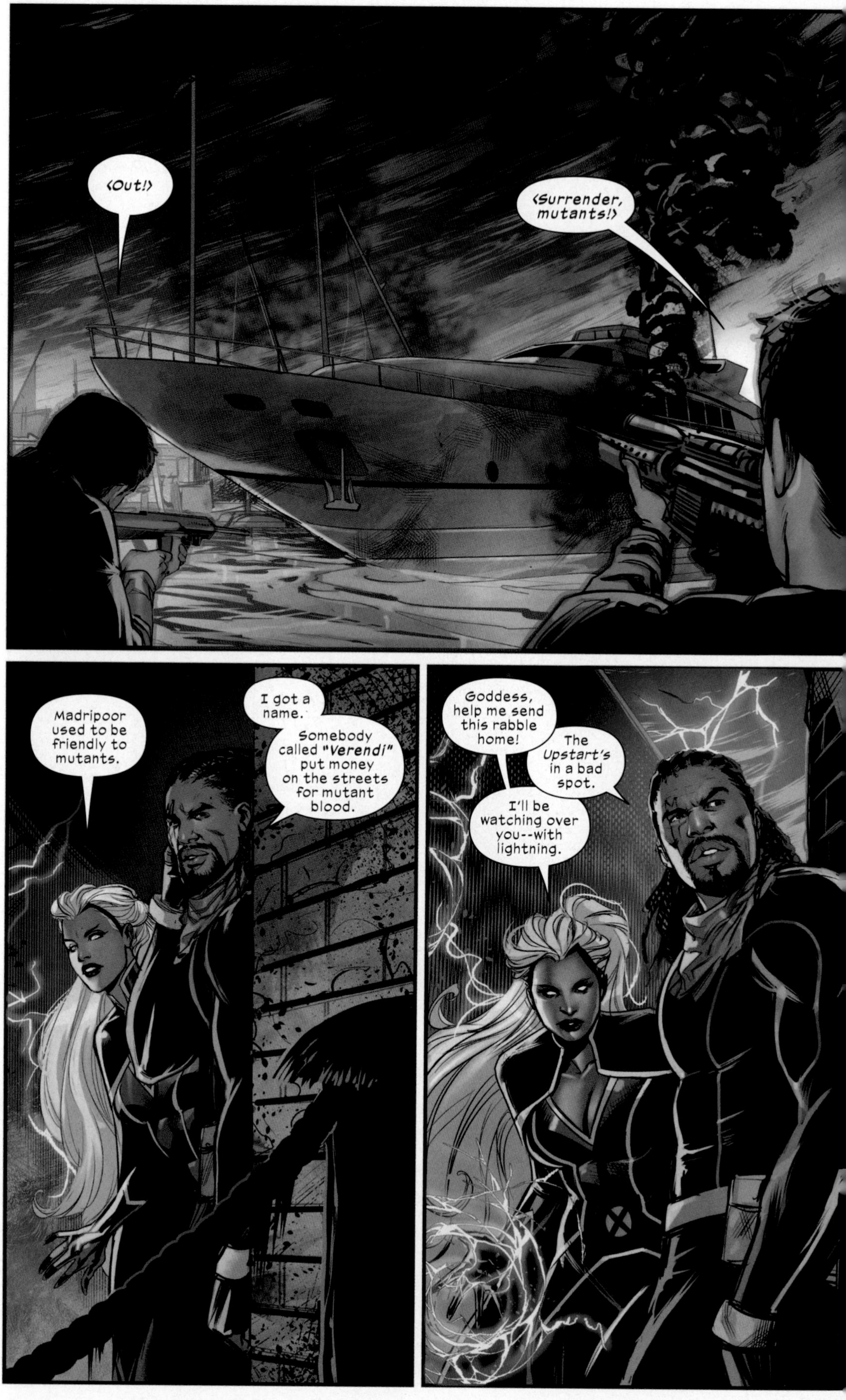
‹Out!›
‹Surrender, mutants!›
Madripoor used to be friendly to mutants.
I got a name.
Somebody called "Verendi" put money on the streets for mutant blood.
Goddess, help me send this rabble home!
The Upstart's in a bad spot.
I'll be watching over you--with lightning.

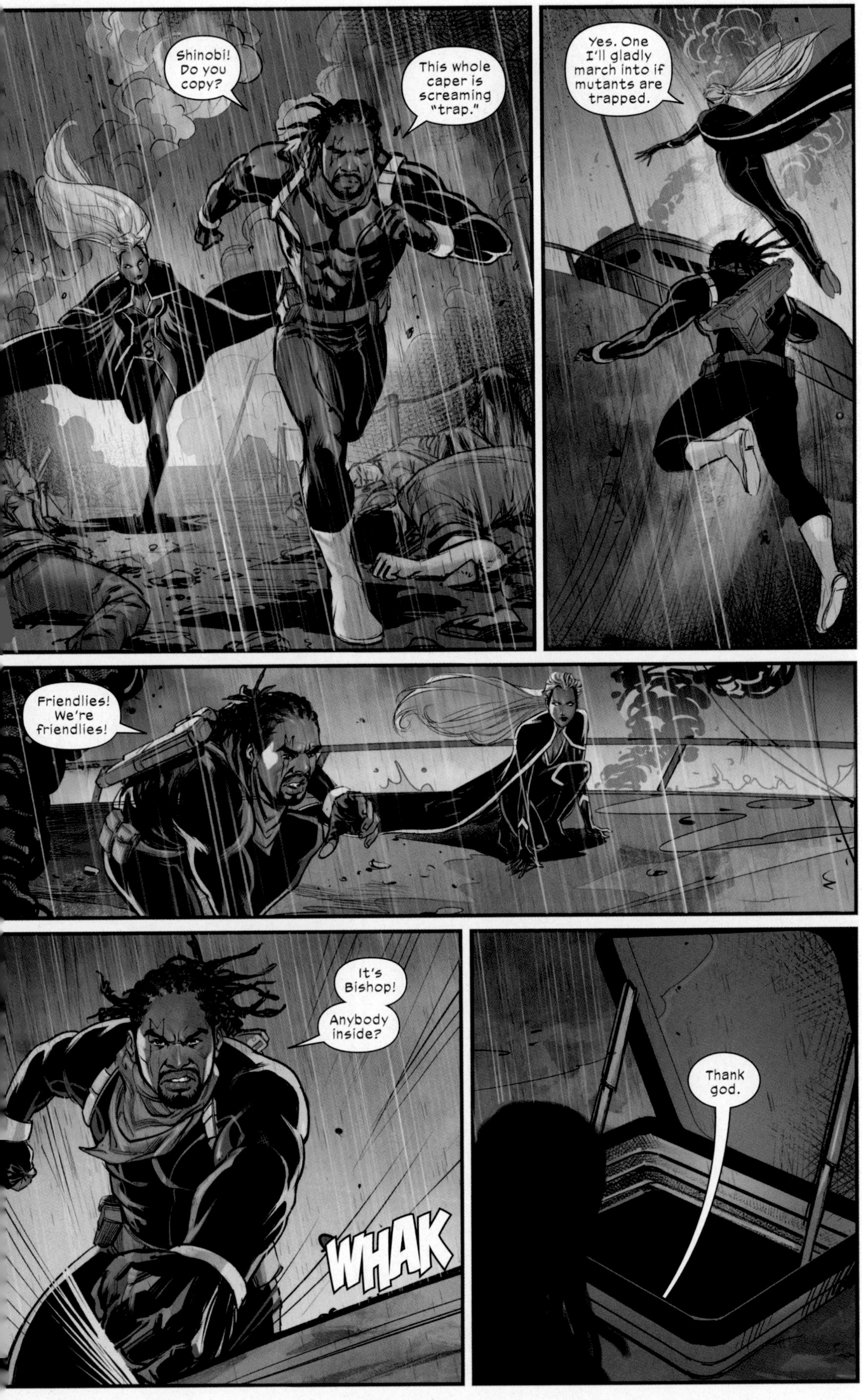
Shinobi! Do you copy?
This whole caper is screaming "trap."
Yes. One I'll gladly march into if mutants are trapped.
Friendlies! We're friendlies!
It's Bishop!
Anybody inside?
WHAK
Thank god.

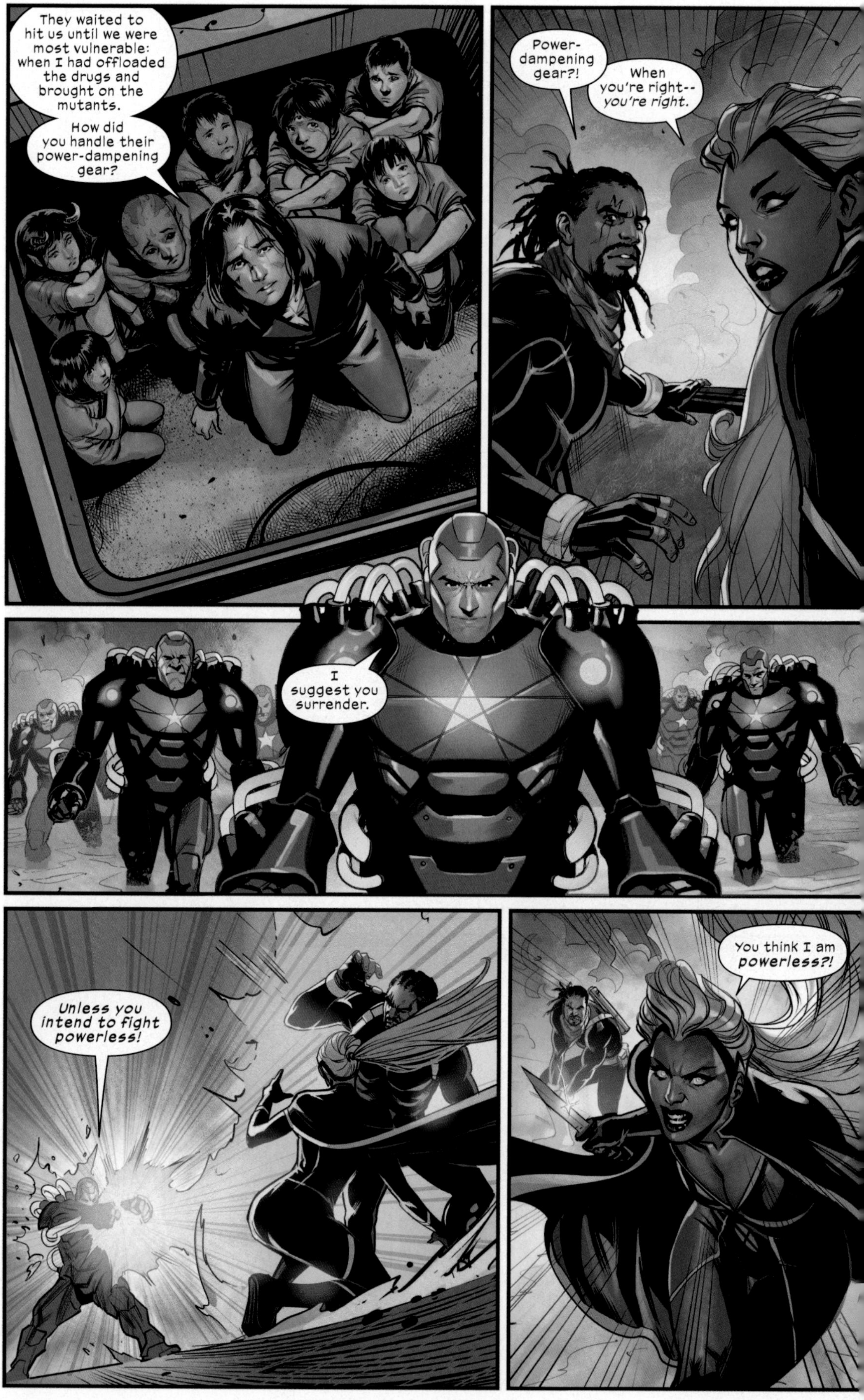
They waited to hit us until we were most vulnerable: when I had offloaded the drugs and brought on the mutants.
How did you handle their power-dampening gear?
Power-dampening gear?!
When you're right-- *you're right.*
I suggest you surrender.
Unless you intend to fight powerless!
You think I am *powerless?!*

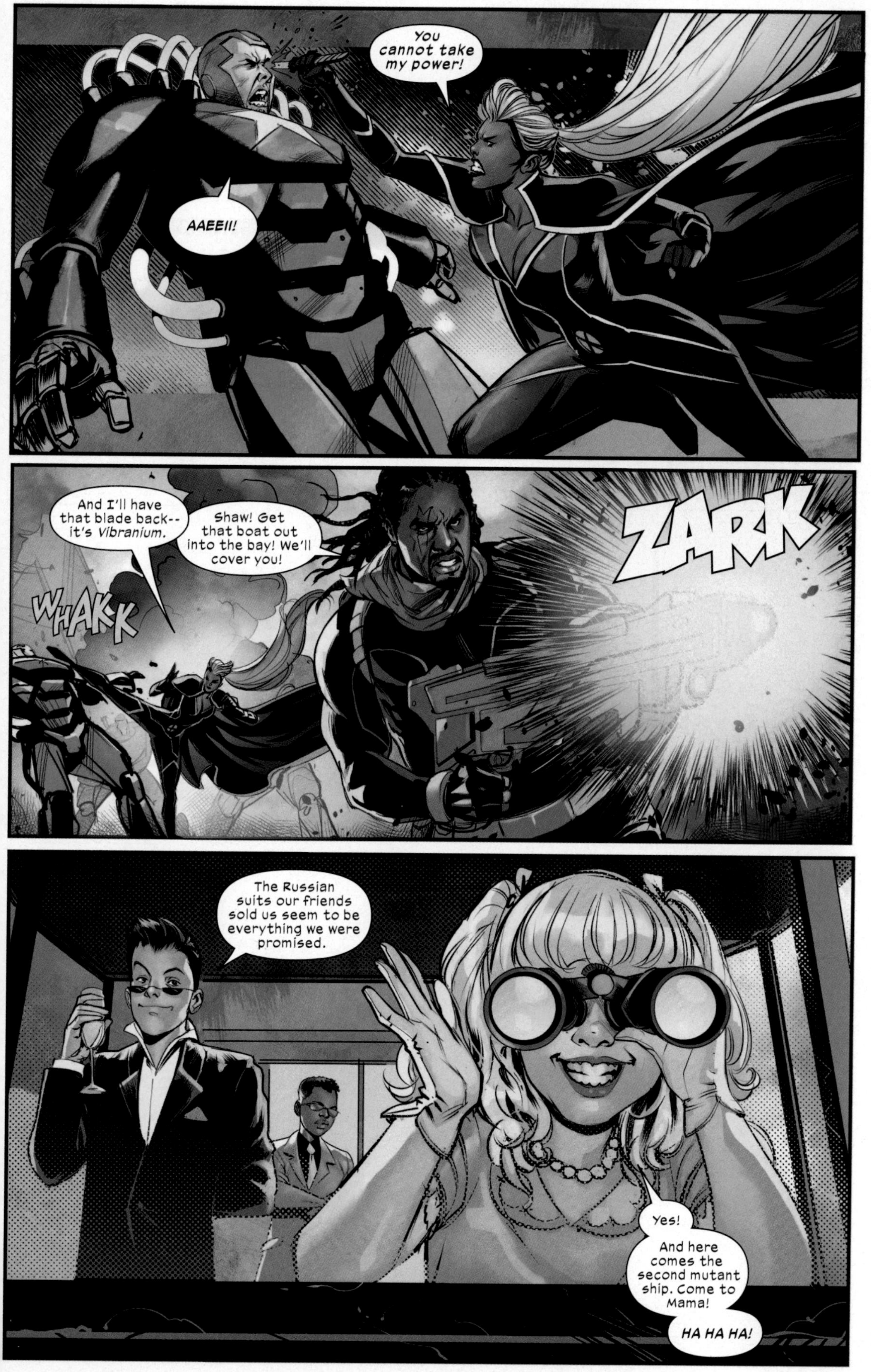
You cannot take my power!
AAEEII!
And I'll have that blade back-- it's Vibranium.
Shaw! Get that boat out into the bay! We'll cover you!
ZARK
WHAKK
The Russian suits our friends sold us seem to be everything we were promised.
Yes!
And here comes the second mutant ship. Come to Mama!
HA HA HA!

HOMINES VERENDI

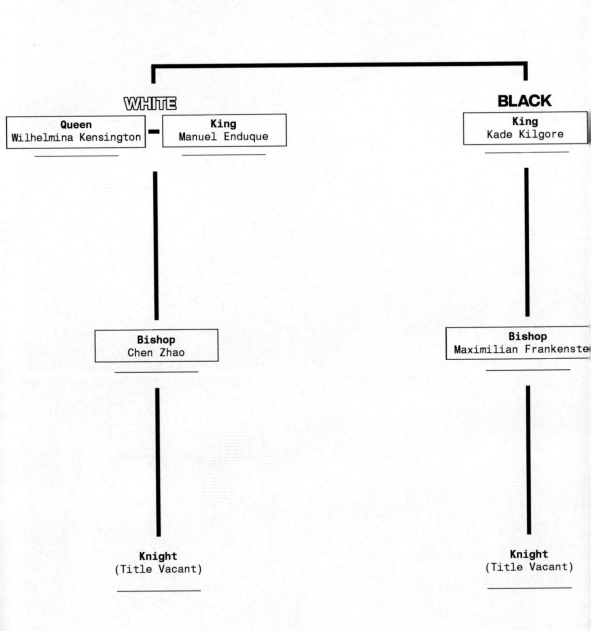

WHITE

Queen
Wilhelmina Kensington

King
Manuel Enduque

BLACK

King
Kade Kilgore

Bishop
Chen Zhao

Bishop
Maximilian Frankenste

Knight
(Title Vacant)

Knight
(Title Vacant)

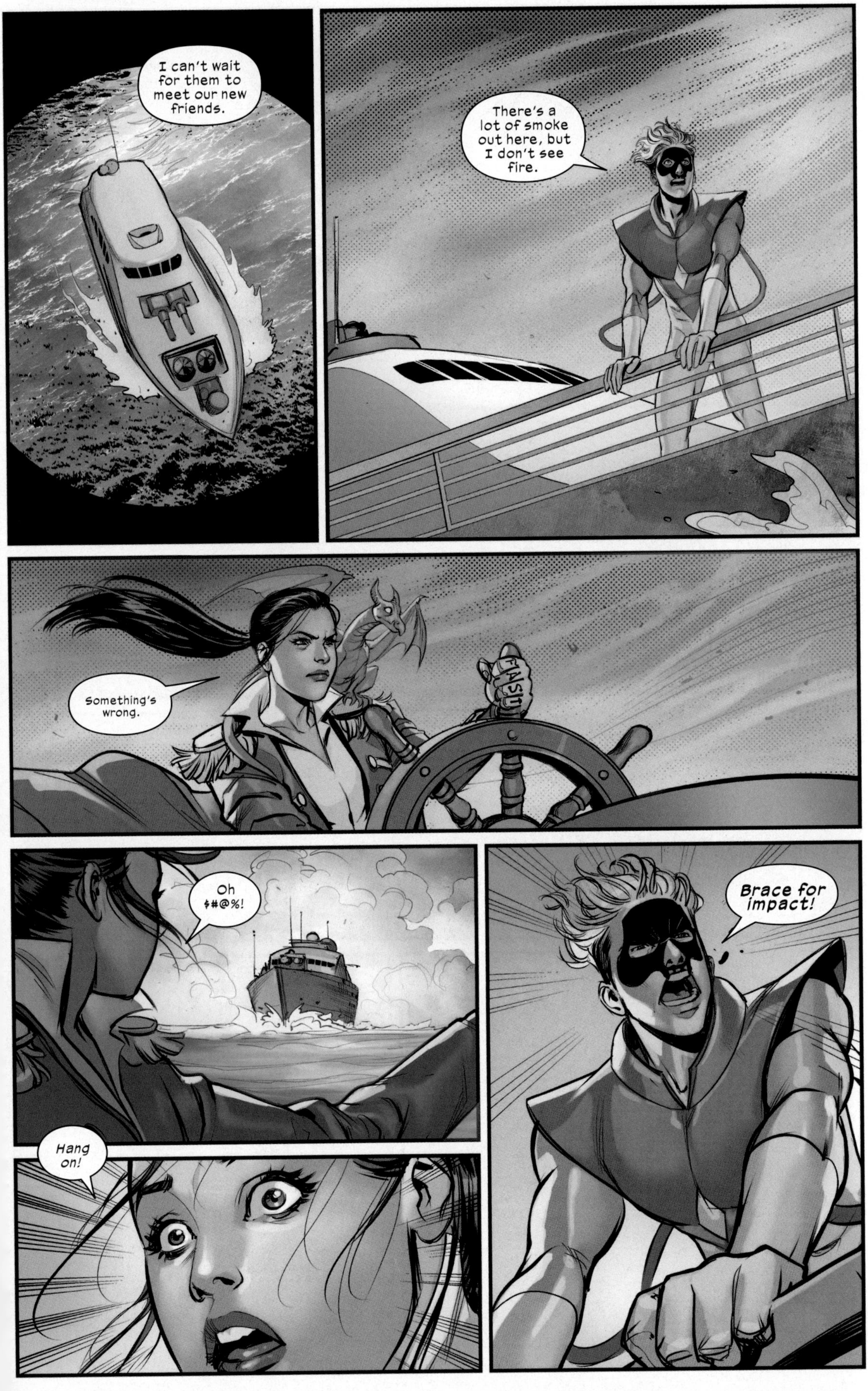

I can't wait for them to meet our new friends.
There's a lot of smoke out here, but I don't see fire.
Something's wrong.
Oh $#@%!
Hang on!
Brace for impact!

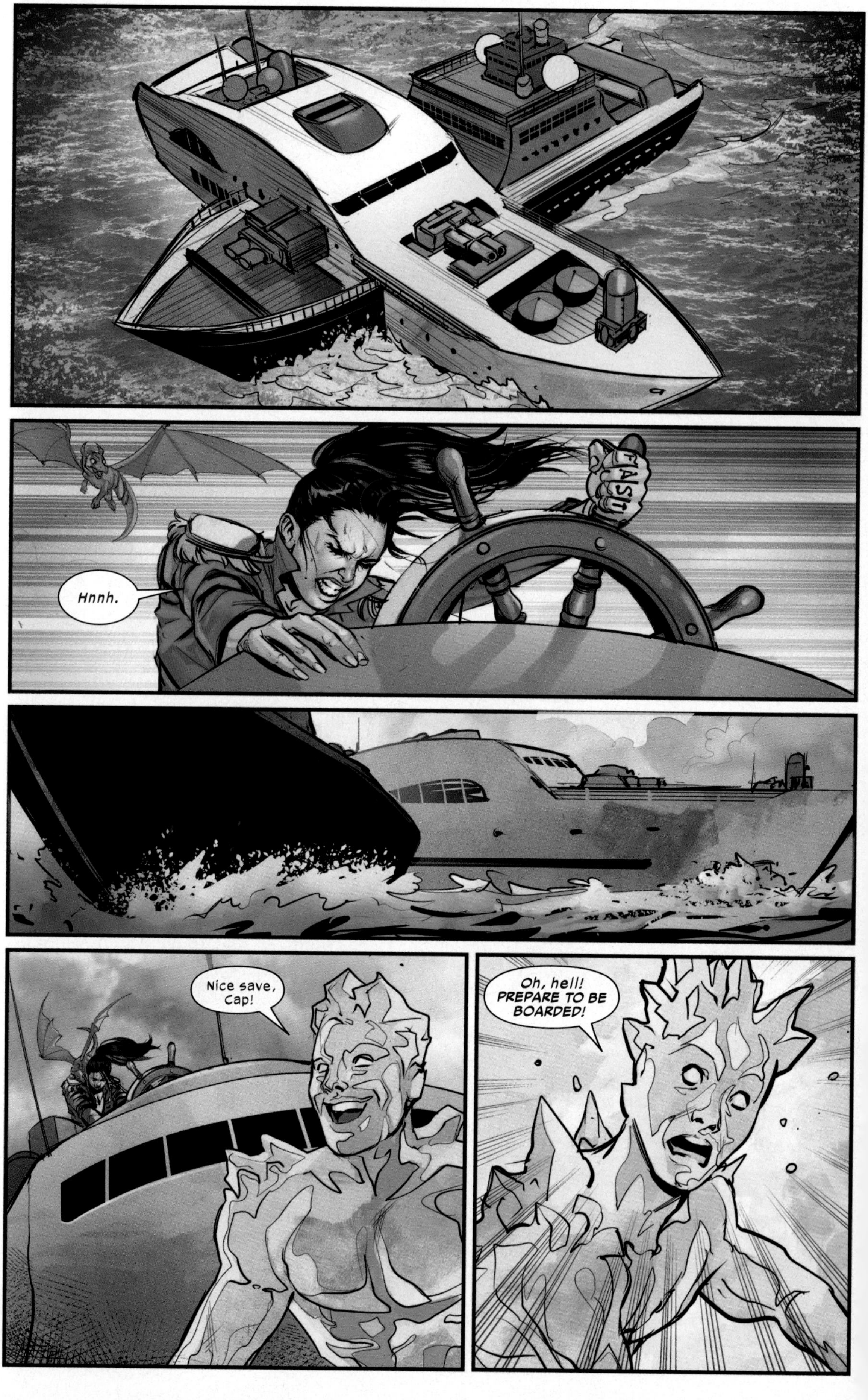
FAST
Hnnh.
Nice save, Cap!
Oh, hell! PREPARE TO BE BOARDED!

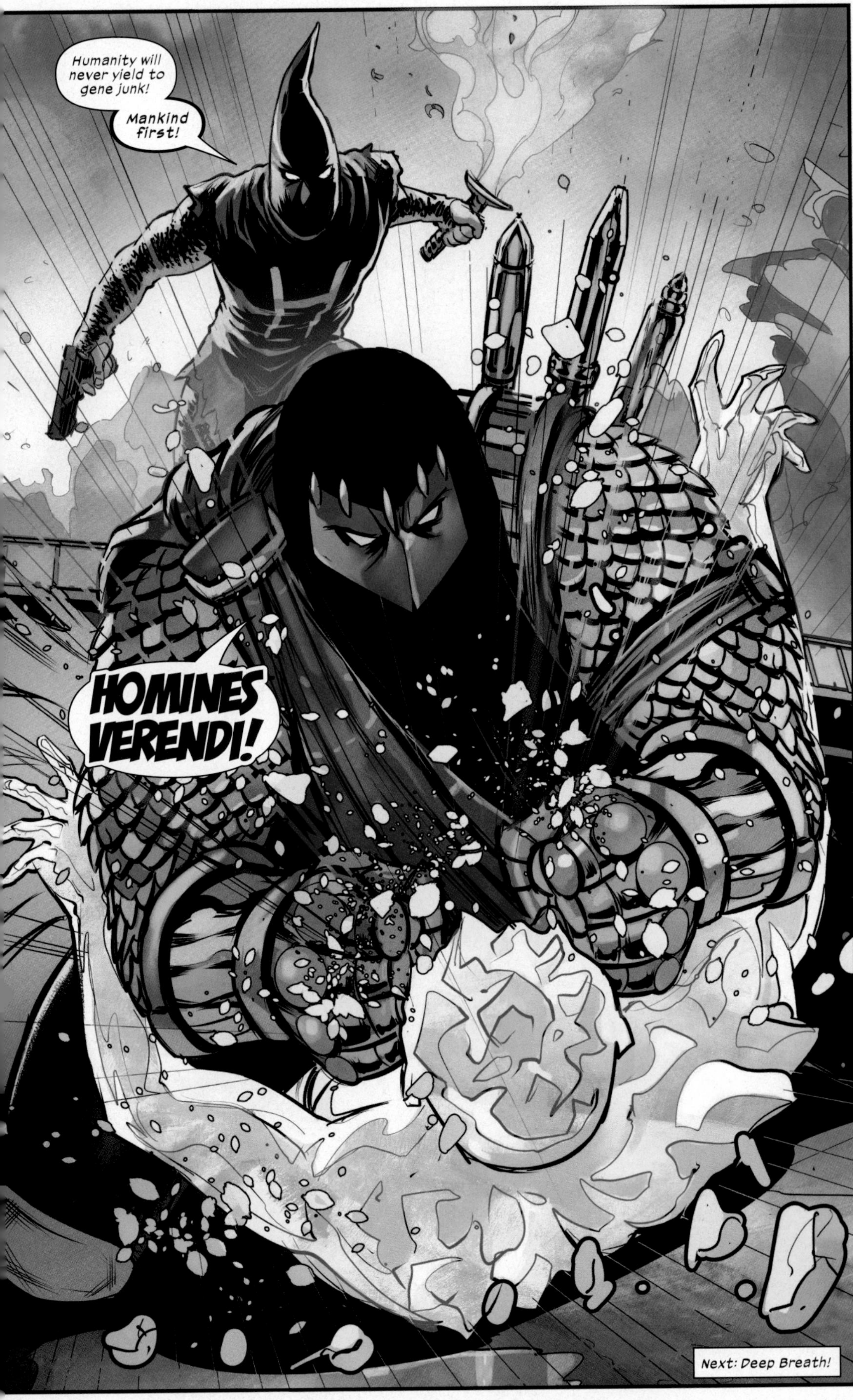
Humanity will never yield to gene junk!
Mankind first!
HOMINES VERENDI!
Next: Deep Breath!

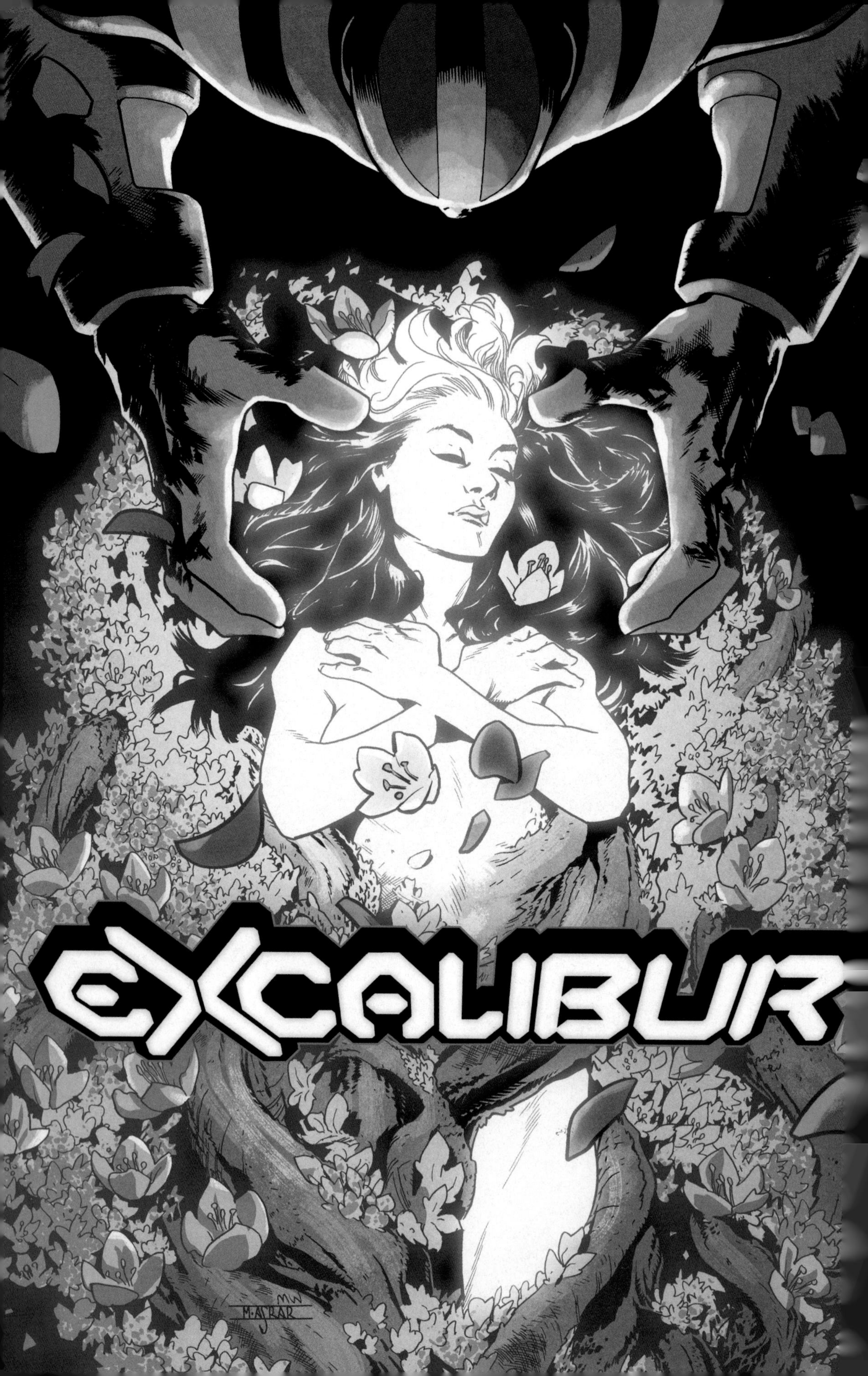
EXCALIBUR

[ava_[0.5]
[lon_[0.5]

[ava_[0.X]
[lon_[0.X]

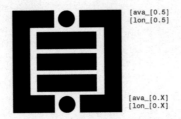

THE VEIL BETWEEN WORLDS

With her brother Brian possessed by an evil sorceress, Betsy Braddock has become Captain Britain -- and must bear the weight of all that name entails! Rogue has been trapped in a mysterious floral stasis, and while Apocalypse has been playing nice, Gambit sees evil lurking beneath the veneer of magic. Jubilee's fears for the safety of her son, Shogo, were relieved when he transfigured into a dragon in Otherworld -- but that relief disappeared when the team learned that his dragonfire dissolves the fragile barrier between Otherworld and their own world.

Now there's nothing to stop all kinds of mystical beasts from coming through...nothing but EXCALIBUR!

Gambit    Rogue   Rictor

Jubilee    Captain
Britain

Pete   Apocalypse
Wisdom

[ava_[0.5]...]
[lon_[0.5]...]

[All....HAIL.]

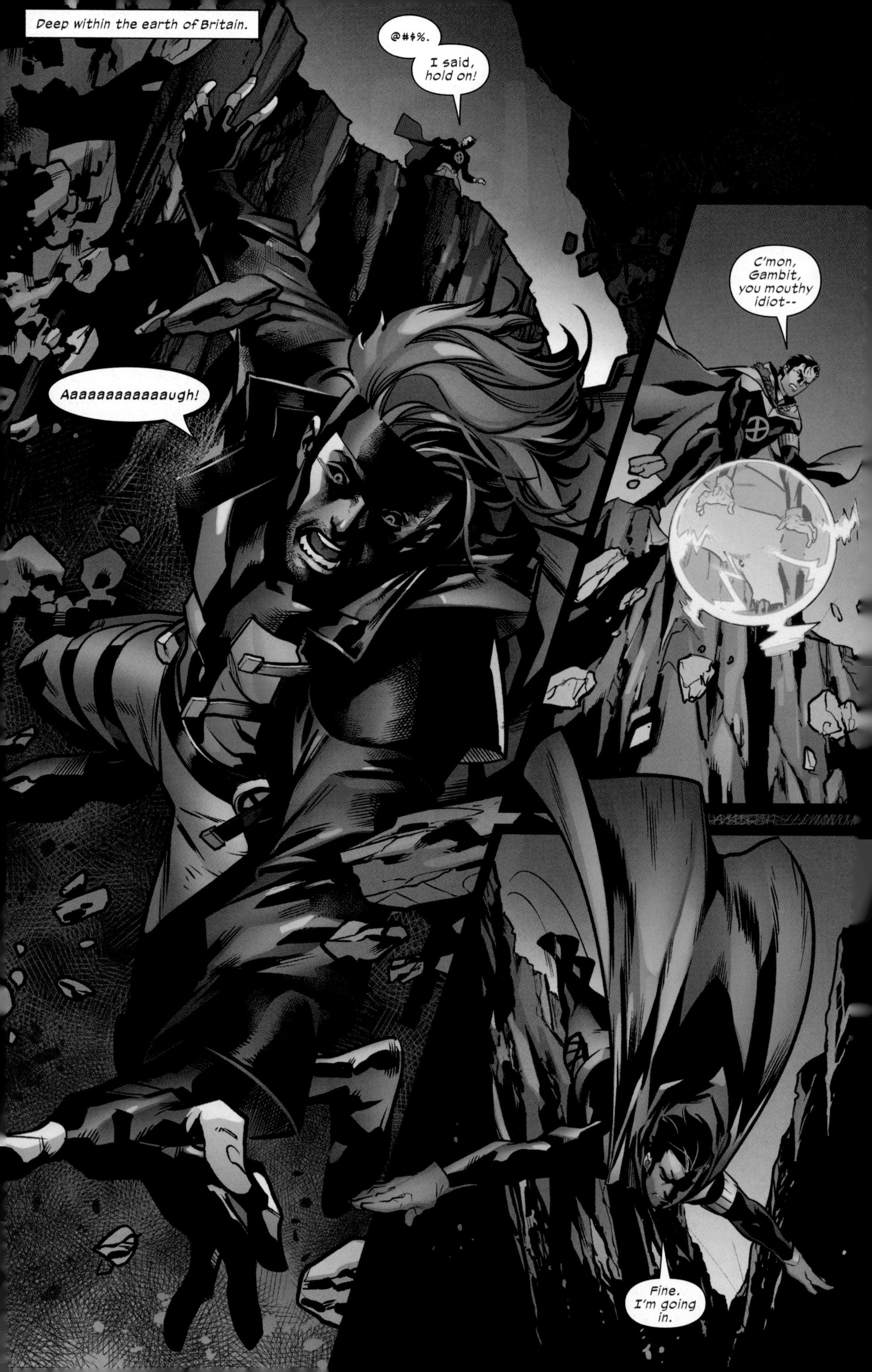
Deep within the earth of Britain.
@#$%.
I said, hold on!
Aaaaaaaaaaaaugh!
C'mon, Gambit, you mouthy idiot--
Fine. I'm going in.

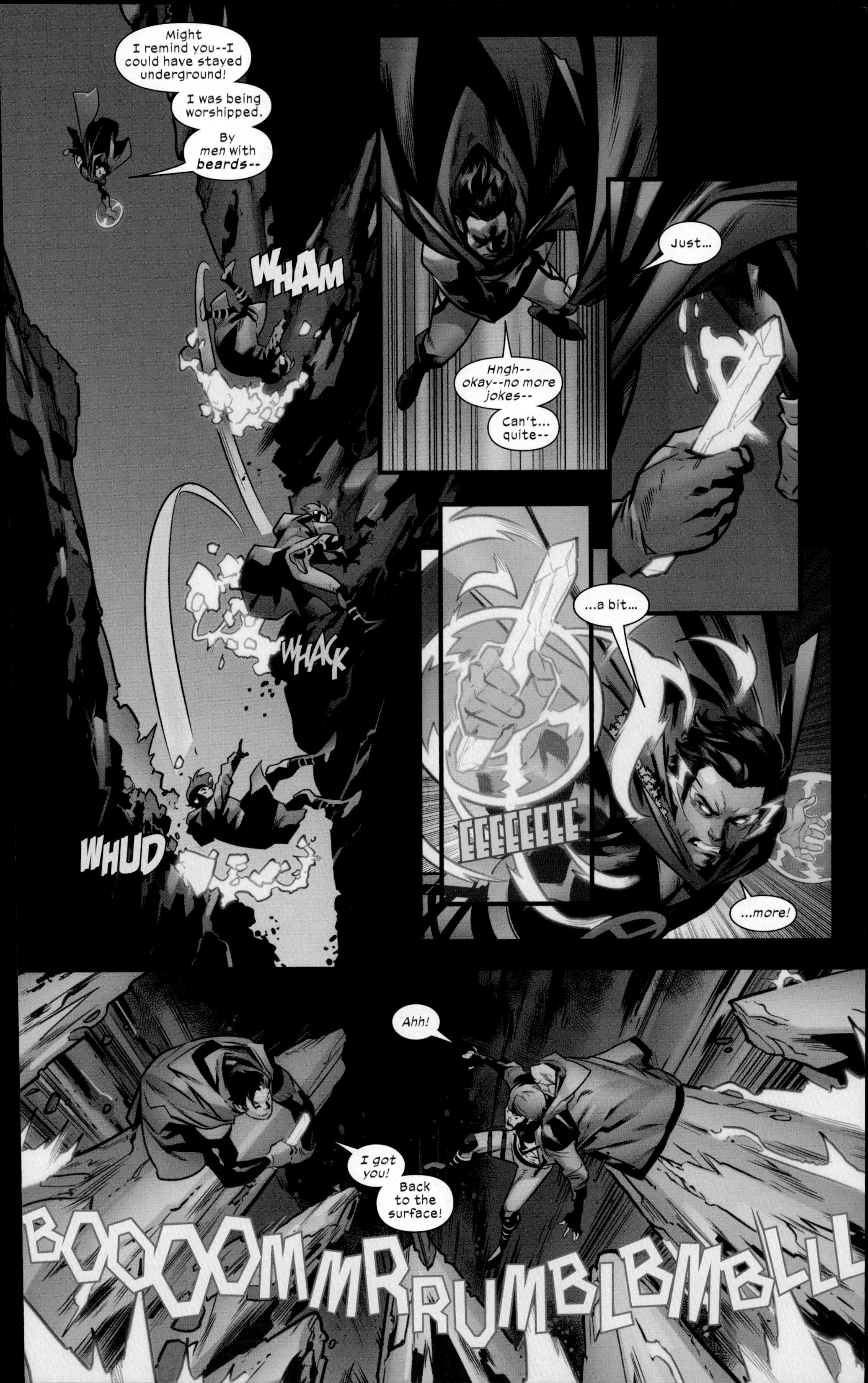
Might I remind you--I could have stayed underground!
I was being worshipped.
By men with beards--
WHAM
WHACK
WHUD
Hngh--okay--no more jokes--
Can't... quite--
Just...
...a bit...
EEEEEEEE
...more!
Ahh!
I got you!
Back to the surface!
BOOOOMMRRUMBLBMBLLL

[00_so_below_X]
[00_as_above_X]

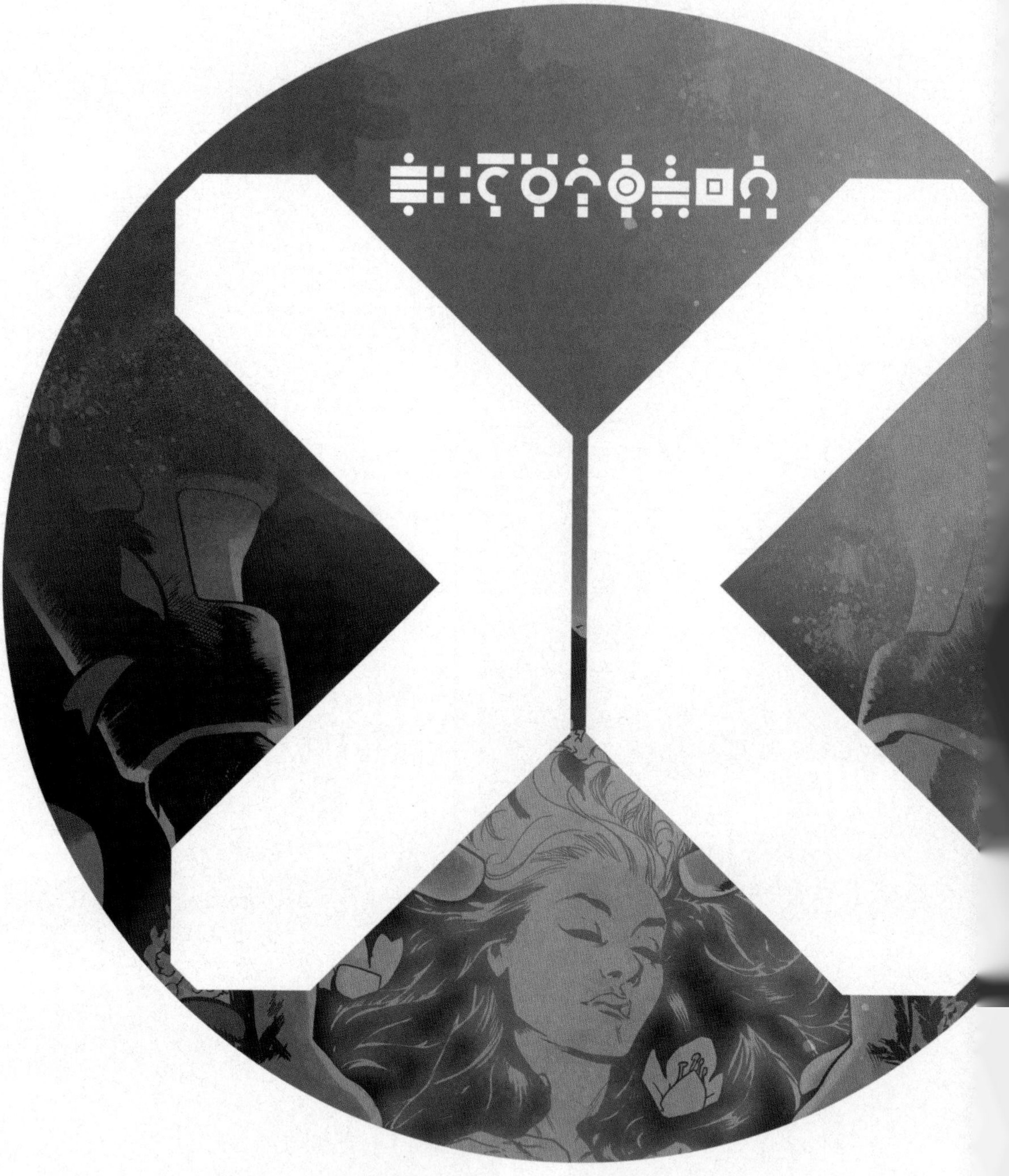

[00_so_below_X
[00_as_above_X]

TINI HOWARD....................................[WRITER]
MARCUS TO......................................[ARTIST]
ERICK ARCINIEGA..........................[COLOR ARTIST]
VC's CORY PETIT..............................[LETTERER]
TOM MULLER.....................................[DESIGN]

MAHMUD ASRAR & MATTHEW WILSON...........[COVER ARTISTS]

WILL SLINEY & DAVID CURIEL; PHILIP TAN & RAIN BEREDO...
...............................[VARIANT COVER ARTISTS]

NICK RUSSELL..............................[PRODUCTION]

JONATHAN HICKMAN............................[HEAD OF X]
ANNALISE BISSA........................[ASSISTANT EDITOR]
JORDAN D. WHITE...............................[EDITOR]
C.B. CEBULSKI.........................[EDITOR IN CHIEF]

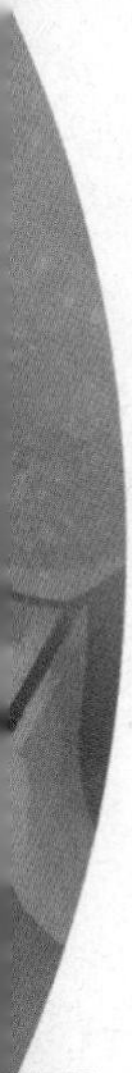

[05] EXCALIBUR

[ISSUE FIVE].....................VERSE V:
...........PANIC ON THE STREETS OF LONDON

[00_so_below_X]
[00_as_above_X]

[00_00.....0]
[00_00.....5]

[00_greater_]
[00_secrets_]

[00________]

[00_exist___]

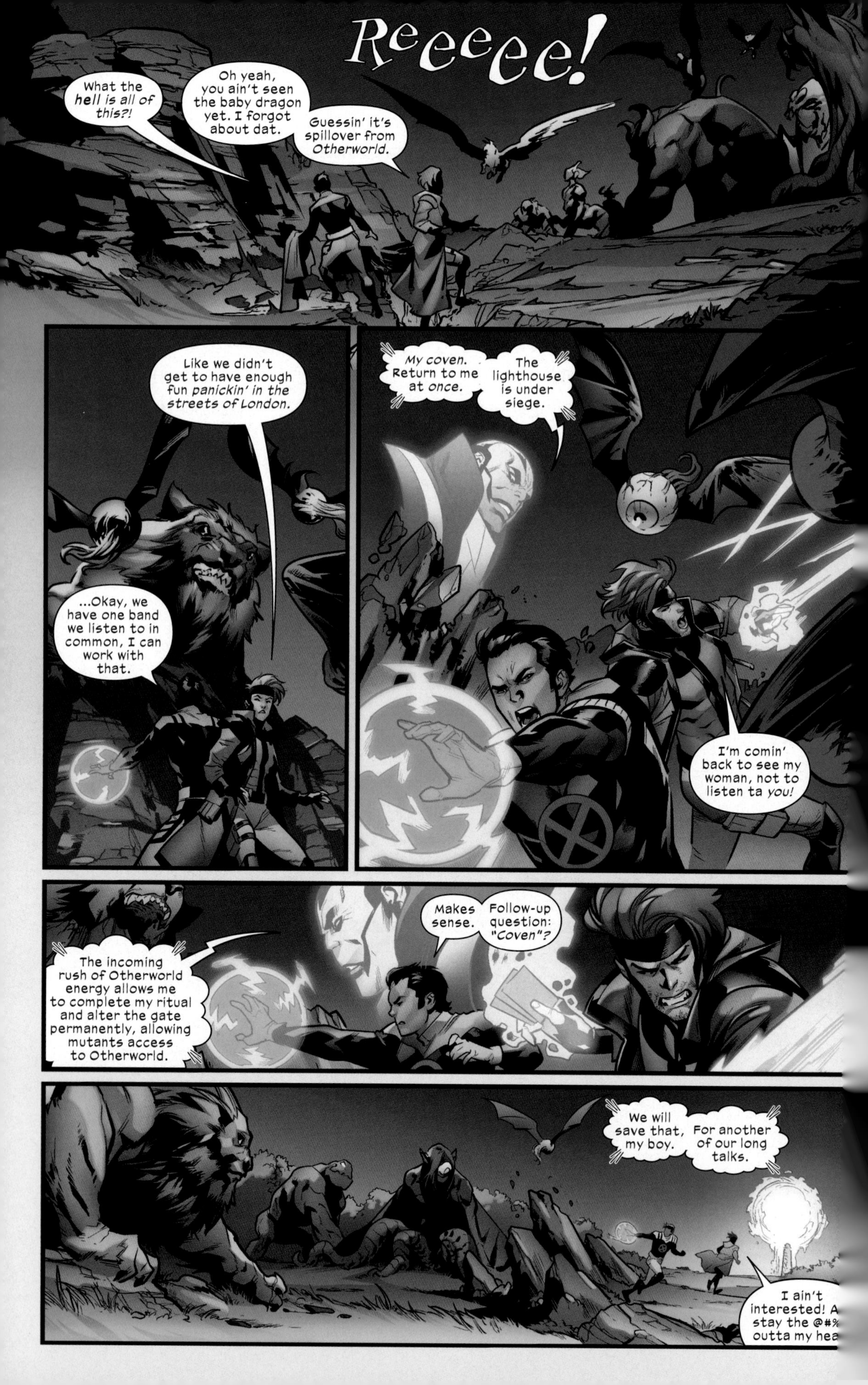
Reeeee!
What the hell is all of this?!
Oh yeah, you ain't seen the baby dragon yet. I forgot about dat.
Guessin' it's spillover from Otherworld.
Like we didn't get to have enough fun panickin' in the streets of London.
...Okay, we have one band we listen to in common, I can work with that.
My coven. Return to me at once.
The lighthouse is under siege.
I'm comin' back to see my woman, not to listen ta you!
The incoming rush of Otherworld energy allows me to complete my ritual and alter the gate permanently, allowing mutants access to Otherworld.
Makes sense.
Follow-up question: "Coven"?
We will save that, my boy.
For another of our long talks.
I ain't interested! A stay the @#% outta my hea

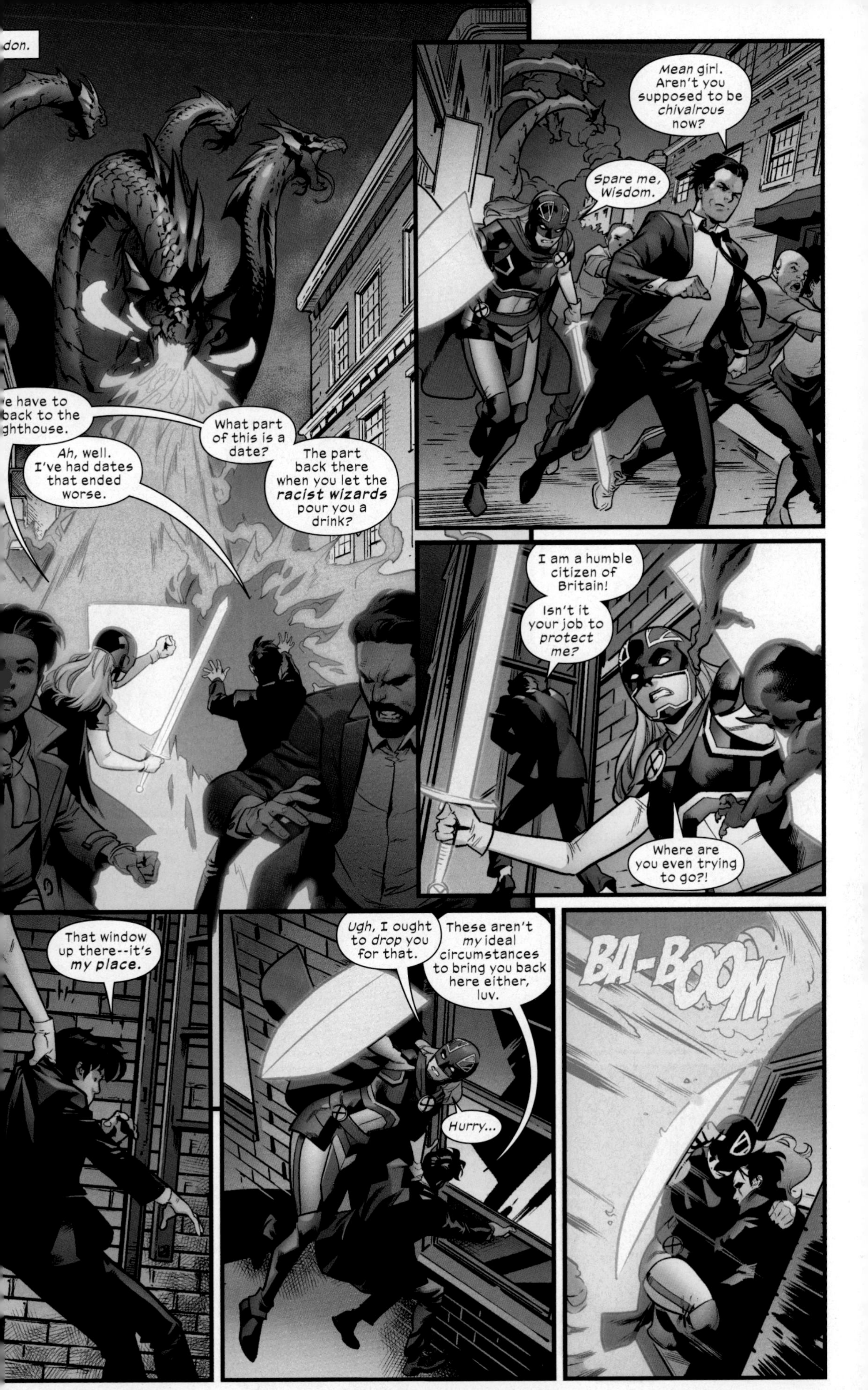
don.
Mean girl. Aren't you supposed to be *chivalrous* now?
Spare me, Wisdom.
e have to back to the ghthouse.
What part of this is a date?
Ah, well. I've had dates that ended worse.
The part back there when you let the ***racist wizards*** pour you a drink?
I am a humble citizen of Britain!
Isn't it your job to *protect* me?
Where are you even trying to go?!
That window up there--it's ***my place.***
Ugh, I ought to *drop* you for that.
These aren't *my* ideal circumstances to bring you back here either, luv.
Hurry...
BA-BOOM

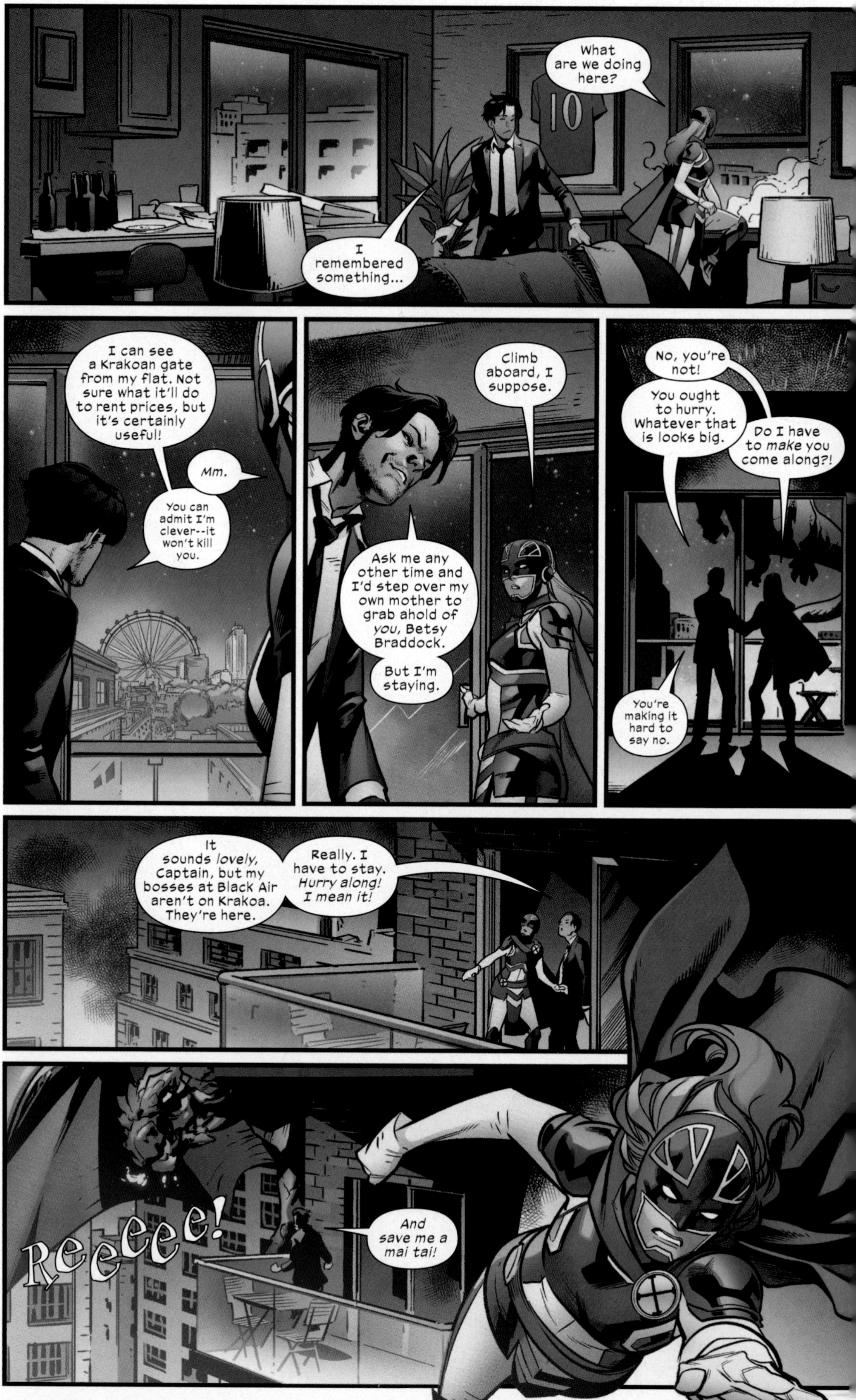
What are we doing here?
I remembered something...
I can see a Krakoan gate from my flat. Not sure what it'll do to rent prices, but it's certainly useful!
Mm.
You can admit I'm clever--it won't kill you.
Climb aboard, I suppose.
Ask me any other time and I'd step over my own mother to grab ahold of *you*, Betsy Braddock.
But I'm staying.
No, you're not!
You ought to hurry. Whatever that is looks big.
Do I have to *make* you come along?!
You're making it hard to say no.
It sounds *lovely*, Captain, but my bosses at Black Air aren't on Krakoa. They're here.
Really. I have to stay. *Hurry along! I mean it!*
Reeeee!
And save me a mai tai!

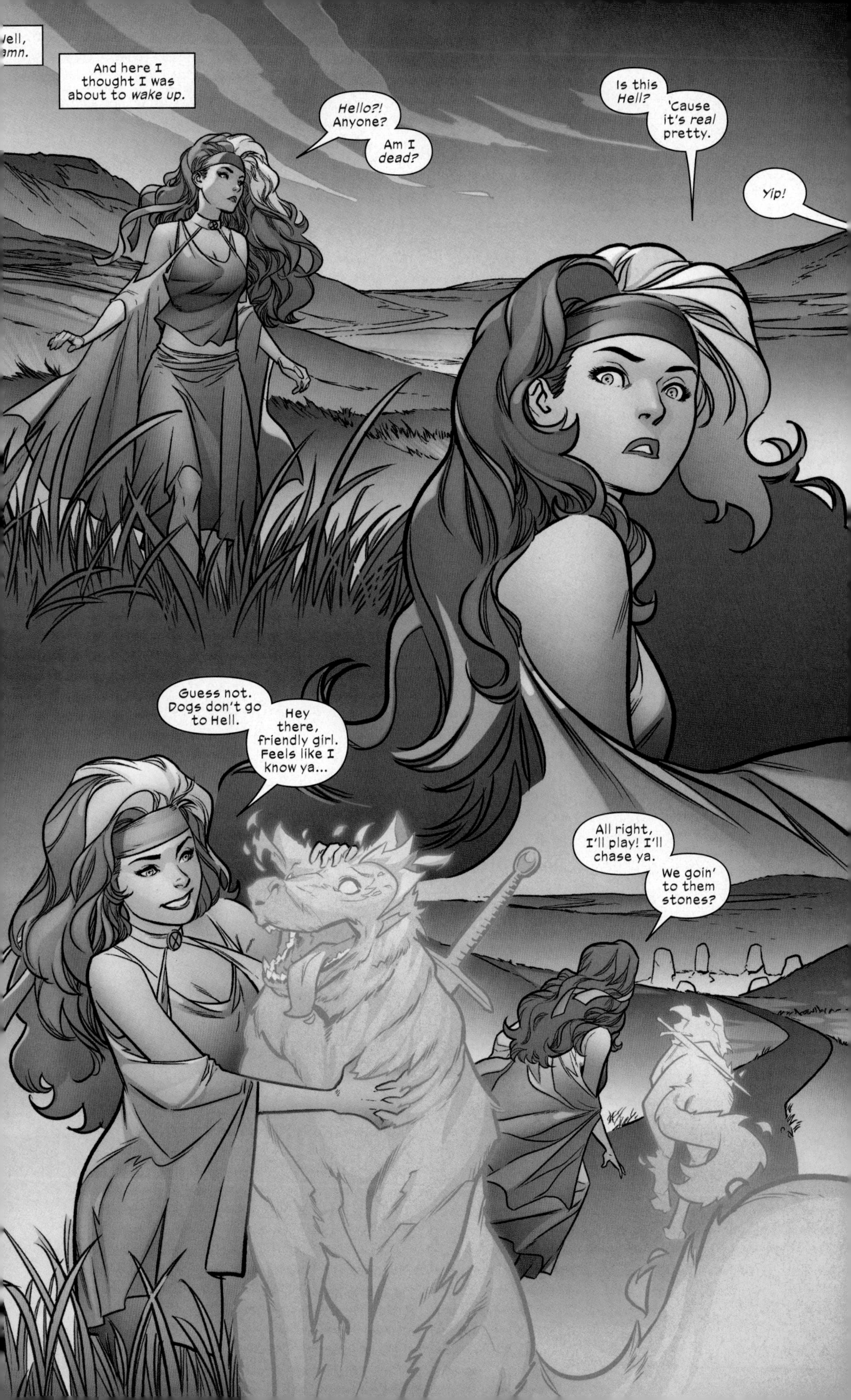
And here I thought I was about to *wake up.*
Hello?! Anyone?
Am I *dead?*
Is this *Hell?*
'Cause it's *real* pretty.
Yip!
Guess not. Dogs don't go to Hell.
Hey there, friendly girl. Feels like I know ya...
All right, I'll play! I'll chase ya.
We goin' to them stones?

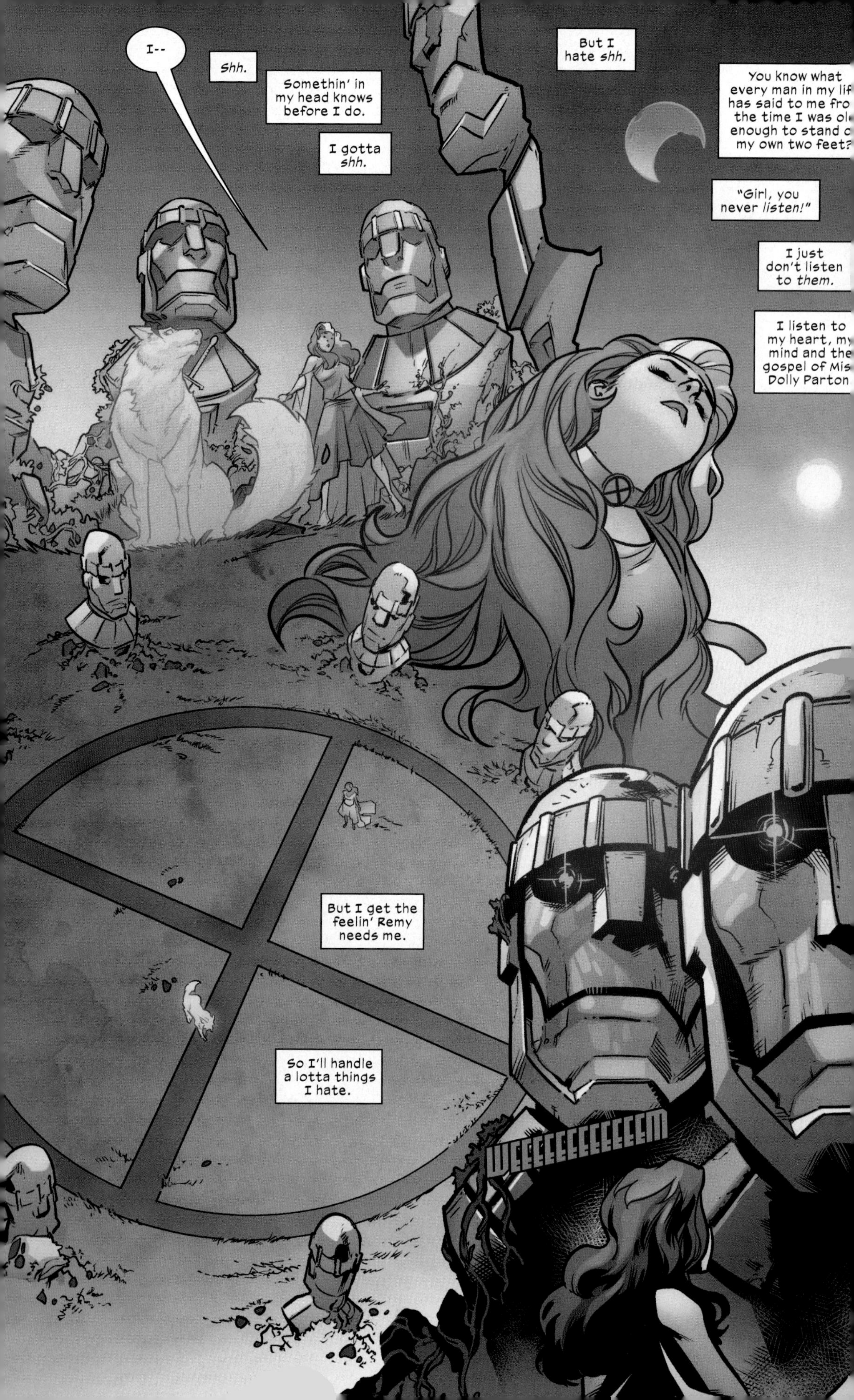
I--
Shh.
Somethin' in my head knows before I do.
I gotta shh.
But I hate shh.
You know what every man in my lif has said to me fro the time I was ol enough to stand c my own two feet?
"Girl, you never listen!"
I just don't listen to them.
I listen to my heart, my mind and the gospel of Mis Dolly Parton
But I get the feelin' Remy needs me.
So I'll handle a lotta things I hate.
WEEEEEEEEEEEEM

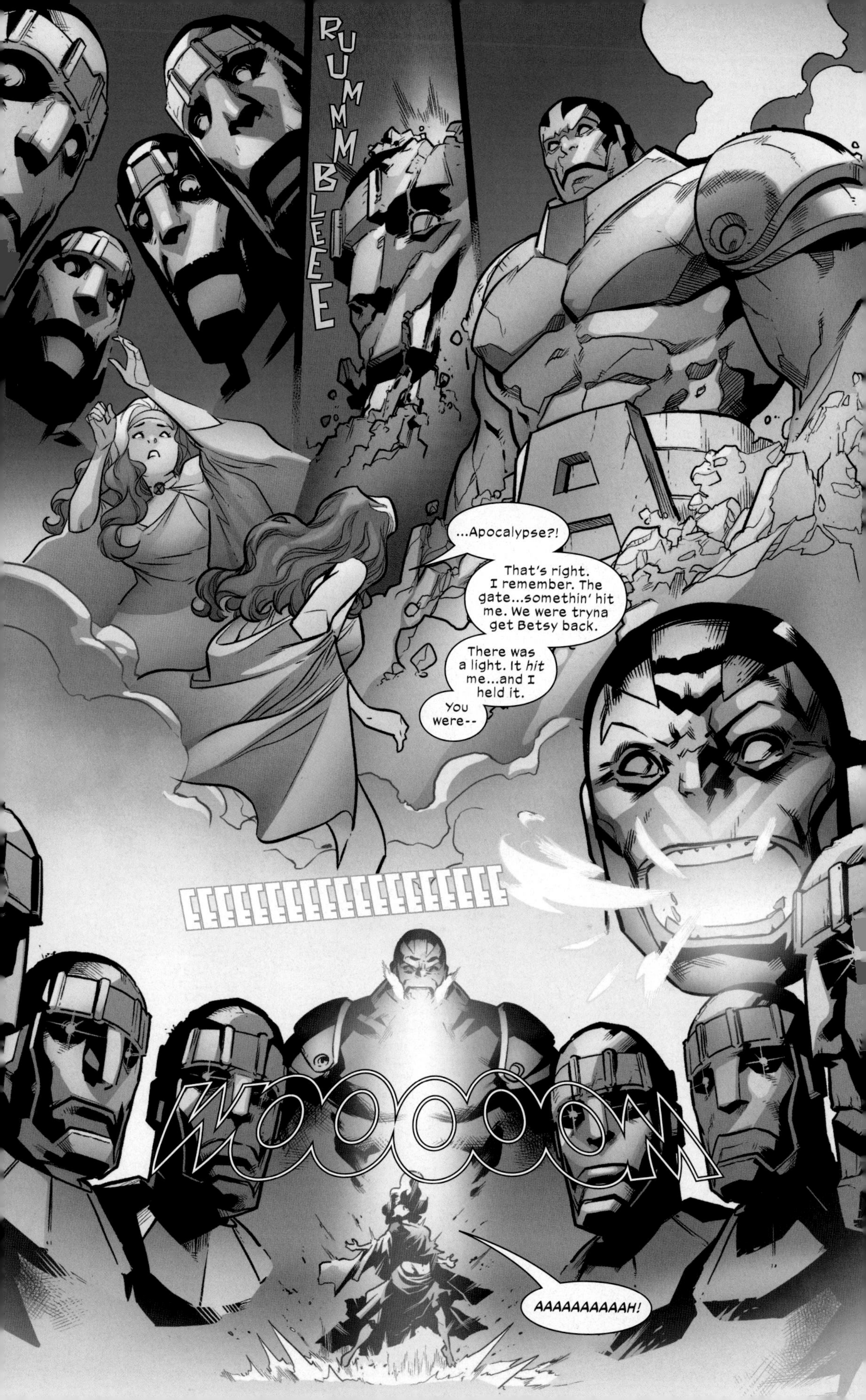
RUMMMBLEEEE
...Apocalypse?!
That's right. I remember. The gate...somethin' hit me. We were tryna get Betsy back.
There was a light. It *hit* me...and I held it.
You were--
EEEEEEEEEEEEEEEEEE
WOOOOOM
AAAAAAAAAAH!

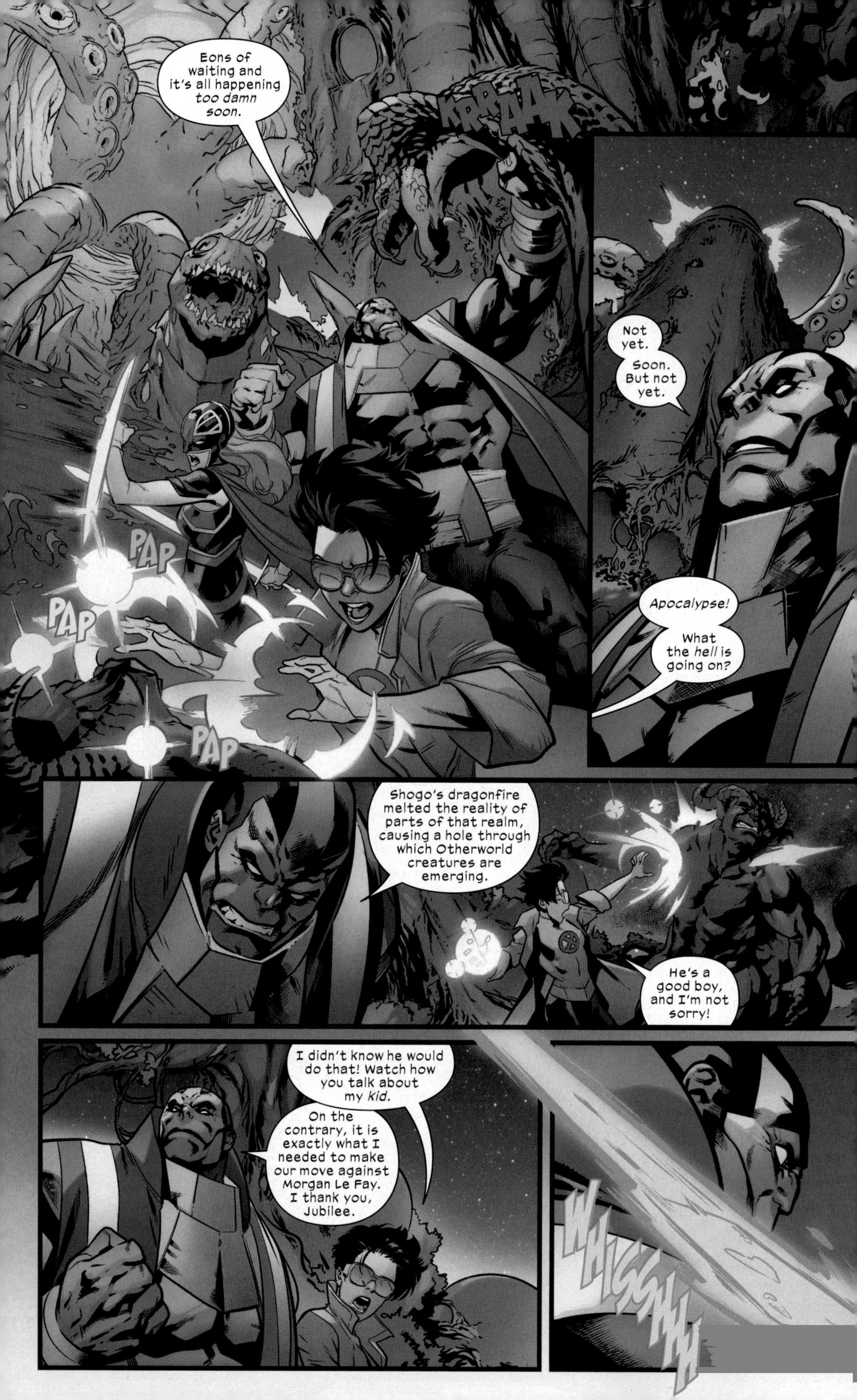
Eons of waiting and it's all happening *too damn* soon.
KRRAAAK
PAP
PAP
PAP
Not yet.
Soon. But not yet.
Apocalypse!
What the *hell* is going on?
Shogo's dragonfire melted the reality of parts of that realm, causing a hole through which Otherworld creatures are emerging.
He's a good boy, and I'm not sorry!
I didn't know he would do that! Watch how you talk about my *kid*.
On the contrary, it is exactly what I needed to make our move against Morgan Le Fay. I thank you, Jubilee.
WHISSHHH

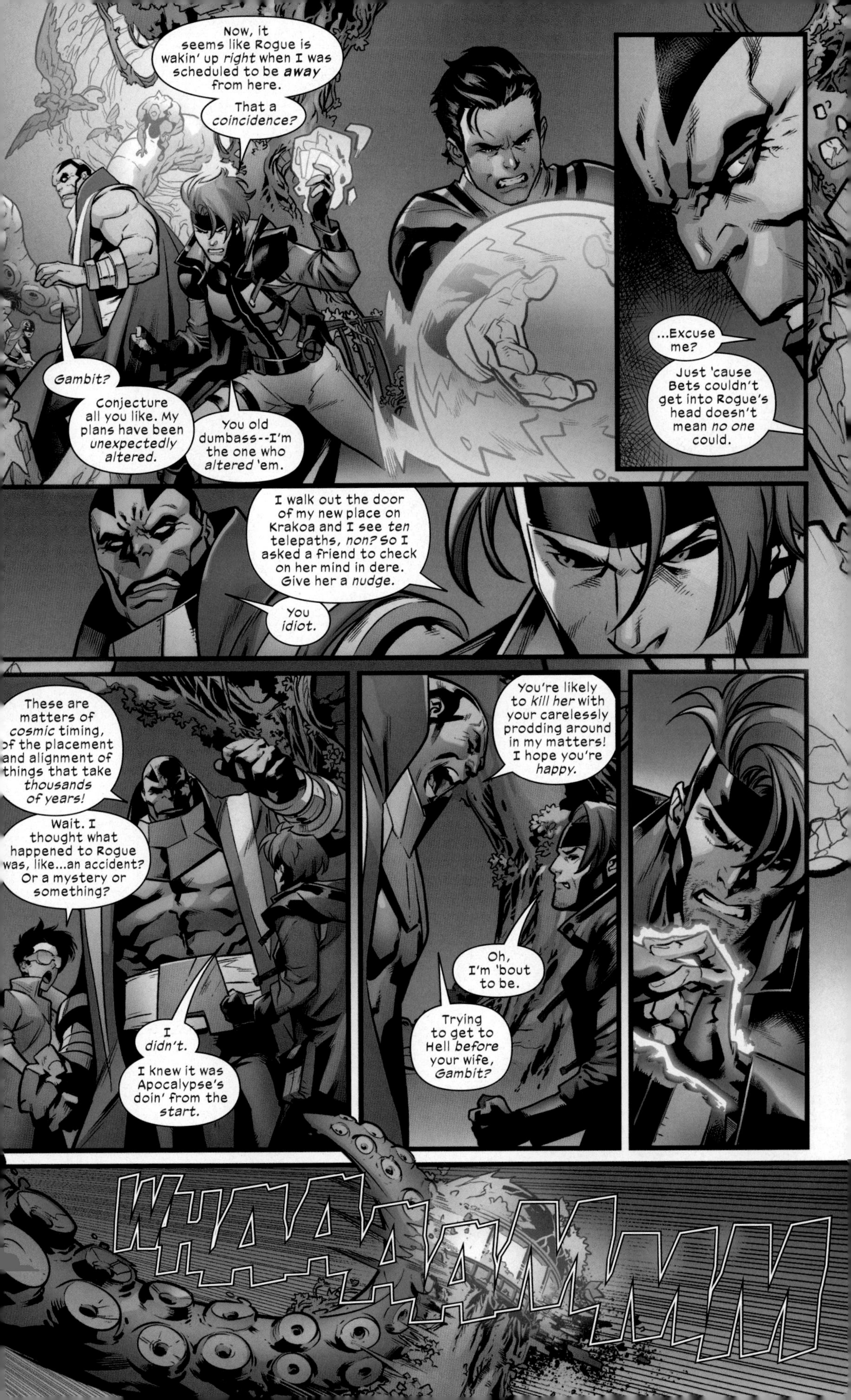

Now, it seems like Rogue is wakin' up *right* when I was scheduled to be *away* from here.
That a *coincidence?*
Gambit?
Conjecture all you like. My plans have been *unexpectedly altered.*
You old dumbass--I'm the one who *altered* 'em.
...Excuse me?
Just 'cause Bets couldn't get into Rogue's head doesn't mean *no one* could.
I walk out the door of my new place on Krakoa and I see *ten* telepaths, *non?* So I asked a friend to check on her mind in dere. Give her a *nudge*.
You *idiot.*
These are matters of *cosmic* timing, of the placement and alignment of things that take *thousands* of years!
Wait. I thought what happened to Rogue was, like...an accident? Or a mystery or something?
I *didn't.*
I knew it was Apocalypse's doin' from the *start.*
You're likely to *kill her* with your carelessly prodding around in my matters! I hope you're *happy.*
Oh, I'm 'bout to be.
Trying to get to Hell *before* your wife, *Gambit?*
WHAAAAMMM

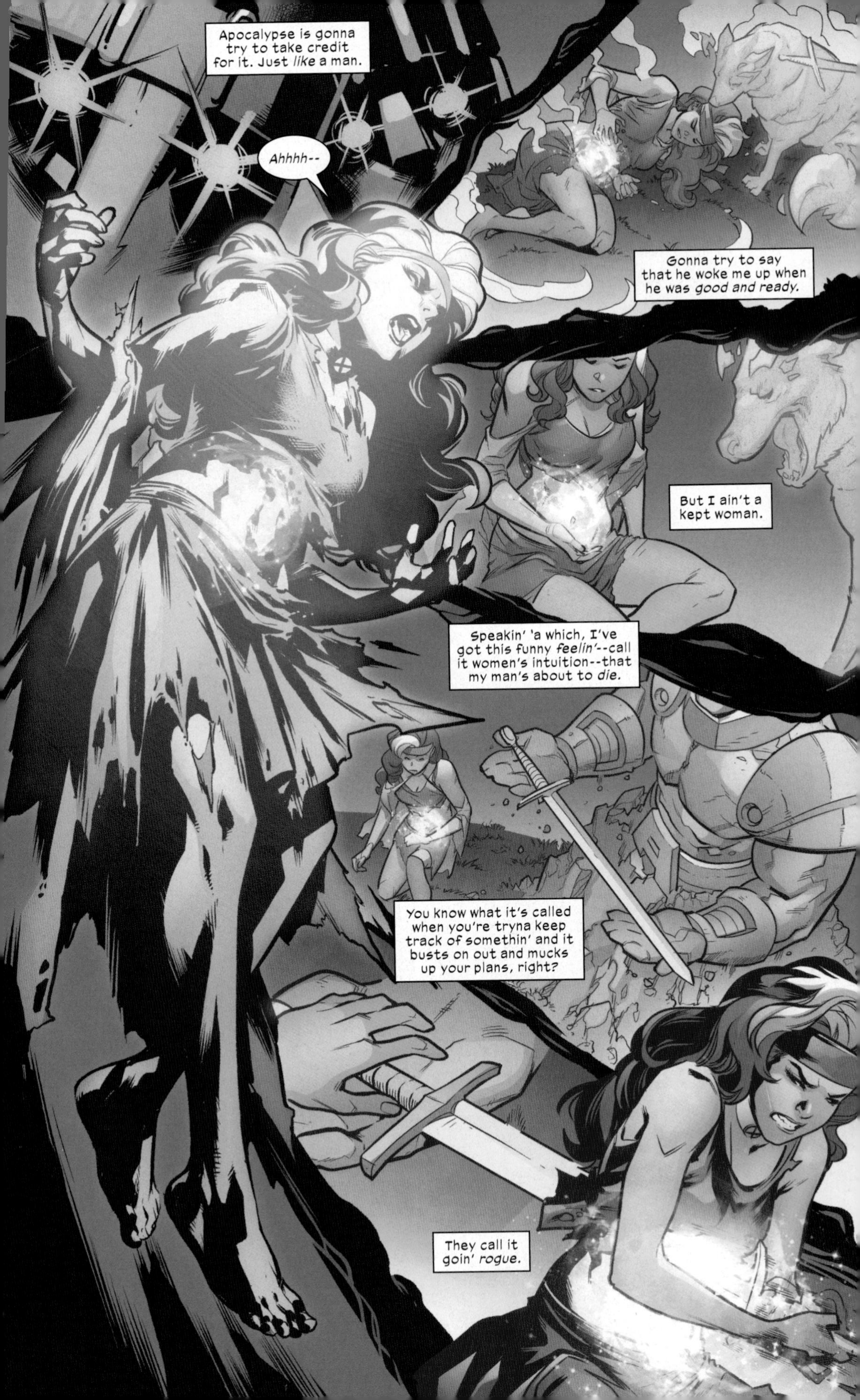
Apocalypse is gonna try to take credit for it. Just *like* a man.
Ahhhh--
Gonna try to say that he woke me up when he was *good and ready.*
But I ain't a kept woman.
Speakin' 'a which, I've got this funny *feelin'*--call it women's intuition--that my man's about to *die.*
You know what it's called when you're tryna keep track of somethin' and it busts on out and mucks up your plans, right?
They call it goin' *rogue.*

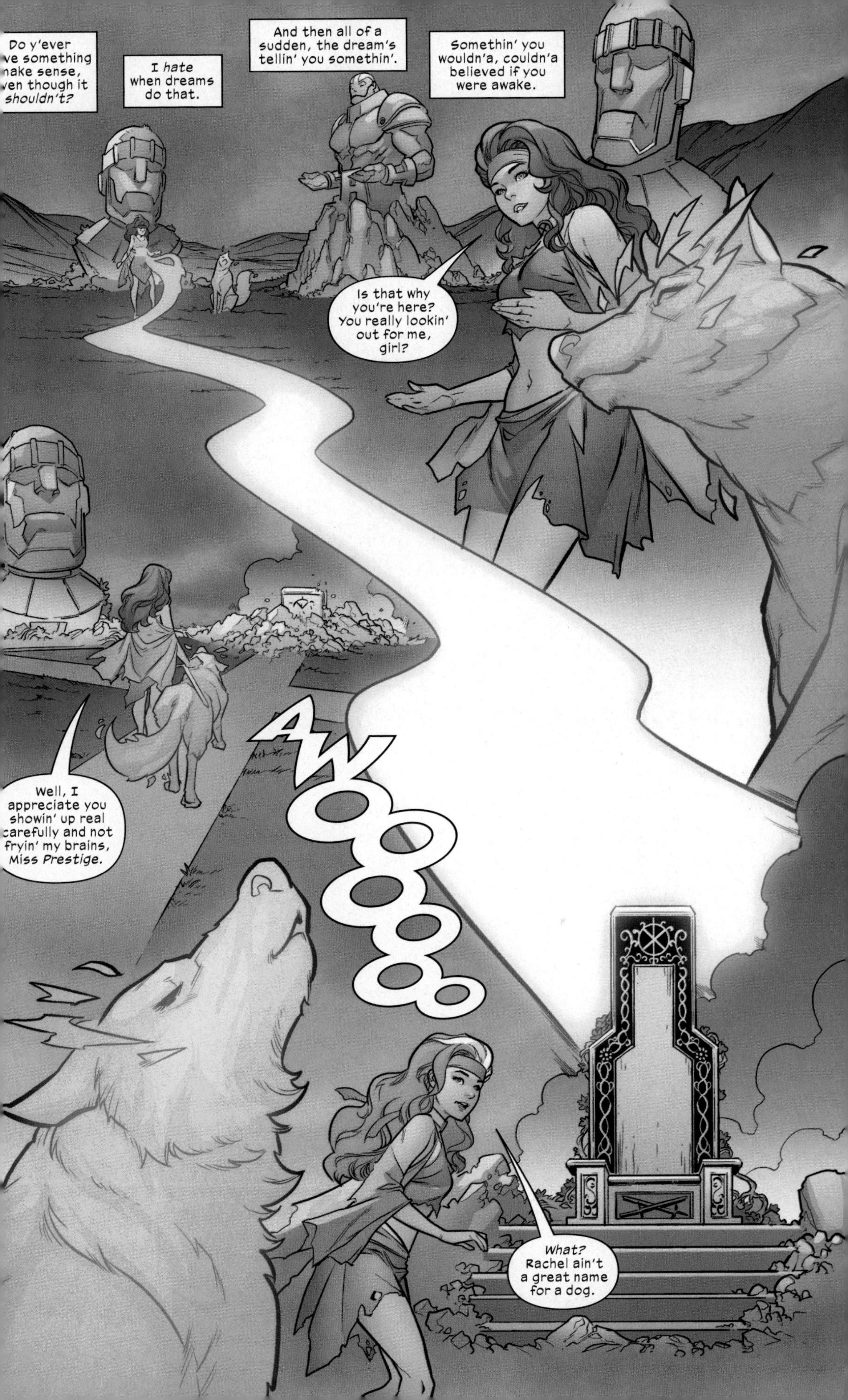

Do y'ever
ve something
nake sense,
ven though it
shouldn't?
I *hate* when dreams do that.
And then all of a sudden, the dream's tellin' you somethin'.
Somethin' you wouldn'a, couldn'a believed if you were awake.
Is that why you're here? You really lookin' out for me, girl?
Well, I appreciate you showin' up real carefully and not fryin' my brains, Miss *Prestige*.
AWOOOOOO
What? Rachel ain't a great name for a dog.

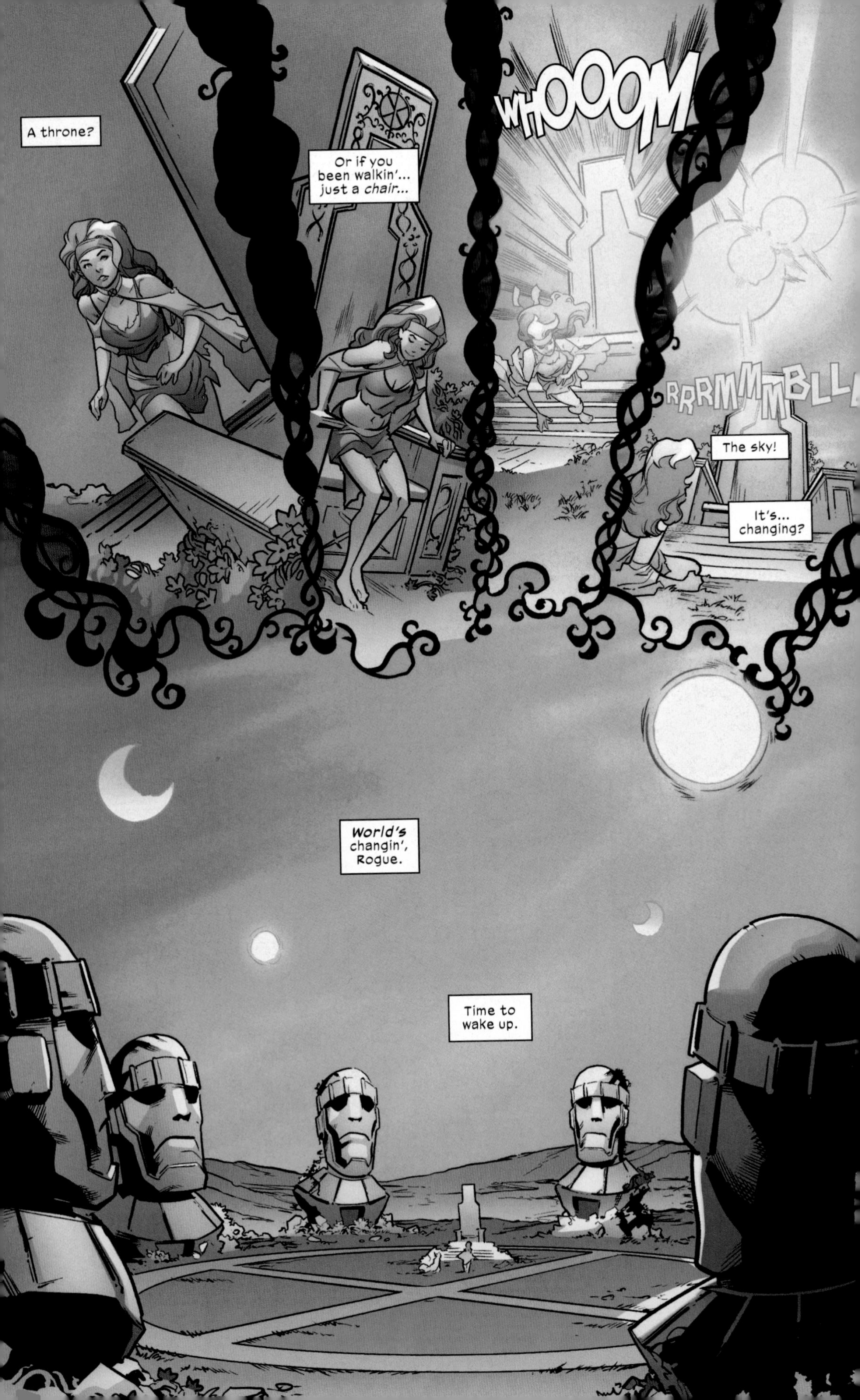
A throne?
Or if you been walkin'... just a chair...
WHOOOM
RRRMMMMBLL
The sky!
It's... changing?
World's changin', Rogue.
Time to wake up.

FROM THE GRIMOIRE OF

EX MAGICA: ALMANAC (Fig. 1)

APEX
CONDUIT

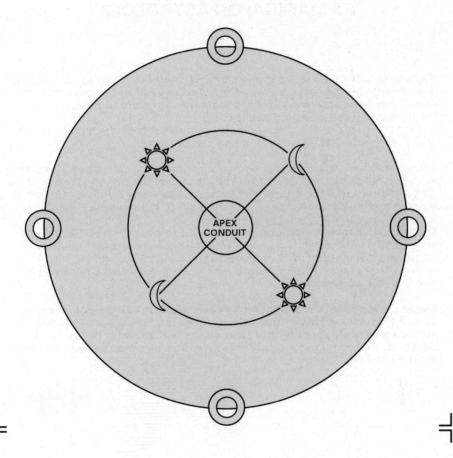

1. :: SUN AND MOON SIMULTANEOUSLY PRESENT IN OPPOSITION

2. :: CONDUIT ARRIVAL TWINS SUN AND MOON

3. :: SUNS AND MOONS TRANSIT TO SQUARE

4. :: CONDUIT FORMS QUINCUNX OF SOLAR/LUNAR SQUARE

[ava_[0.5]...]
[lon_[0.5]...]

[GRIMOIRE....]

FROM THE GRIMOIRE OF

EX MAGICA: ON ASTROLOGY

Regarding astrology: It is beyond the knowledge of stars to attempt to divine the actions of others or foreknow future events; the use of cosmic knowledge and placement for such matters of ego are foolish, likened to the lightning itself worrying about the preference of the grain of sand it might strike. It is in this that ego poisons the magic of the individual, the magic of the mortal and the magic of the *Sapiens*.

Among mortals, the sentiment of being "under the same sky" persists in the form of modern romantic folly, culturally seeking to comfort a perceived distance by a reminder of shared heavenly bodies. However, modern human settlements know very little of community.

The earliest human communities recalled the ego-destroying power of sky and, prior to the building of settlement walls, had no place upon which to stack a ceiling. But with the walls that divided humankind came the ceilings that blocked them from the sky, the most exact almanac given to *creatures of every realm*.

Theory: X-gene possession inherently seeks quincunx alignment for higher power formation. This is the true purpose of *Homo superior*. Mutant abilities are purely phenotypical expressions that allow for higher survival capability and an increased ability to exist as a communal organism with shared interest.

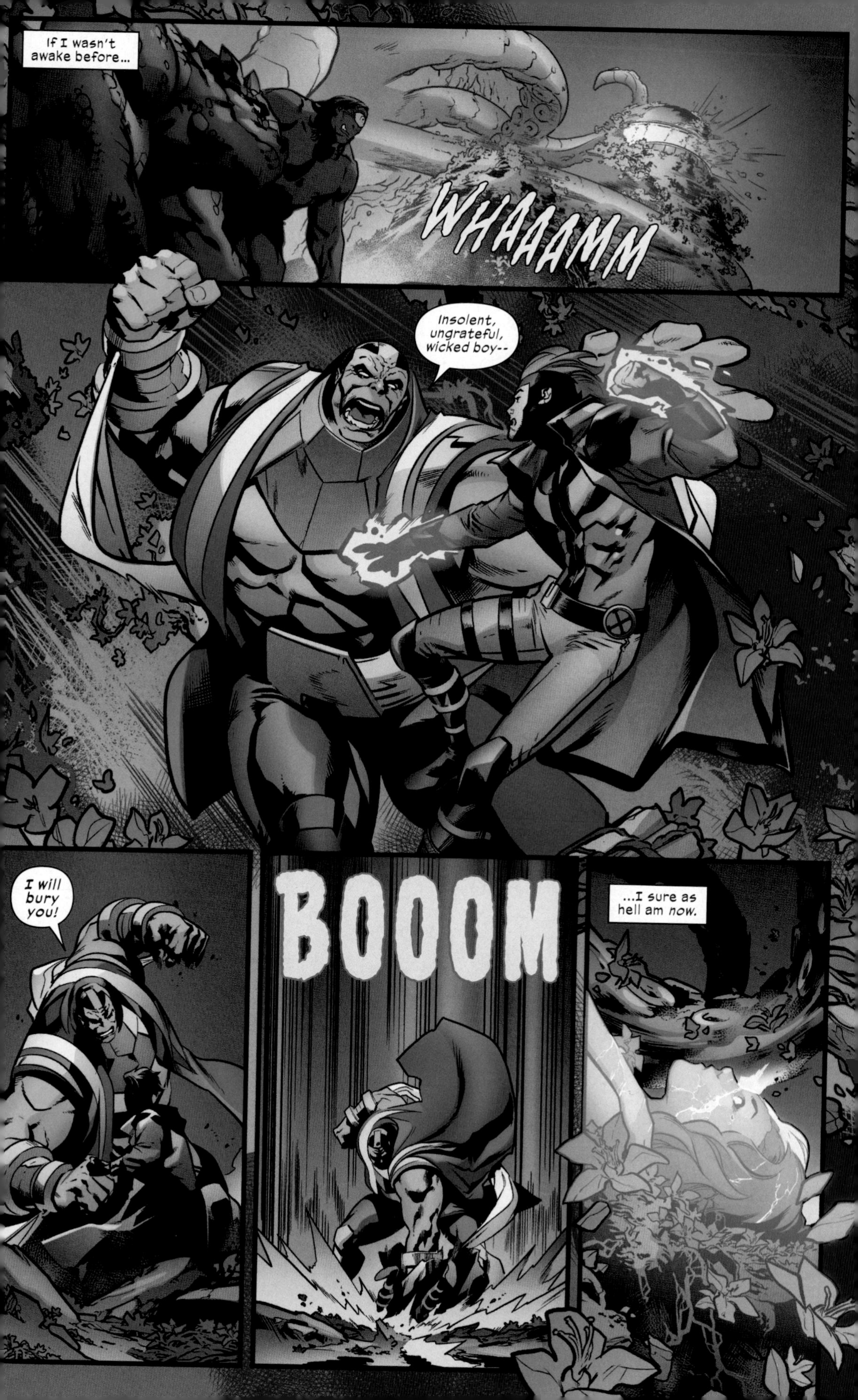
If I wasn't awake before...
WHAAAMM
Insolent, ungrateful, wicked boy--
I will bury you!
BOOOM
...I sure as hell am now.

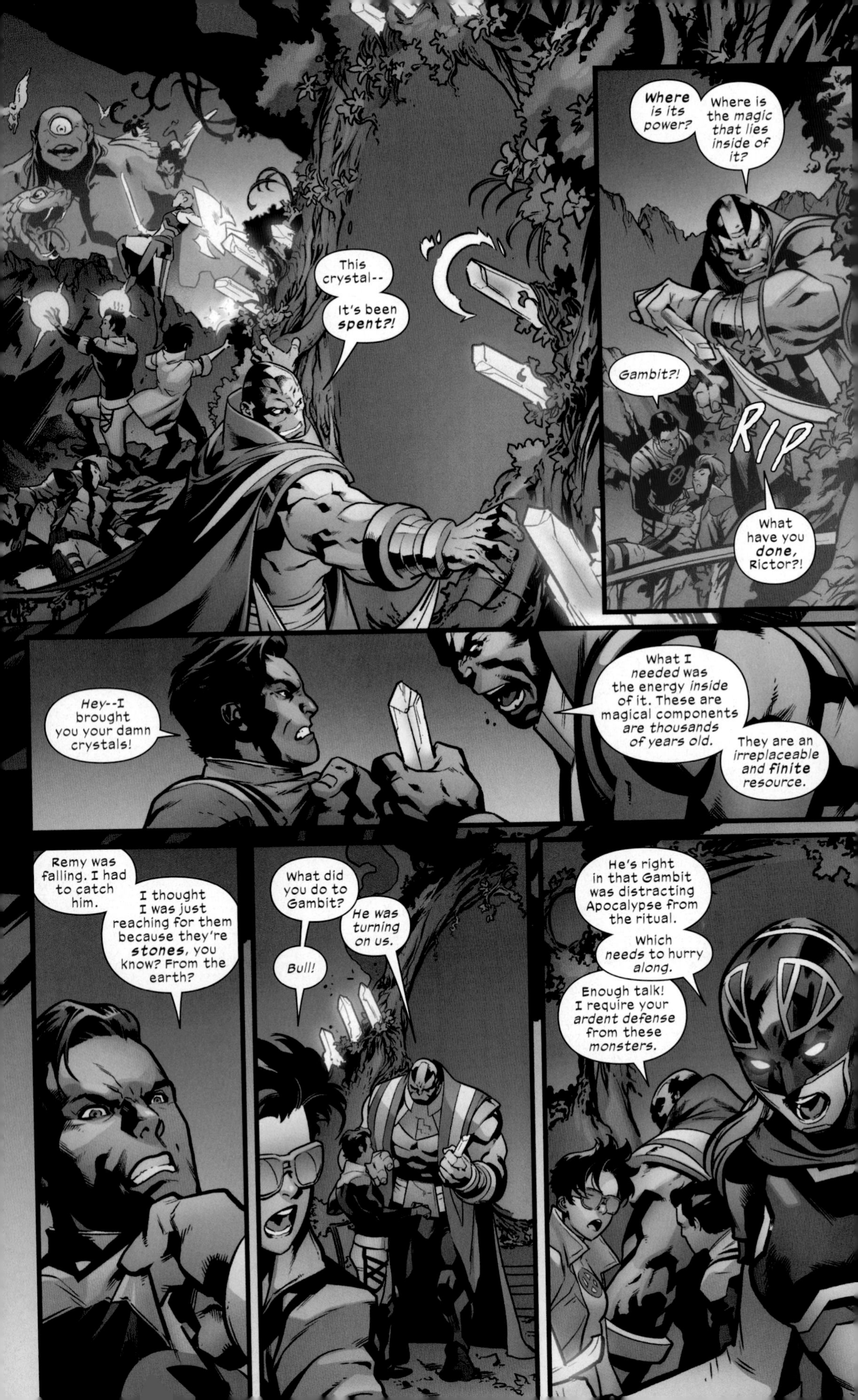
This crystal--
It's been *spent?!*
Where is its power?
Where is the *magic* that lies inside of it?
Gambit?!
RIP
What have you *done,* Rictor?!
Hey--I brought you your damn crystals!
What I *needed* was the energy *inside* of it. These are magical components *are thousands of years old.*
They are an *irreplaceable* and **finite** resource.
Remy was falling. I had to catch him.
I thought I was just reaching for them because they're **stones**, you know? From the earth?
What did you do to Gambit?
He was turning on us.
Bull!
He's right in that Gambit was distracting Apocalypse from the ritual.
Which *needs* to hurry *along.*
Enough talk! I require your *ardent defense* from these *monsters.*

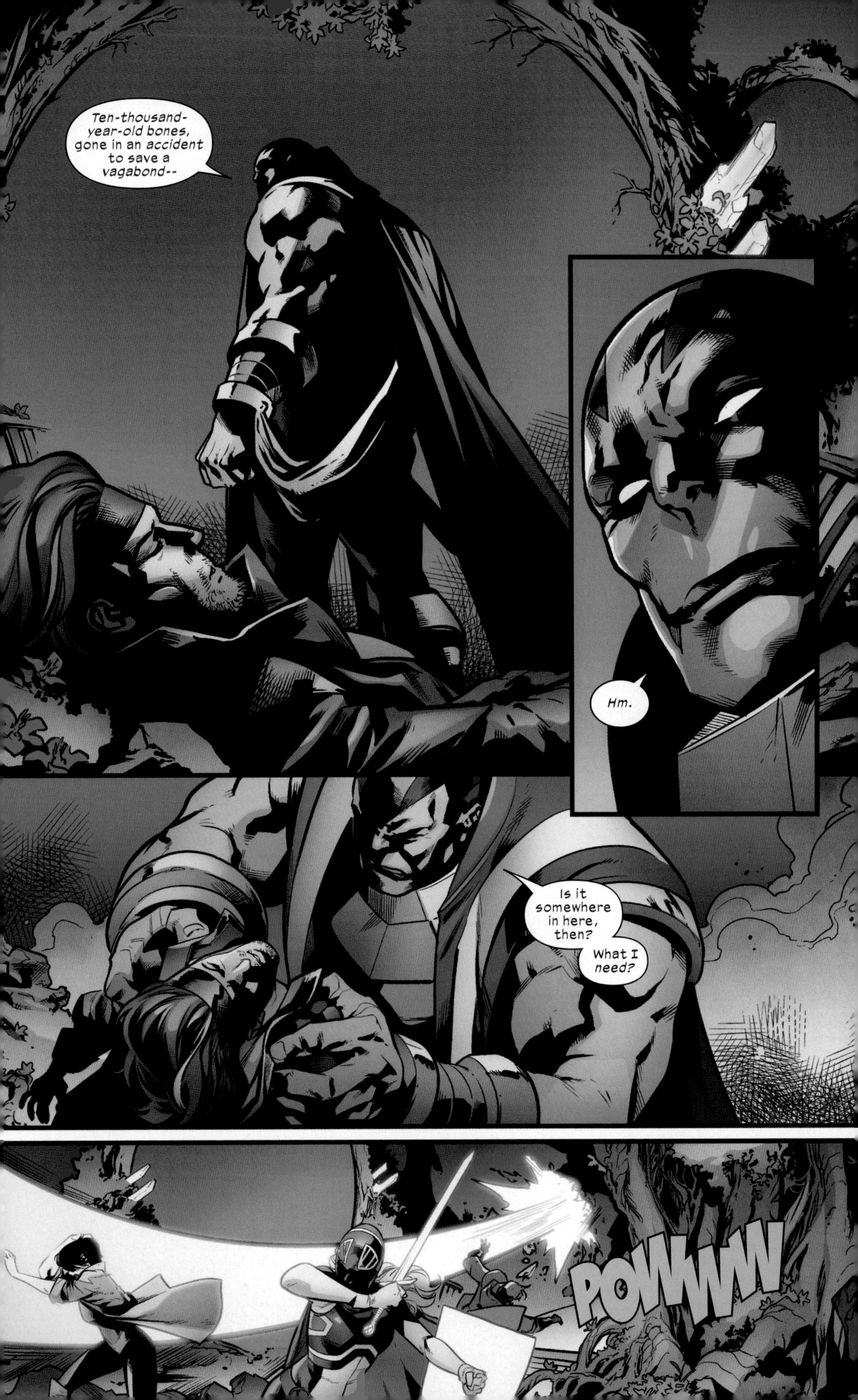
Ten-thousand-year-old bones, gone in an accident to save a vagabond--
Hm.
Is it somewhere in here, then?
What I need?
POWWW

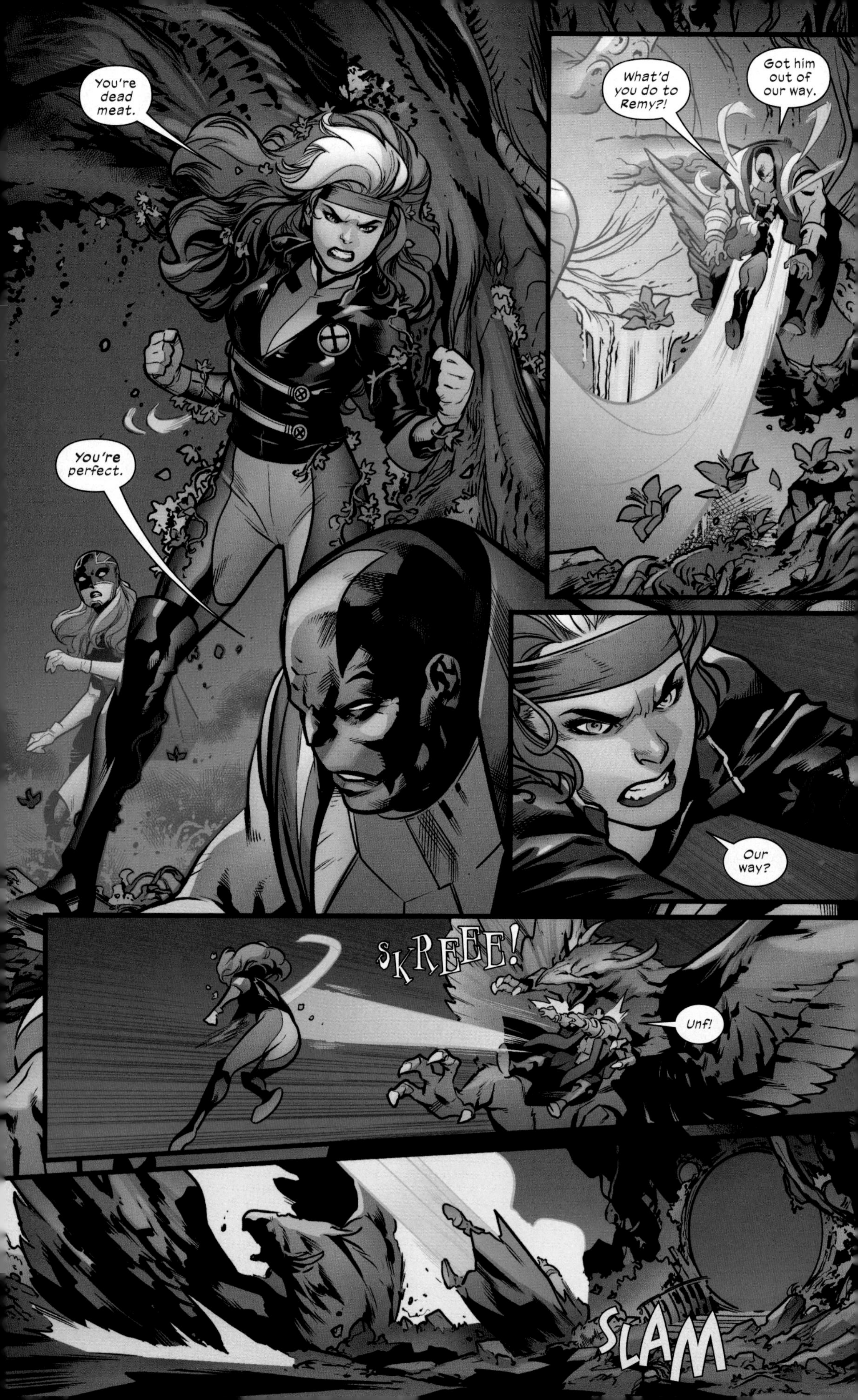
You're dead meat.
You're perfect.
What'd you do to Remy?!
Got him out of our way.
Our way?
SKREEE!
Unf!
SLAM

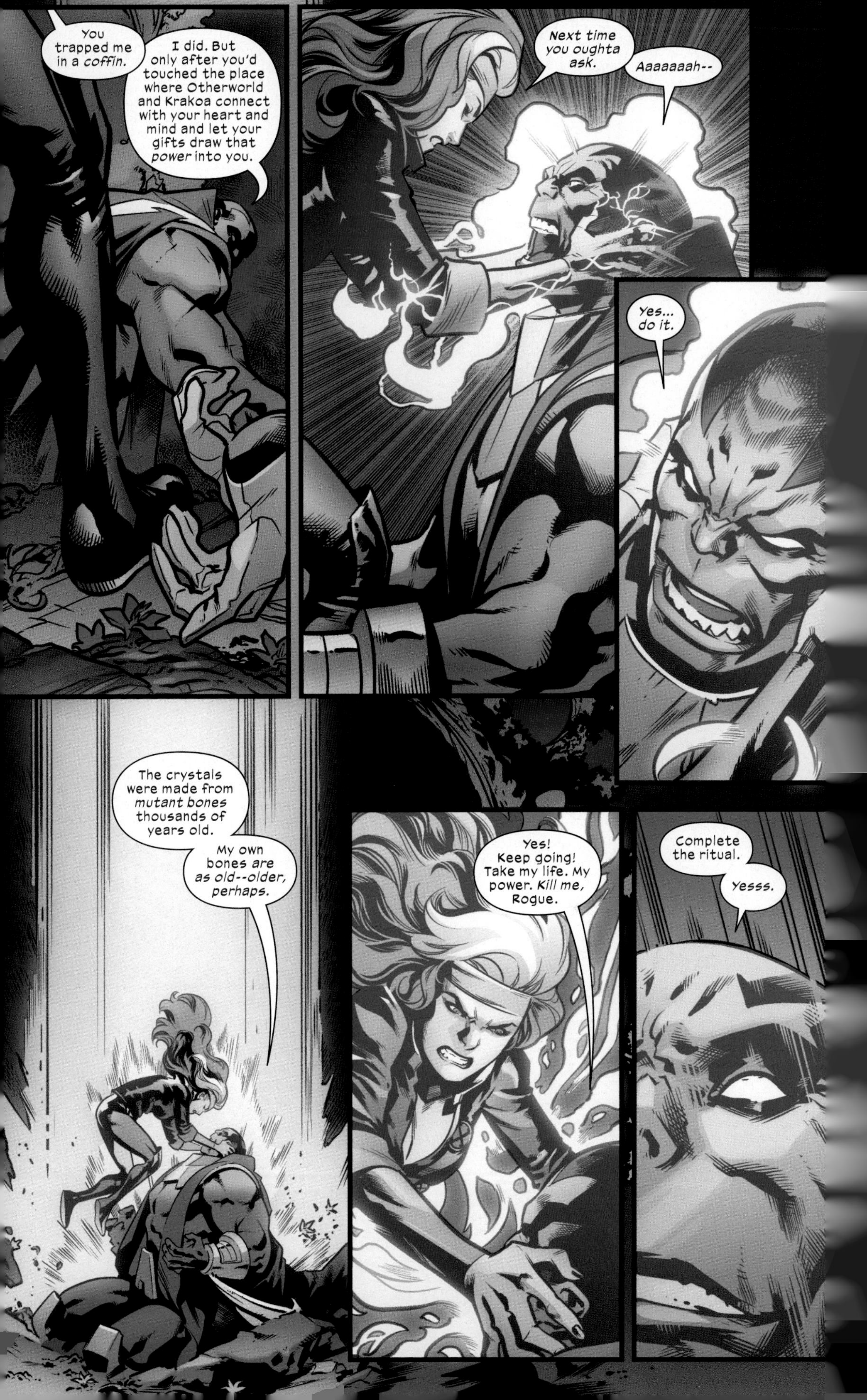
You trapped me in a *coffin.*
I did. But only after you'd touched the place where Otherworld and Krakoa connect with your heart and mind and let your gifts draw that *power* into you.
Next time you oughta ask.
Aaaaaaah--
Yes... do it.
The crystals were made from *mutant bones* thousands of years old.
My own bones *are* as *old*--*older*, perhaps.
Yes! Keep going! Take my life. My power. *Kill me,* Rogue.
Complete the ritual.
Yesss.

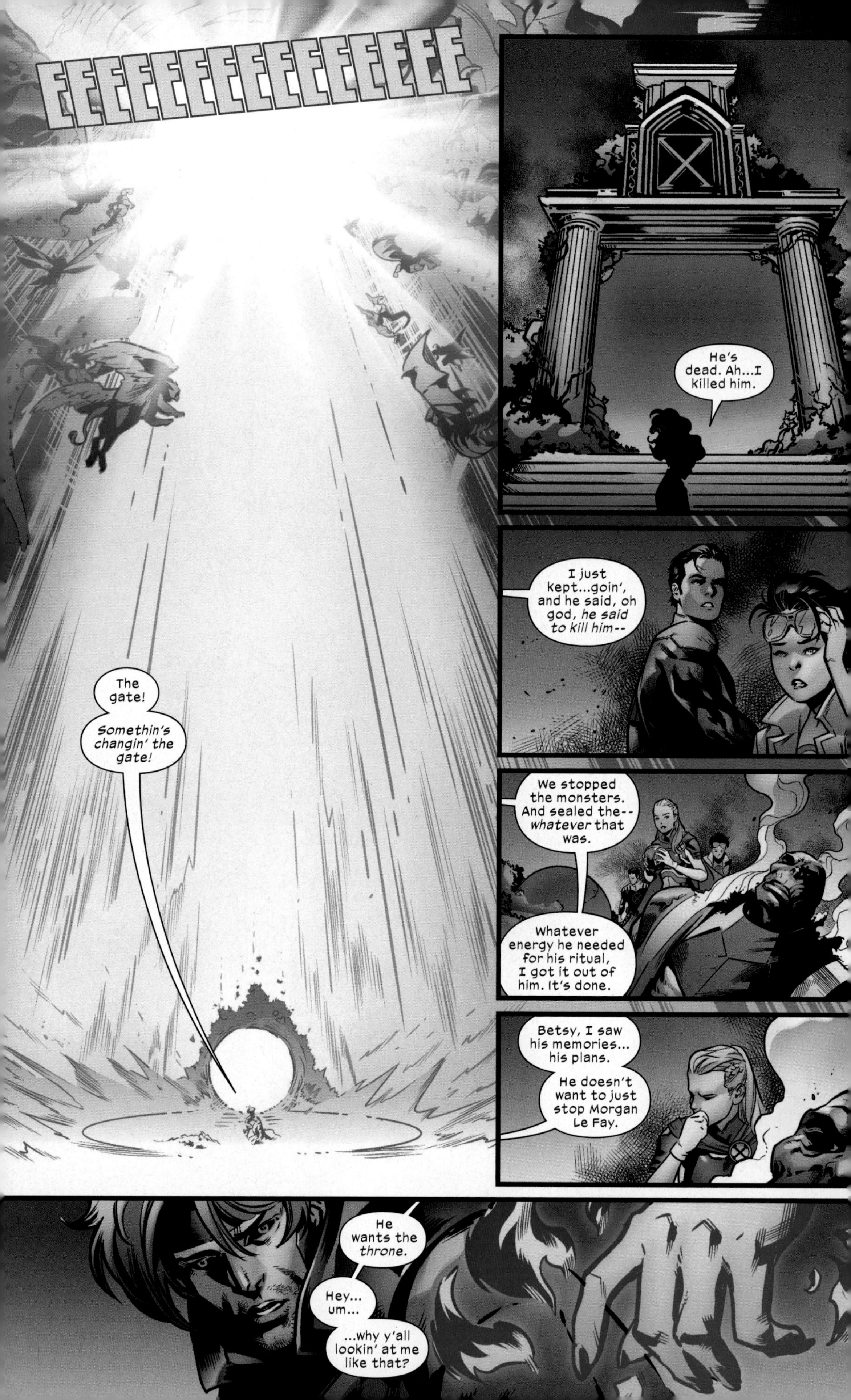
EEEEEEEEEEEEEEEE
He's dead. Ah...I killed him.
I just kept...goin', and he said, oh god, *he said to kill him--*
We stopped the monsters. And sealed the-- *whatever* that was.
Whatever energy he needed for his ritual, I got it out of him. It's done.
Betsy, I saw his memories... his plans.
He doesn't want to just stop Morgan Le Fay.
The gate!
Somethin's changin' the gate!
He wants the *throne.*
Hey... um...
...why y'all lookin' at me like that?

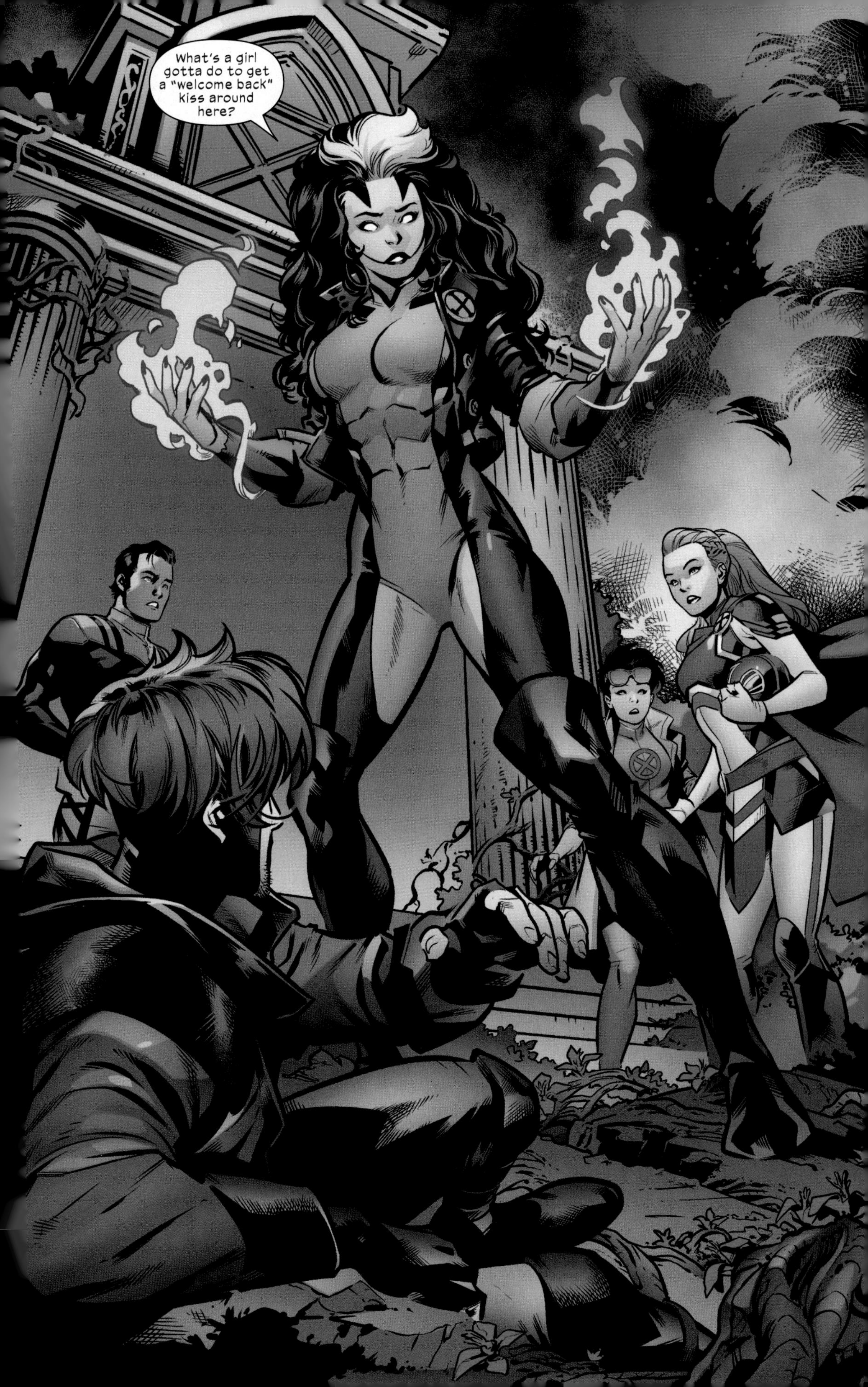
What's a girl gotta do to get a "welcome back" kiss around here?

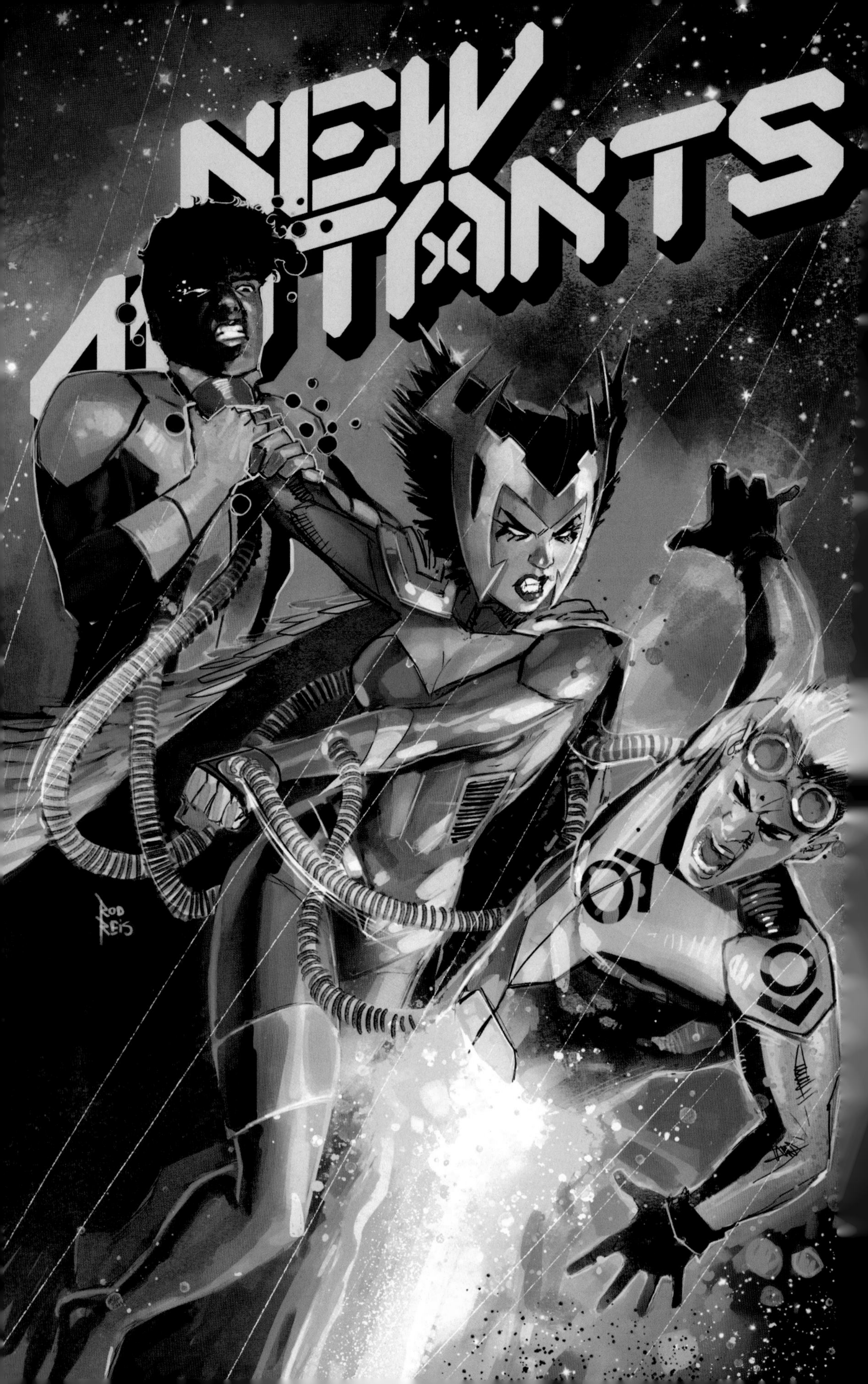
NEW MUTANTS
ROD REIS

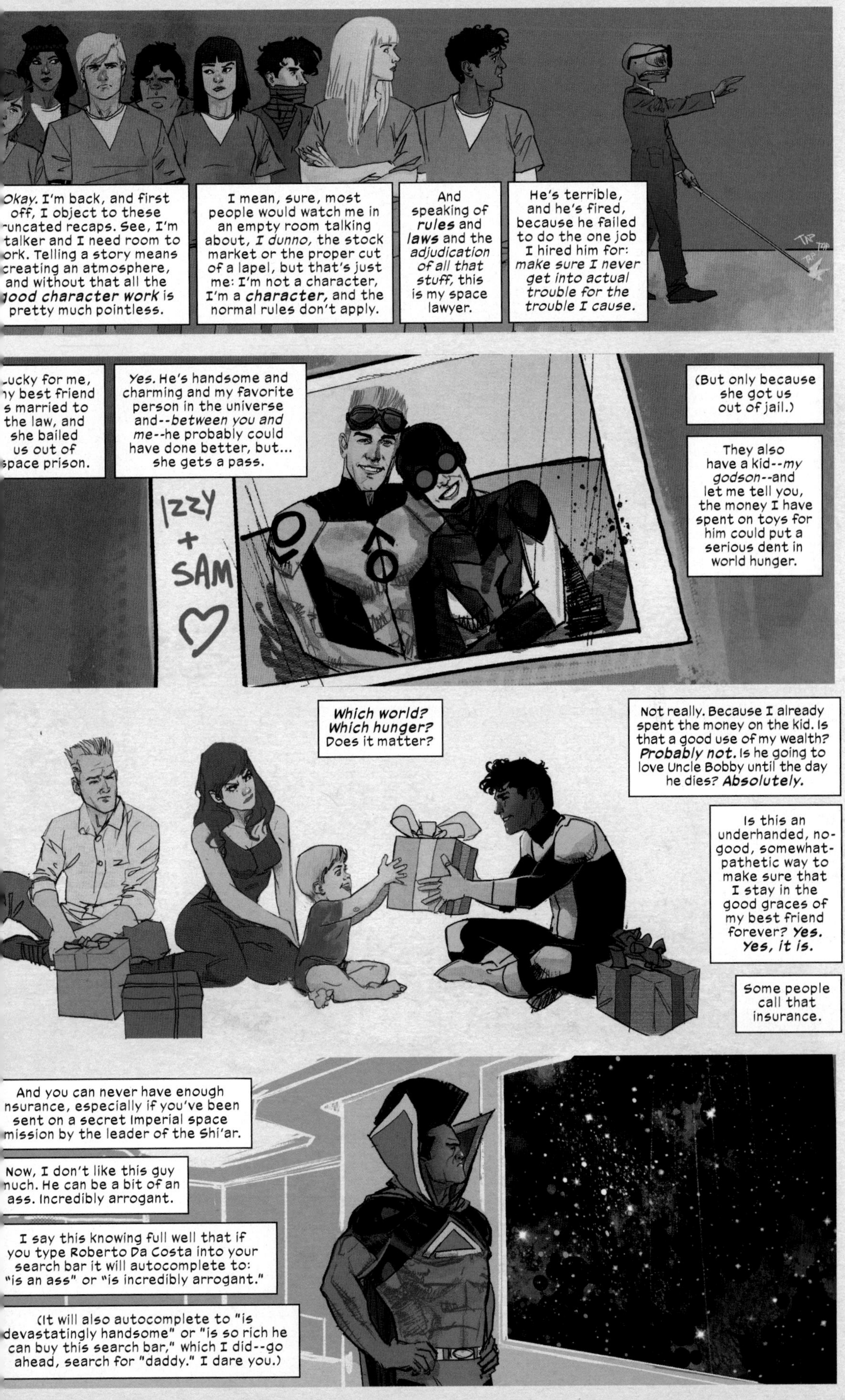

Okay. I'm back, and first off, I object to these runcated recaps. See, I'm talker and I need room to ork. Telling a story means creating an atmosphere, and without that all the good character work is pretty much pointless.
I mean, sure, most people would watch me in an empty room talking about, I dunno, the stock market or the proper cut of a lapel, but that's just me: I'm not a character, I'm a character, and the normal rules don't apply.
And speaking of rules and laws and the adjudication of all that stuff, this is my space lawyer.
He's terrible, and he's fired, because he failed to do the one job I hired him for: make sure I never get into actual trouble for the trouble I cause.
TAP TAP TAP
ucky for me, ny best friend s married to the law, and she bailed us out of space prison.
Yes. He's handsome and charming and my favorite person in the universe and--between you and me--he probably could have done better, but... she gets a pass.
IZZY + SAM
(But only because she got us out of jail.)
They also have a kid--my godson--and let me tell you, the money I have spent on toys for him could put a serious dent in world hunger.
Which world? Which hunger? Does it matter?
Not really. Because I already spent the money on the kid. Is that a good use of my wealth? Probably not. Is he going to love Uncle Bobby until the day he dies? Absolutely.
Is this an underhanded, no-good, somewhat-pathetic way to make sure that I stay in the good graces of my best friend forever? Yes. Yes, it is.
Some people call that insurance.
And you can never have enough nsurance, especially if you've been sent on a secret Imperial space mission by the leader of the Shi'ar.
Now, I don't like this guy nuch. He can be a bit of an ass. Incredibly arrogant.
I say this knowing full well that if you type Roberto Da Costa into your search bar it will autocomplete to: "is an ass" or "is incredibly arrogant."
(It will also autocomplete to "is devastatingly handsome" or "is so rich he can buy this search bar," which I did--go ahead, search for "daddy." I dare you.)

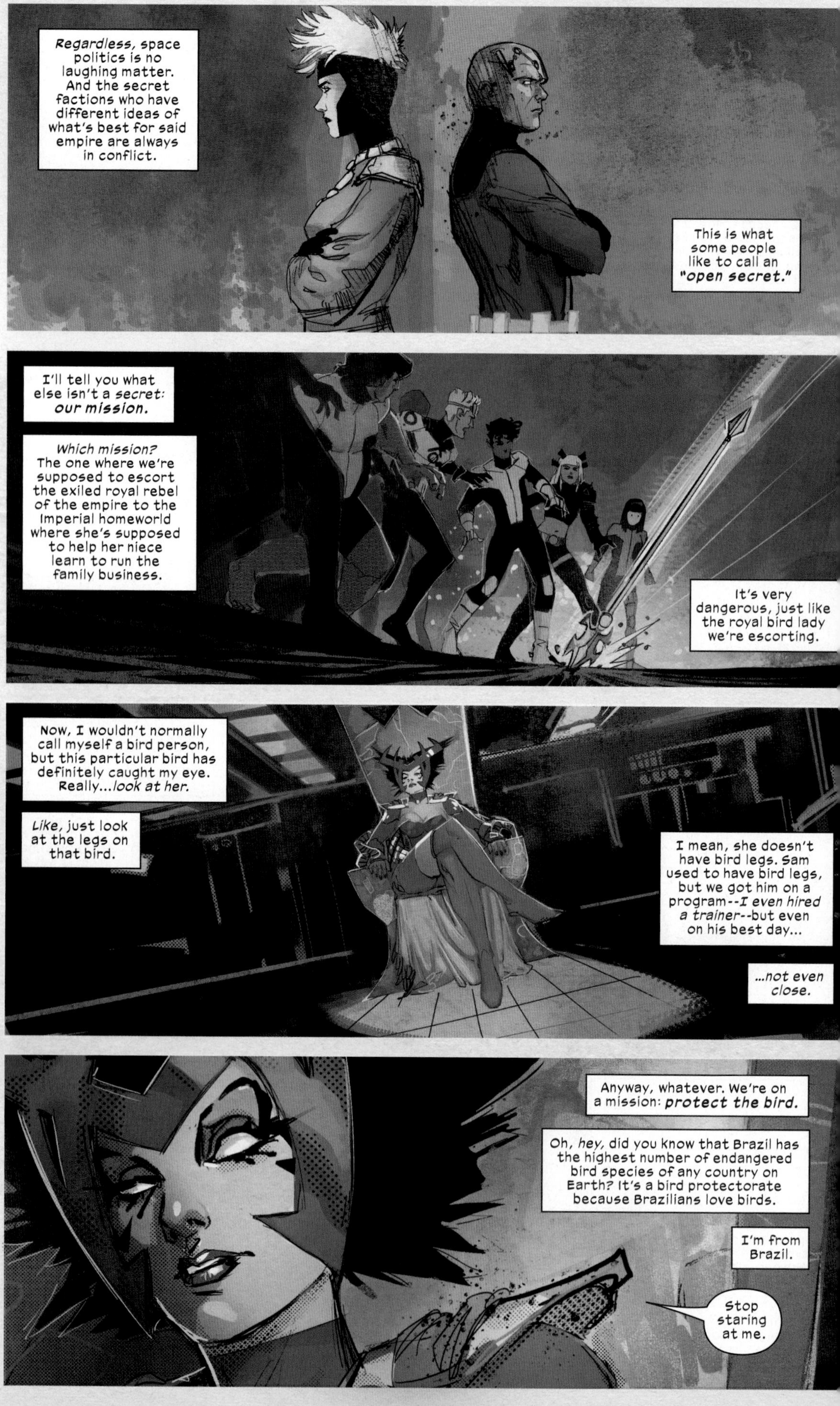
Regardless, space politics is no laughing matter. And the secret factions who have different ideas of what's best for said empire are always in conflict.
This is what some people like to call an ***"open secret."***
I'll tell you what else isn't a *secret:* ***our mission.***
Which mission? The one where we're supposed to escort the exiled royal rebel of the empire to the Imperial homeworld where she's supposed to help her niece learn to run the family business.
It's very dangerous, just like the royal bird lady we're escorting.
Now, I wouldn't normally call myself a bird person, but this particular bird has definitely caught my eye. Really...*look at her.*
Like, just look at the legs on that bird.
I mean, she doesn't have bird legs. Sam used to have bird legs, but we got him on a program--*I even hired a trainer*--but even on his best day...
...not even close.
Anyway, whatever. We're on a mission: ***protect the bird.***
Oh, *hey,* did you know that Brazil has the highest number of endangered bird species of any country on Earth? It's a bird protectorate because Brazilians love birds.
I'm from Brazil.
Stop staring at me.

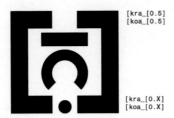

[kra_[0.5]
[koa_[0.5]

[kra_[0.X]
[koa_[0.X]

TROUBLE FOLLOWS THEM

Like Sunspot said -- space jail, space war, space romance.

NEW MUTANTS.

| Karma |  Wolfsbane |  Mondo | Cypher |  Mirage |

| Sunspot |  Chamber |  Magik | 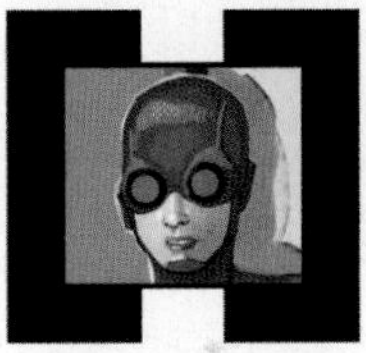 Smasher | Cannonball |

| Gladiator |  Mentor |  Oracle | Deathbird |

[kra_[0.5]...]
[koa_[0.5]...]

[And..beyond.]

[00_lets_go____X]
[00_to_space___X]

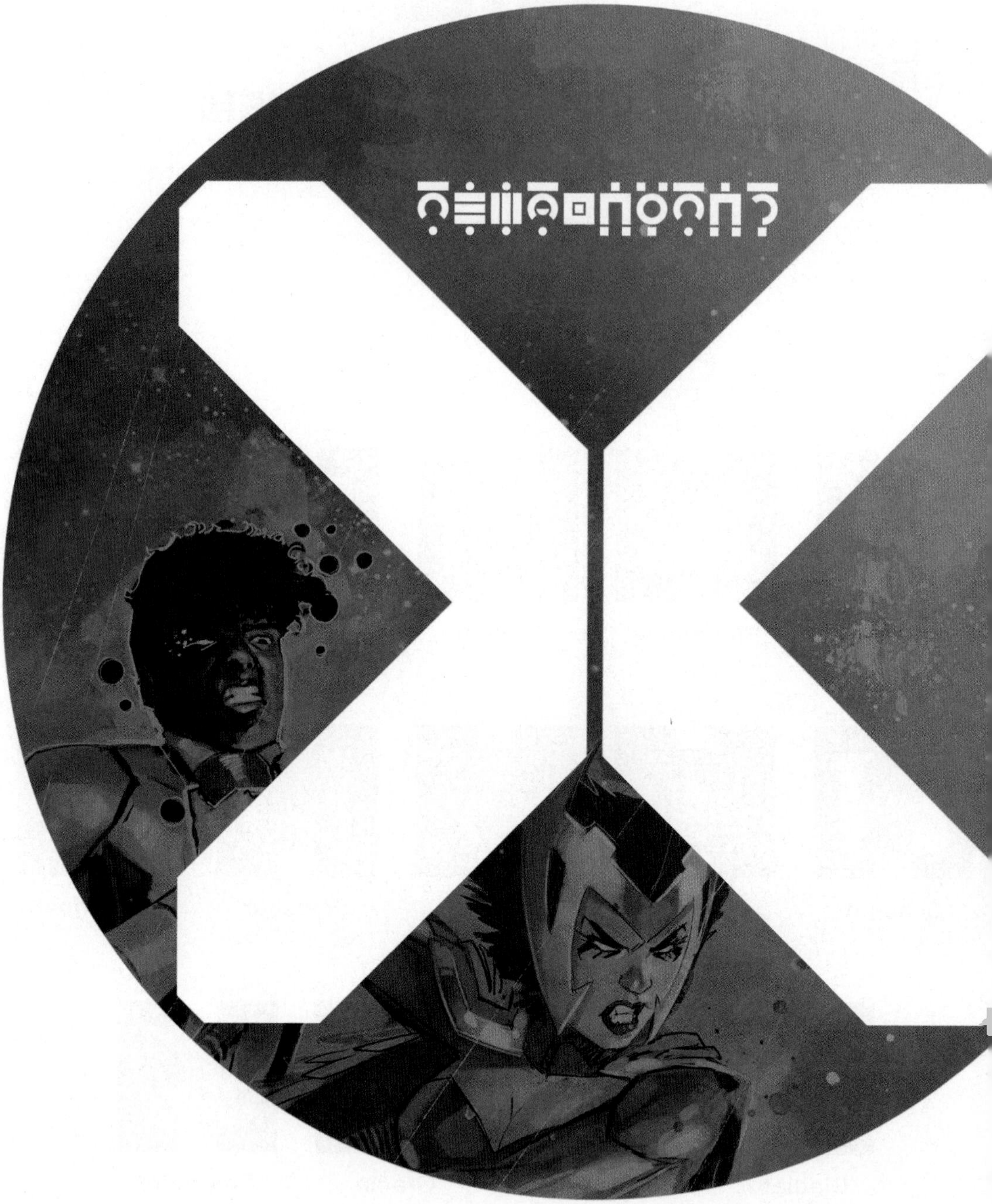

JONATHAN HICKMAN.................................[WRITER]
ROD REIS..[ARTIST]
VC's TRAVIS LANHAM..............................[LETTERER]
TOM MULLER......................................[DESIGN]

ROD REIS..................................[COVER ARTIST]

JUAN JOSÉ RYP & JESUS ABURTOV...[VARIANT COVER ARTISTS]

NICK RUSSELL..............................[PRODUCTION]

JONATHAN HICKMAN...........................[HEAD OF X]
ANNALISE BISSA................................[EDITOR]
JORDAN D. WHITE........................[SENIOR EDITOR]
C.B. CEBULSKI.......................[EDITOR IN CHIEF]

[05] NEW MUTANTS

[ISSUE FIVE]...........ENDANGERED BIRDS

[00_lets_go__X]
[00_to_space_X]

[00_00.....0]
[00_00.....5]

[00_good____]
[00_times___]

[00_in_____]

[00_space___]

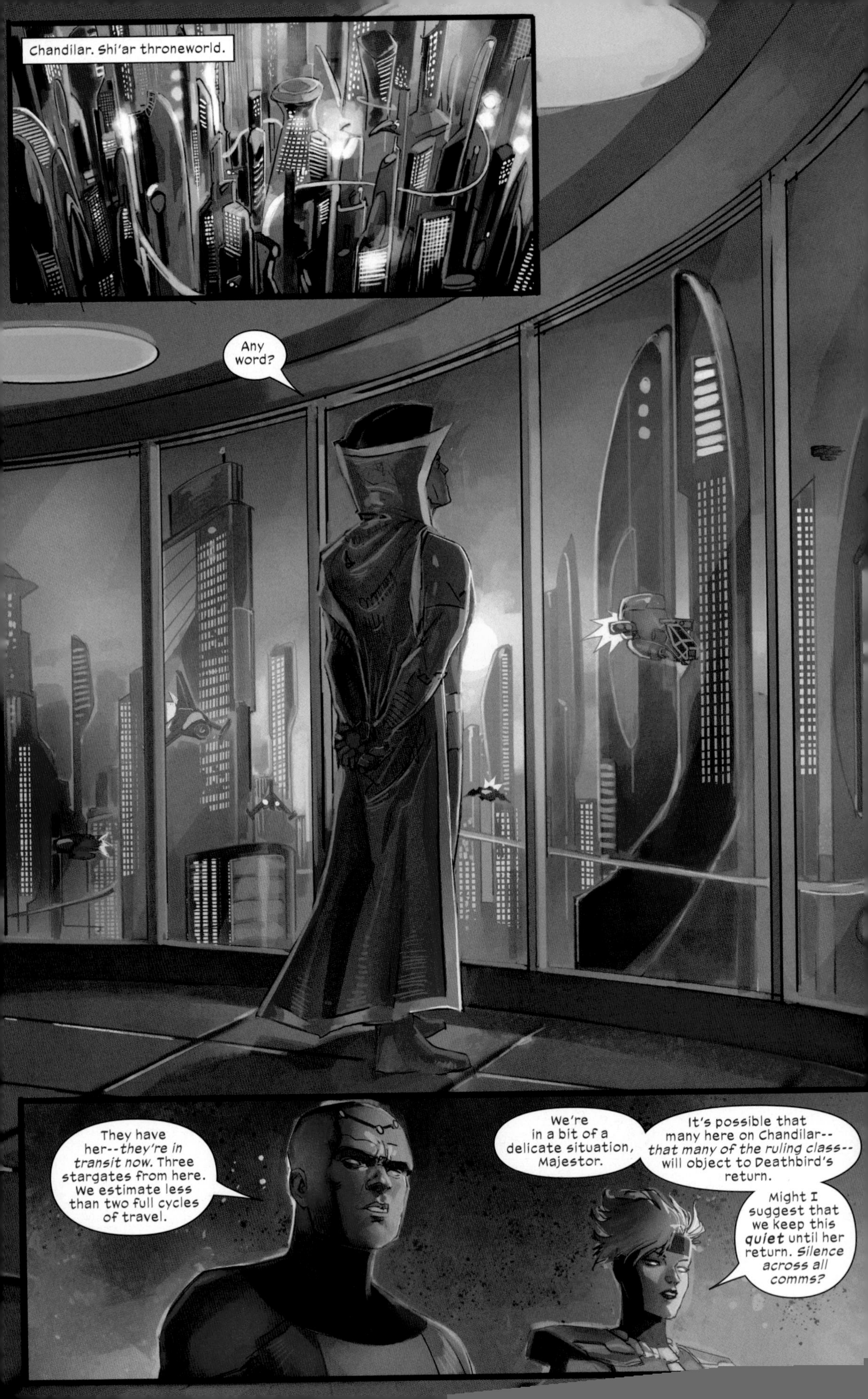
Chandilar. Shi'ar throneworld.
Any word?
They have her--*they're in transit now.* Three stargates from here. We estimate less than two full cycles of travel.
We're in a bit of a delicate situation, Majestor.
It's possible that many here on Chandilar--*that many of the ruling class*--will object to Deathbird's return.
Might I suggest that we keep this ***quiet*** until her return. *Silence across all comms?*

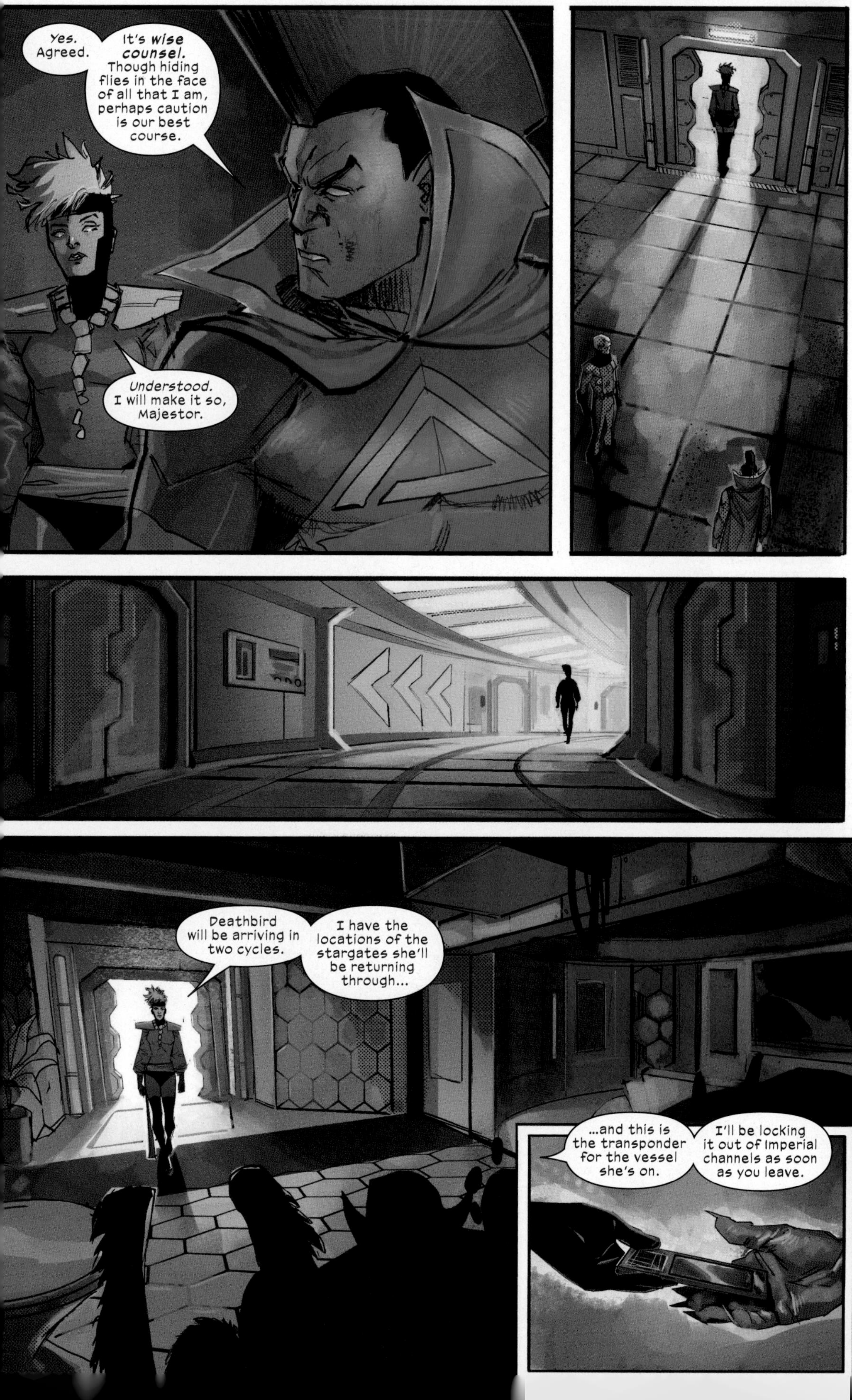
Yes. Agreed.
It's wise counsel. Though hiding flies in the face of all that I am, perhaps caution is our best course.
Understood. I will make it so, Majestor.
Deathbird will be arriving in two cycles.
I have the locations of the stargates she'll be returning through...
...and this is the transponder for the vessel she's on.
I'll be locking it out of Imperial channels as soon as you leave.

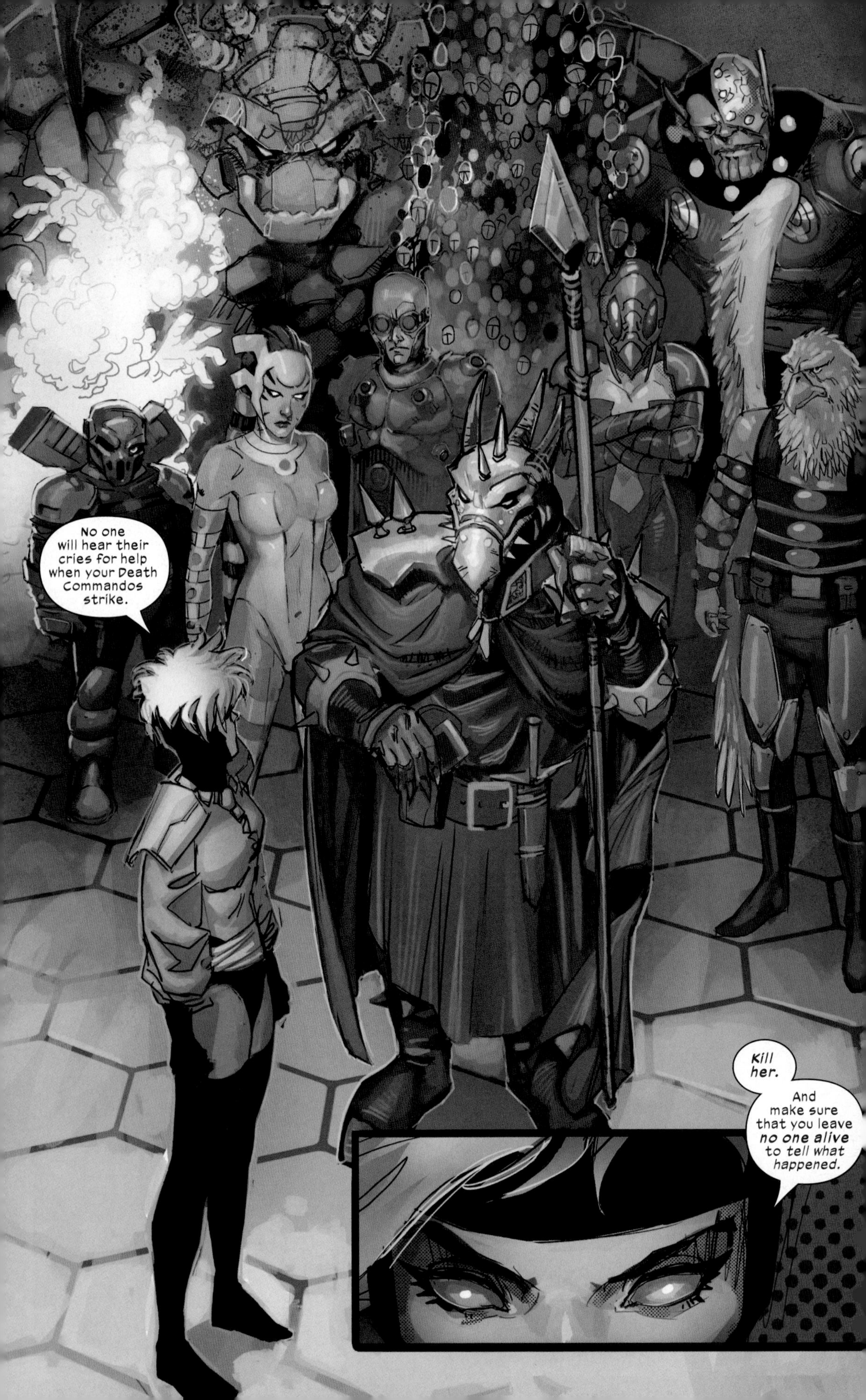
No one will hear their cries for help when your Death Commandos strike.
Kill her.
And make sure that you leave *no one alive* to tell what happened.

SHI'AR DEATH COMMANDOS

Existing outside the traditional Superguardian/guardian military structure, Shi'ar Death Commandos are an elite, black-book, group of mercenaries that mostly come from races that operate outside the normal political arena of the Shi'ar Empire. The Death Commandos often handle missions that have a low percentage of success or are deemed too politically problematic for the Imperial Guard.

Unlike the Imperial Guards, the Death Commandos have no institutional replacement program. So if a Krait dies on a mission, there is no secondary Krait waiting to replace him, and a new Death Commando member must be recruited. The only exception to this is Black Cloak, who is rumored to always come from Superguardian/guardian stock. There is always a Black Cloak.

CURRENT MEMBERS:

BLACK CLOAK [COMMANDER]
Black Cloak is the commander of the Shi'ar Death Commandos and its chief strategist. Believed to have been trained in the Shi'ar war colleges, a Black Cloak often displays advanced tactics and a ruthless efficiency that is the trademark of such an education. The weapons of a Black Cloak are the D'Kere spear, which is both a blade and an energy weapon, and a containment cloak, which can send an adversary into a temporary stasis void.

FLAW [FIELD LEADER]
Flaw is a biologically converted Warskrull and the field leader of the Shi'ar Death Commandos. He possesses minimal shape-shifting abilities due to the natural incompatibility of his Shi'ar brain and Skrull body but is a proven warrior and ruthless killer. Flaw is also a practitioner of third-stage Shi'ar meditation techniques and, for ethical reasons, does not eat solid food.

D'EVO
D'Evo is a classical biological predator who creates his own capture mechanism in the form of an impenetrable force-field, along with an acidic digestive in the form of a gas that reduces his prey into an easily consumable, high-protein goo. Therefore he also does not eat solids but not for ethical reasons.

HYPERNOVA
Hypernova is a failed Shi'ar guardian of the Hussar class who can fire energy blasts that disintegrate her target on impact. Hypernova's inability to control the lethality of her powers is believed to be the reason she failed her guardianship. Despite this, she believes that she has always been too good to be a Death Commando and has total contempt for her companions.

KRAIT

Krait is a biological experiment of the religious scientists of the Sharra sect. Once a standard-type Shi'ar commoner, Krait underwent years of experiments and surgery to become a bird of prey with wings and large, sharp claws. Krait can fly at speeds approaching escape velocity and has superior strength and endurance. After the Sharran scientists revealed to Krait that the process was irreversible, Krait murdered them and converted to the cult of K'ythri, which violently rejects the duality of the Shi'ar godhead.

OFFSET

Offset is from a subterranean species of mantis-like insectoids with six limbs. She has a dislocatable jaw with retractable teeth and possesses a neurotoxin that neutralizes the superhuman abilities of others with a touch. She can also gain the memories of her victims by severing and injecting their brains. Her species is entirely female and reproduces by laying eggs in the decapitated bodies of her victims. Offset has terrible breath.

SEGA

Sega is a being in a gaseous cloud form who serves as a scout for the Death Commandos. Sega is a coward and, in a fight, cannot be depended upon.

SHELL

Shell is an Orthoxalith, an alien species composed of rock and bred to be a subservient labor class that traditionally operates in high-radiation, high-gravity worlds. Medically modified for limited cognitive thought, Shell possesses super-strength and -endurance and can produce containment exo-shells.

WARSHOT

Warshot is an exiled Kree weaponsmaster who specializes in advanced energy weapons. Like all Kree weaponsmasters, he is a skilled sharp-shooter/gunman and long-range marksman and capable of advanced combat in most scenarios. Warshot was exiled from New Hala 60 cycles ago for the crimes of rebellion, sedition and illegal arms trade.

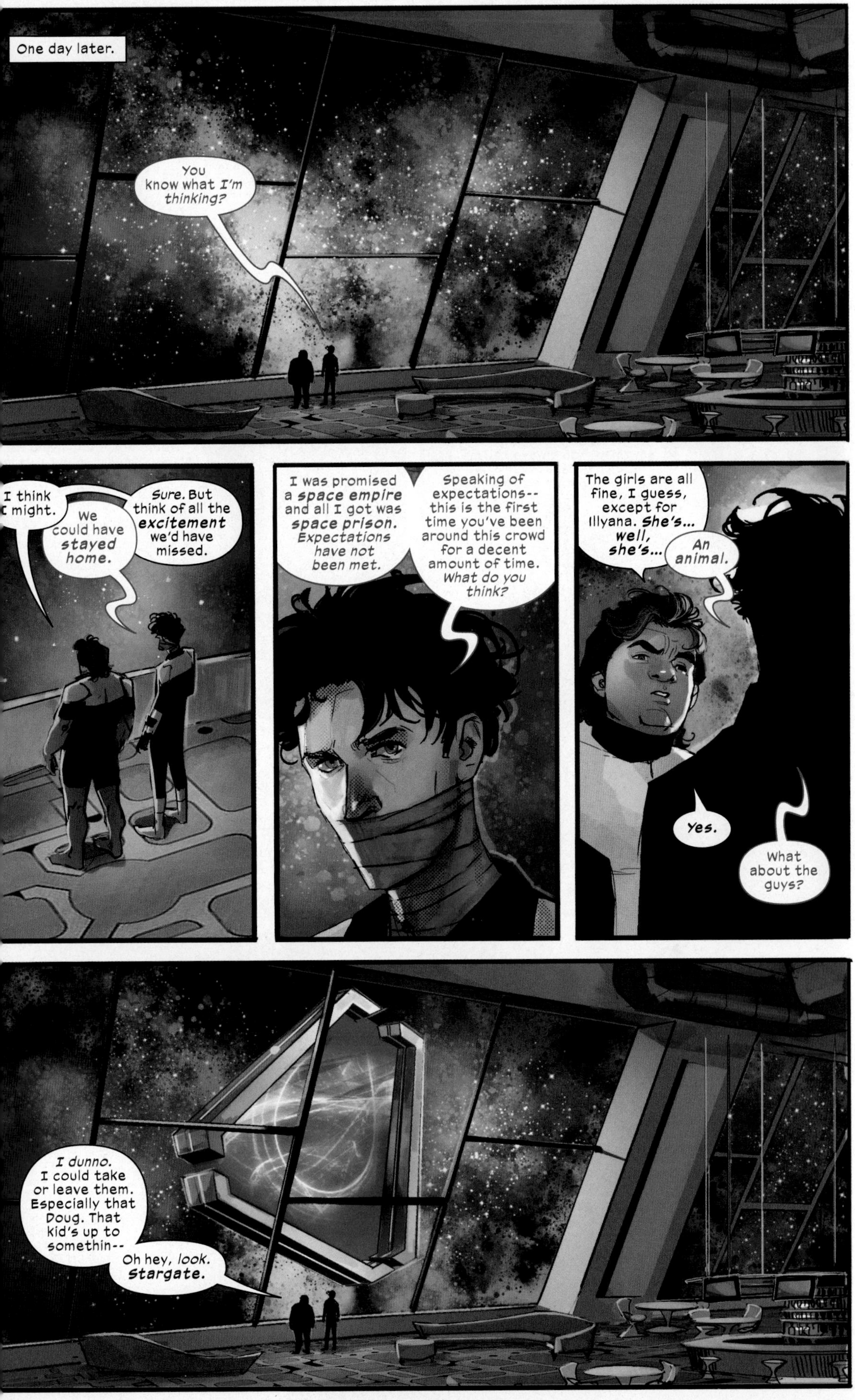

One day later.
You know what I'm thinking?
We could have stayed home.
Sure. But think of all the excitement we'd have missed.
I think
might.
I was promised a space empire and all I got was space prison. Expectations have not been met.
Speaking of expectations-- this is the first time you've been around this crowd for a decent amount of time. What do you think?
The girls are all fine, I guess, except for Illyana. She's... well, she's...
An animal.
Yes.
What about the guys?
I dunno. I could take or leave them. Especially that Doug. That kid's up to somethin--
Oh hey, look. Stargate.

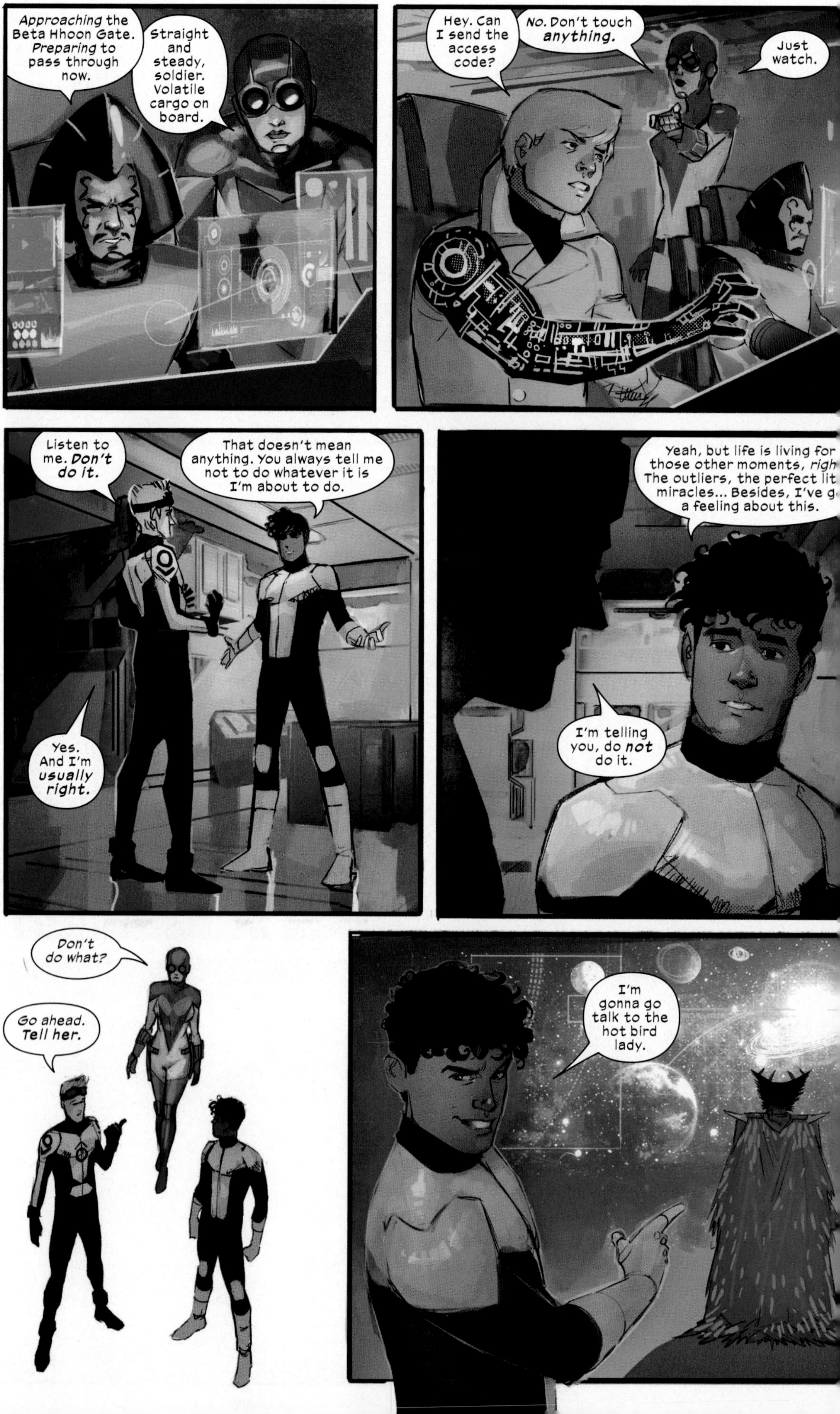

Approaching the Beta Hhoon Gate. Preparing to pass through now.
Straight and steady, soldier. Volatile cargo on board.
Hey. Can I send the access code?
No. Don't touch anything.
Just watch.
Listen to me. Don't do it.
That doesn't mean anything. You always tell me not to do whatever it is I'm about to do.
Yes. And I'm usually right.
Yeah, but life is living for those other moments, righ
The outliers, the perfect lit miracles... Besides, I've g a feeling about this.
I'm telling you, do not do it.
Don't do what?
Go ahead. Tell her.
I'm gonna go talk to the hot bird lady.

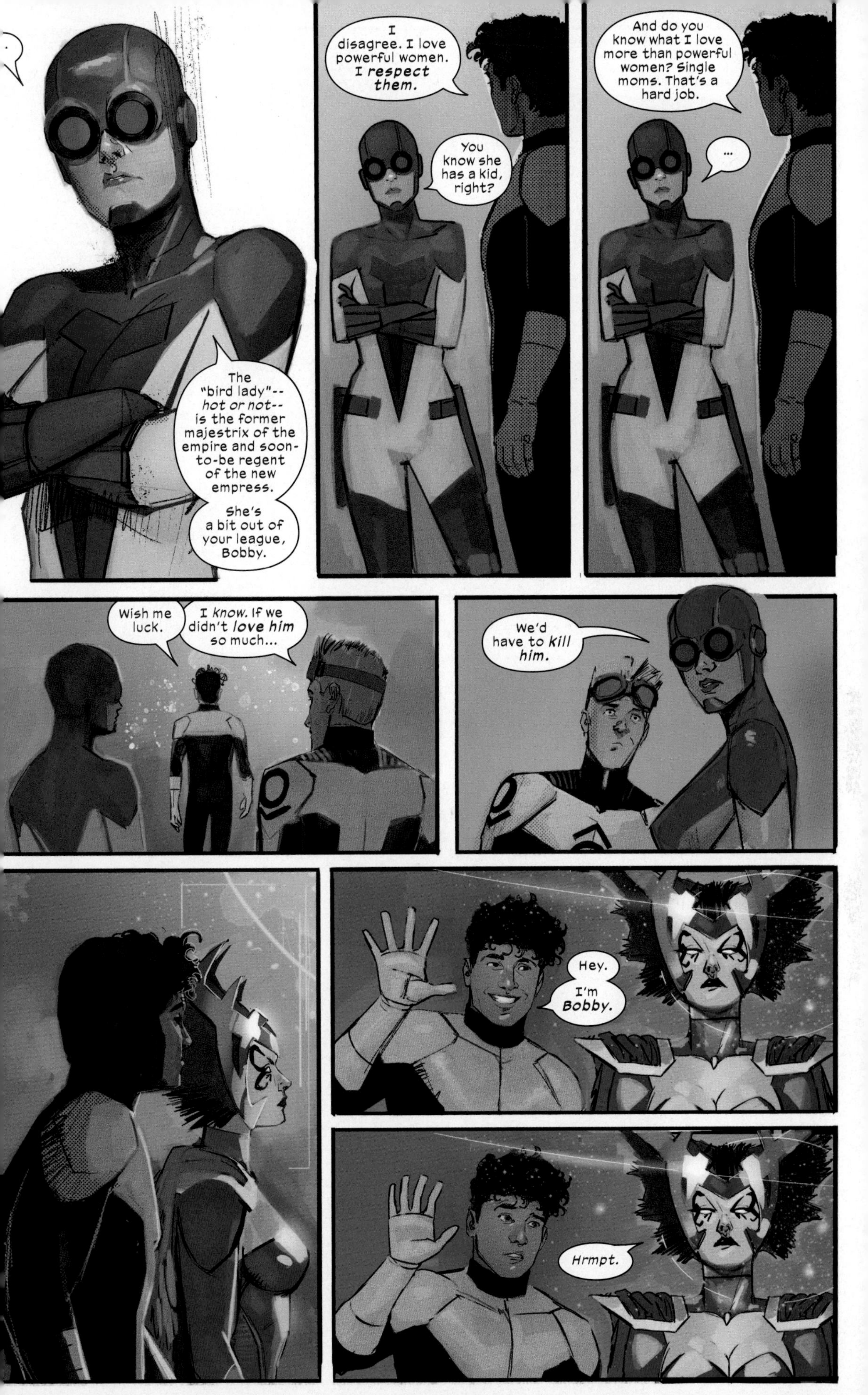
The "bird lady"-- *hot or not*-- is the former majestrix of the empire and soon-to-be regent of the new empress.
She's a bit out of your league, Bobby.
I disagree. I love powerful women. I ***respect them.***
You know she has a kid, right?
And do you know what I love more than powerful women? Single moms. That's a hard job.
...
Wish me luck.
I *know.* If we didn't ***love him*** so much...
We'd have to ***kill him.***
Hey.
I'm ***Bobby.***
Hrmpt.

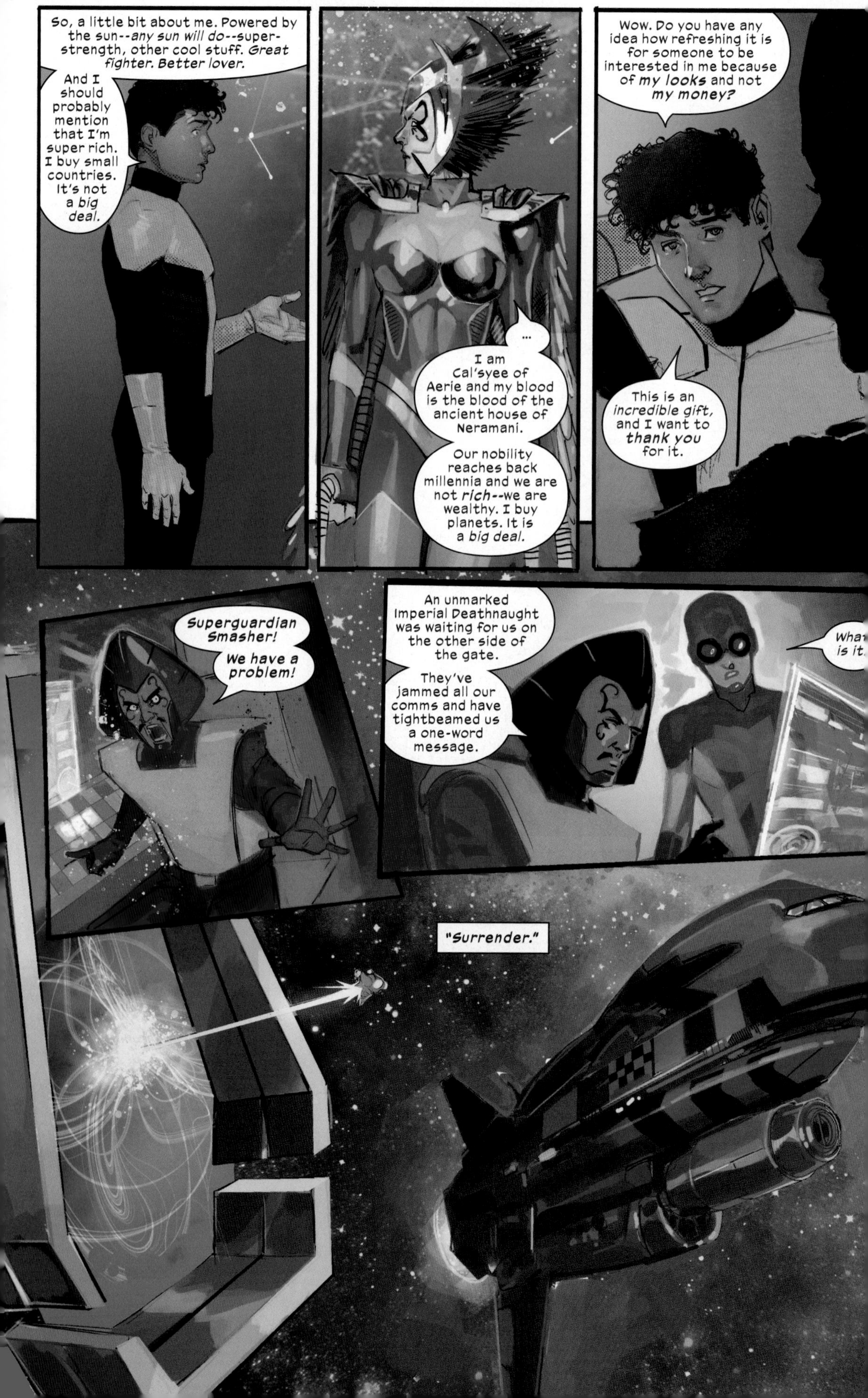
So, a little bit about me. Powered by the sun--*any sun will do*--super-strength, other cool stuff. *Great fighter. Better lover.*
And I should probably mention that I'm super rich. I buy small countries. It's not a *big deal.*
...
I am Cal'syee of Aerie and my blood is the blood of the ancient house of Neramani.
Our nobility reaches back millennia and we are not *rich*--we are wealthy. I buy planets. It is a *big deal.*
Wow. Do you have any idea how refreshing it is for someone to be interested in me because of *my looks* and not *my money?*
This is an *incredible gift,* and I want to ***thank you*** for it.
Superguardian Smasher!
We have a problem!
An unmarked Imperial Deathnaught was waiting for us on the other side of the gate.
They've jammed all our comms and have tightbeamed us a one-word message.
"*Surrender.*"

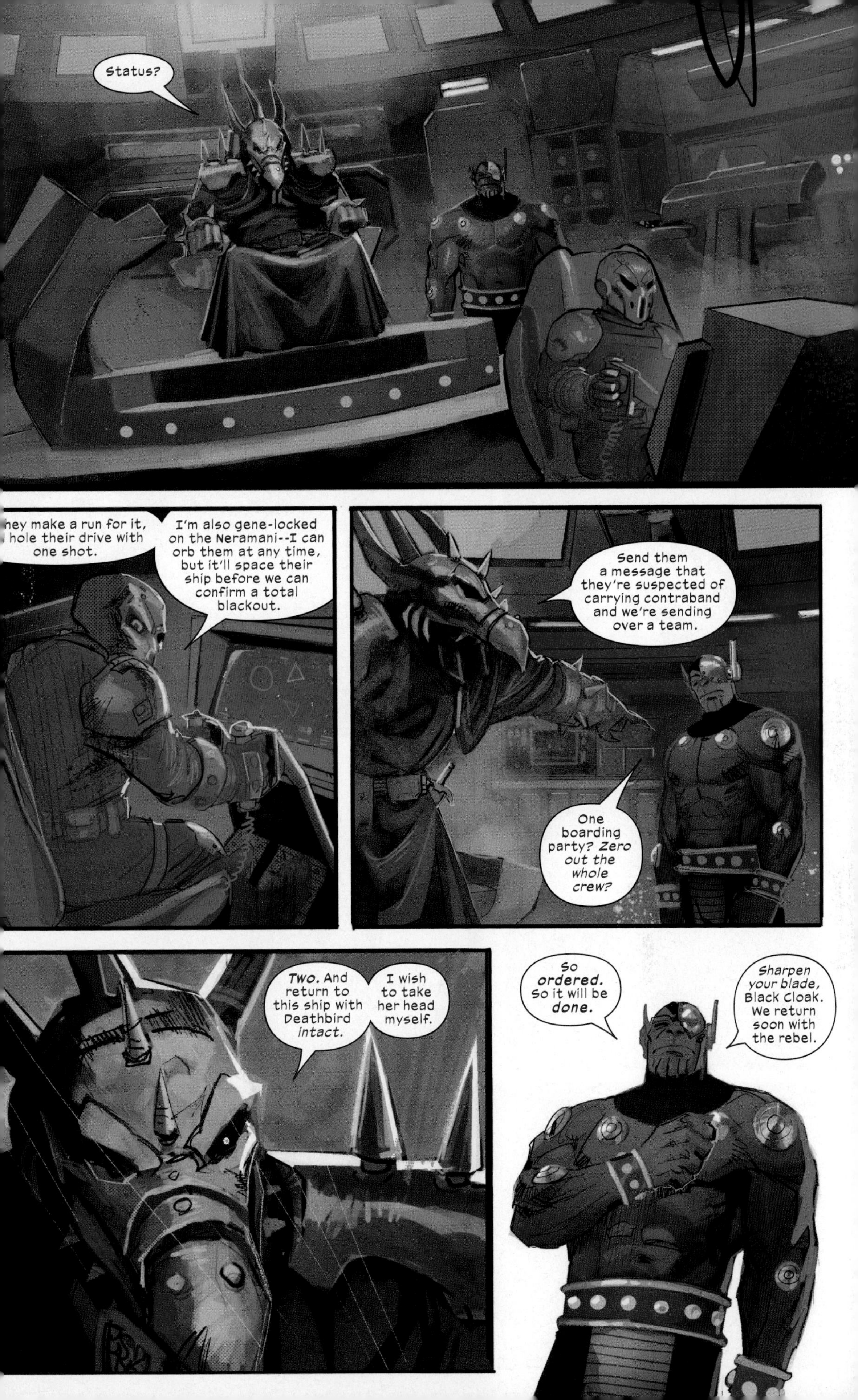
Status?
hey make a run for it, hole their drive with one shot.
I'm also gene-locked on the Neramani--I can orb them at any time, but it'll space their ship before we can confirm a total blackout.
Send them a message that they're suspected of carrying contraband and we're sending over a team.
One boarding party? Zero out the whole crew?
Two. And return to this ship with Deathbird intact.
I wish to take her head myself.
So ordered. So it will be done.
Sharpen your blade, Black Cloak. We return soon with the rebel.

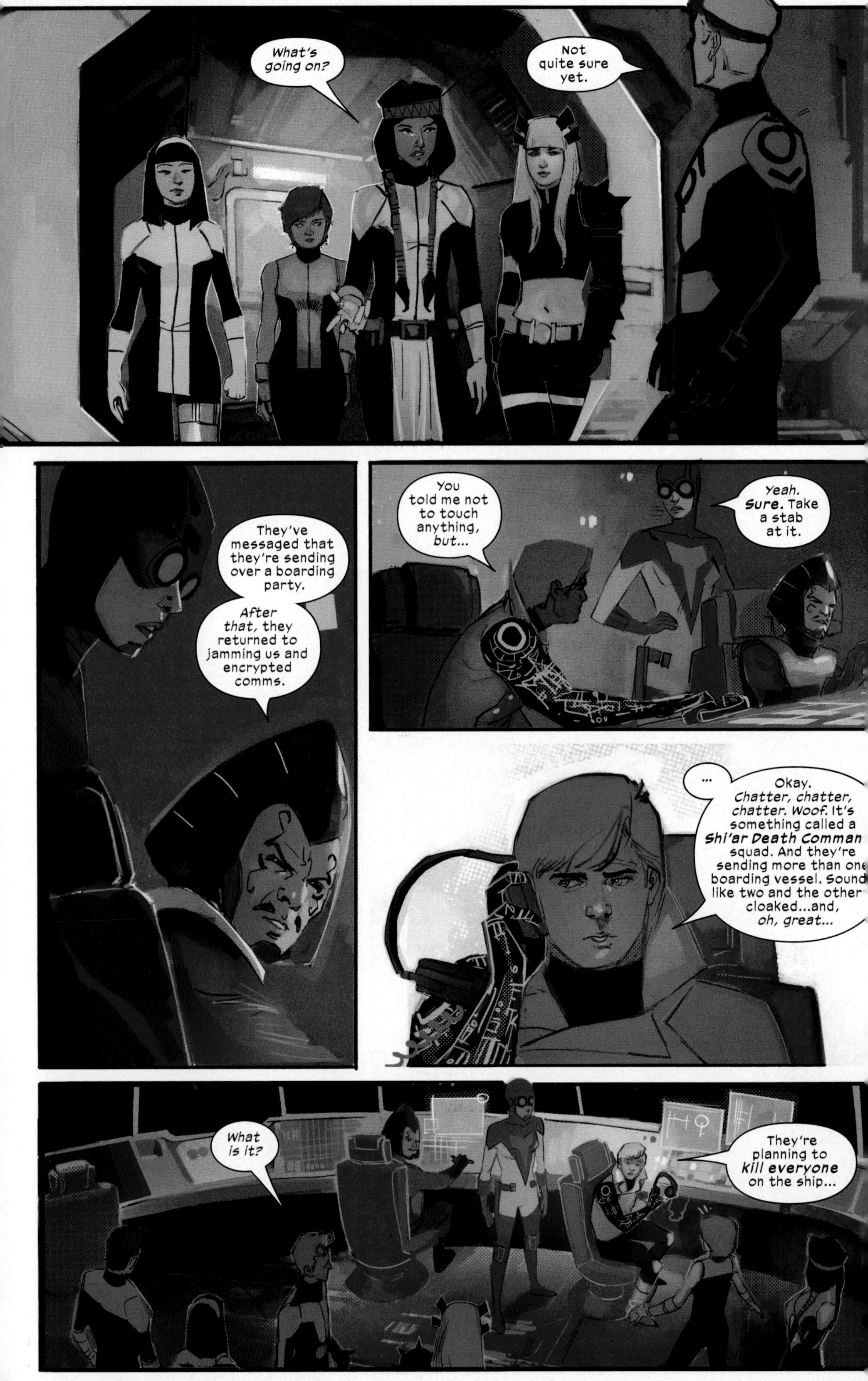
What's going on?
Not quite sure yet.
They've messaged that they're sending over a boarding party.
After that, they returned to jamming us and encrypted comms.
You told me not to touch anything, but...
Yeah. Sure. Take a stab at it.
...
Okay. Chatter, chatter, chatter. Woof. It's something called a Shi'ar Death Comman squad. And they're sending more than one boarding vessel. Sound like two and the other cloaked...and, oh, great...
What is it?
They're planning to kill everyone on the ship...

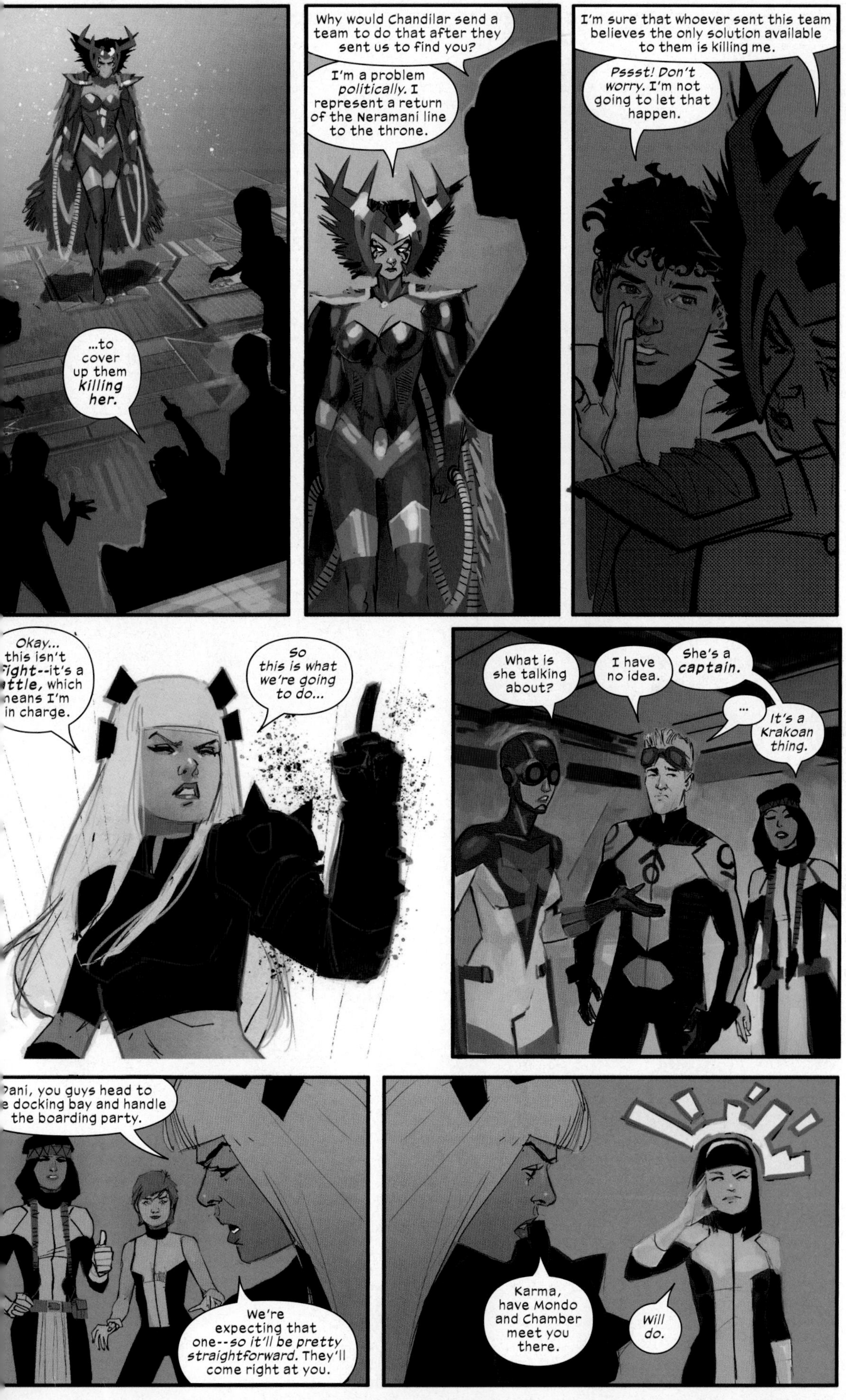
...to cover up them *killing her.*
Why would Chandilar send a team to do that after they sent us to find you?
I'm a problem *politically.* I represent a return of the Neramani line to the throne.
I'm sure that whoever sent this team believes the only solution available to them is killing me.
Pssst! Don't worry. I'm not going to let that happen.
Okay... this isn't *fight*--it's a *ttle,* which neans I'm in charge.
So this is what we're going to do...
What is she talking about?
I have no idea.
She's a *captain.*
...
It's a Krakoan thing.
Dani, you guys head to e docking bay and handle the boarding party.
We're expecting that one--*so it'll be pretty straightforward.* They'll come right at you.
Karma, have Mondo and Chamber meet you there.
Will do.

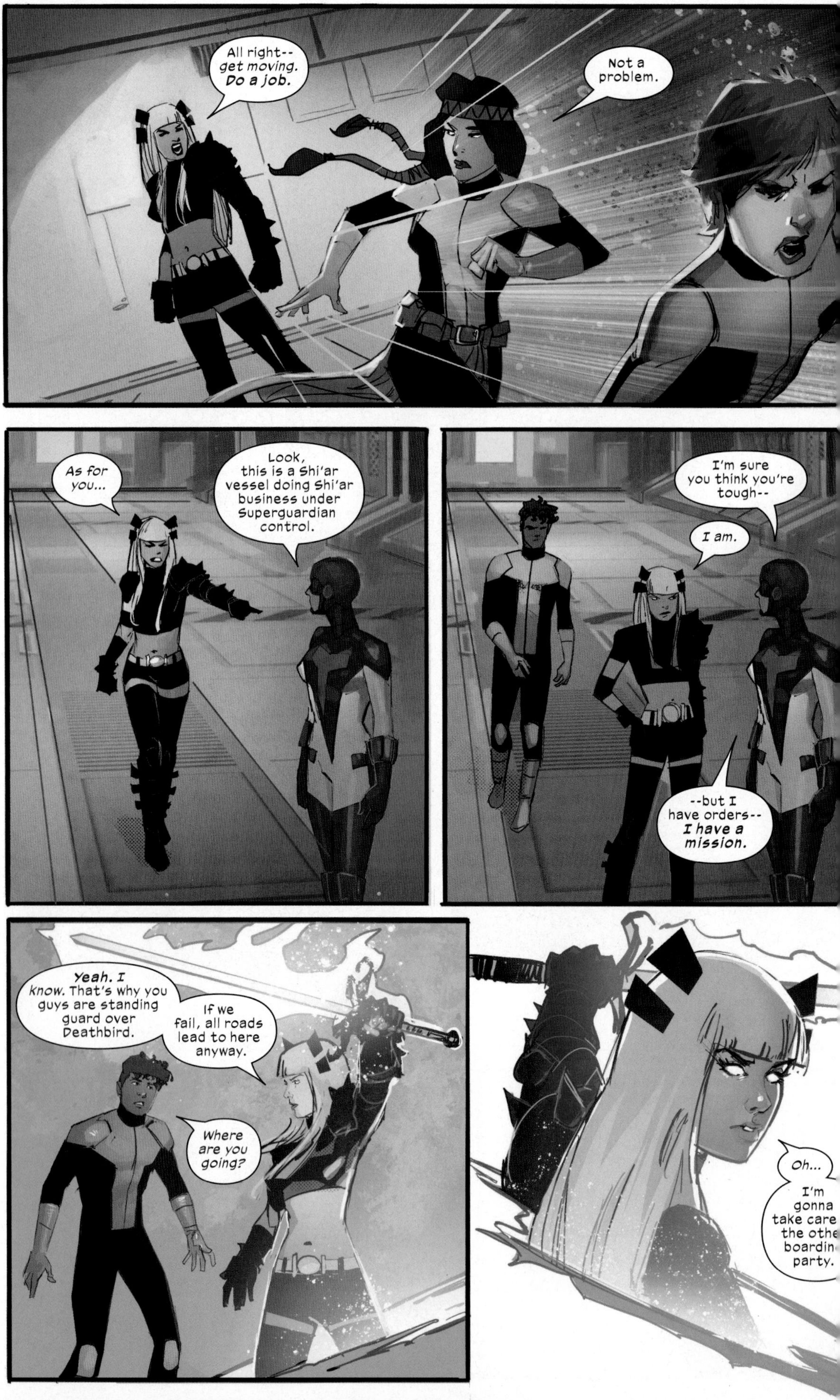

All right--
get moving.
Do a job.
Not a
problem.
As for
you...
Look,
this is a Shi'ar
vessel doing Shi'ar
business under
Superguardian
control.
I'm sure
you think you're
tough--
I am.
--but I
have orders--
I have a
mission.
Yeah. I
know. That's why you
guys are standing
guard over
Deathbird.
If we
fail, all roads
lead to here
anyway.
Where
are you
going?
Oh...
I'm
gonna
take care
the othe
boardin
party.

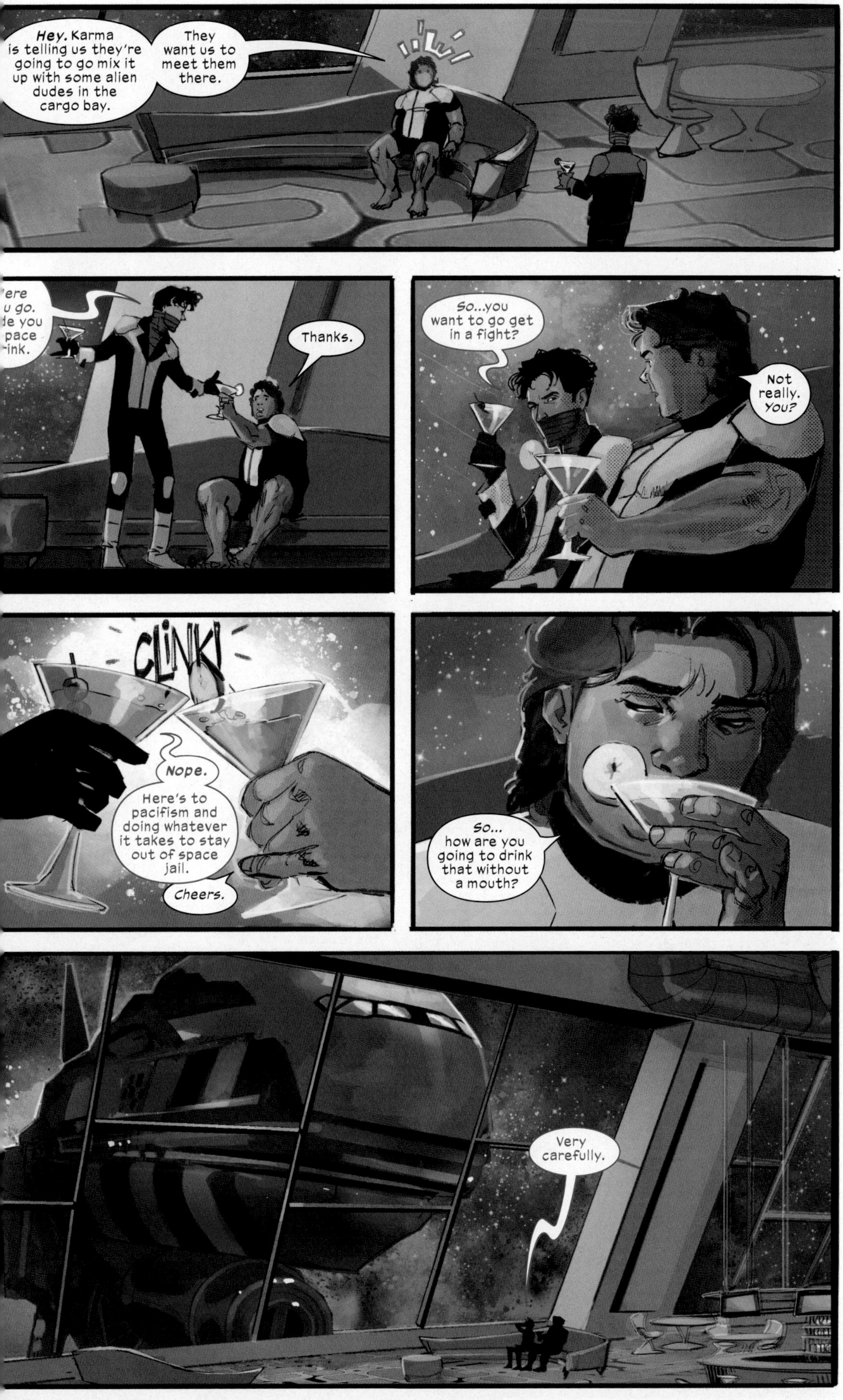
Hey. Karma is telling us they're going to go mix it up with some alien dudes in the cargo bay.
They want us to meet them there.
Thanks.
So...you want to go get in a fight?
Not really. You?
CLINK!
Nope.
Here's to pacifism and doing whatever it takes to stay out of space jail.
Cheers.
So... how are you going to drink that without a mouth?
Very carefully.

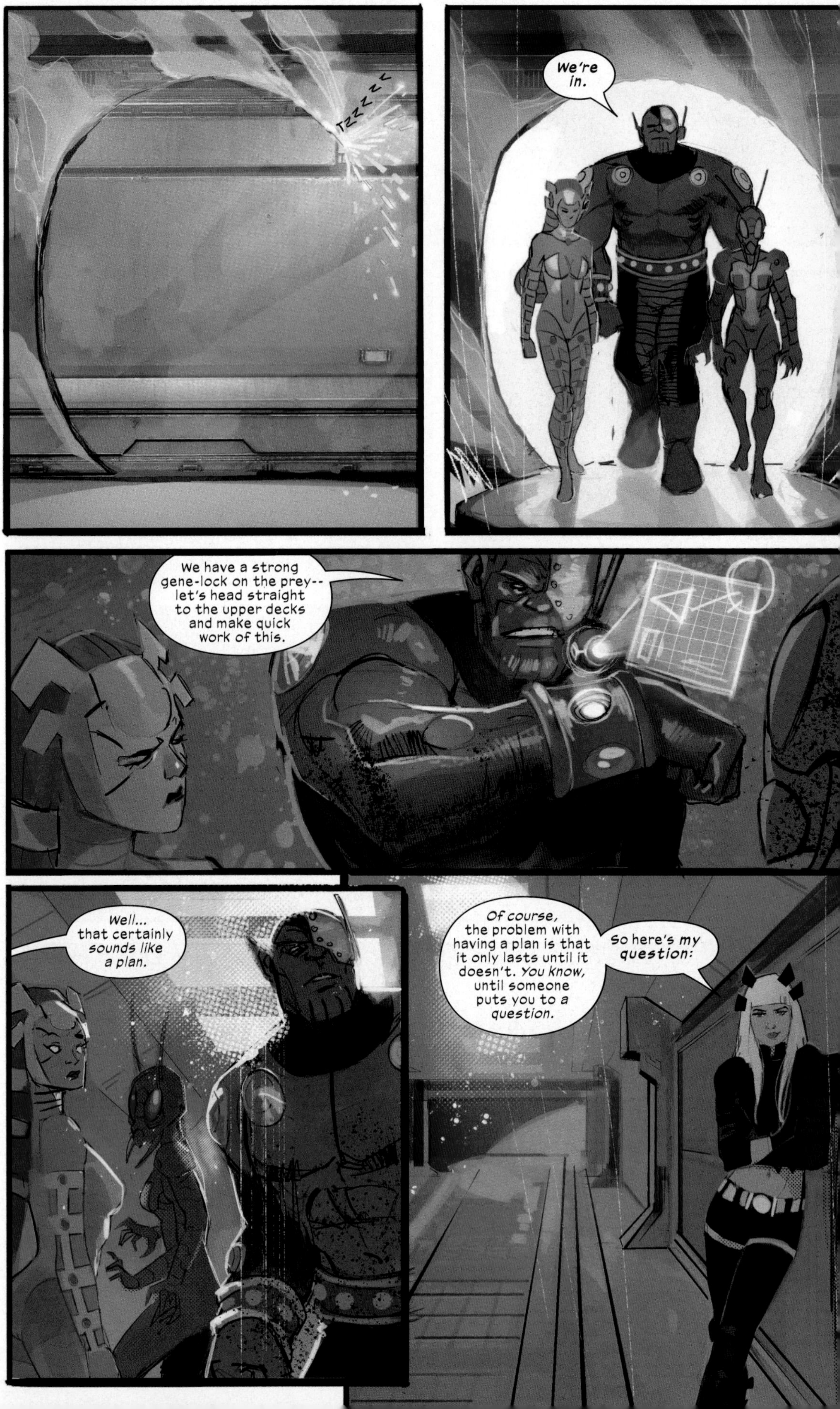
TZZZZZ
We're in.
We have a strong gene-lock on the prey-- let's head straight to the upper decks and make quick work of this.
Well... that certainly sounds like a plan.
Of course, the problem with having a plan is that it only lasts until it doesn't. You know, until someone puts you to a question.
So here's my question:

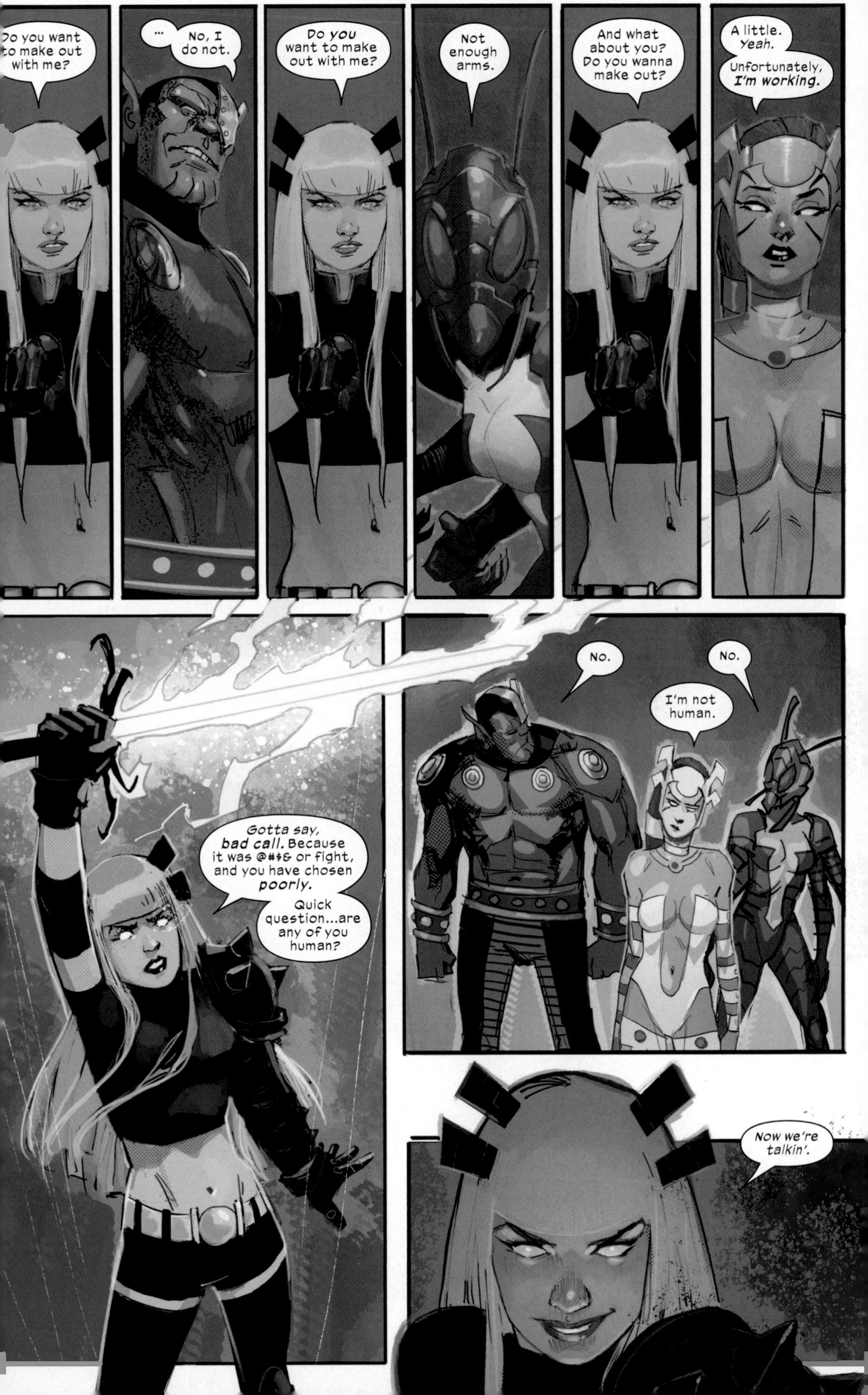
Do you want to make out with me?
... No, I do not.
Do *you* want to make out with me?
Not enough arms.
And what about you? Do you wanna make out?
A little. *Yeah.*
Unfortunately, ***I'm working.***
Gotta say, **bad call.** Because it was @#$& or fight, and you have chosen ***poorly.***
Quick question...are any of you human?
No.
I'm not human.
No.
Now we're talkin'.

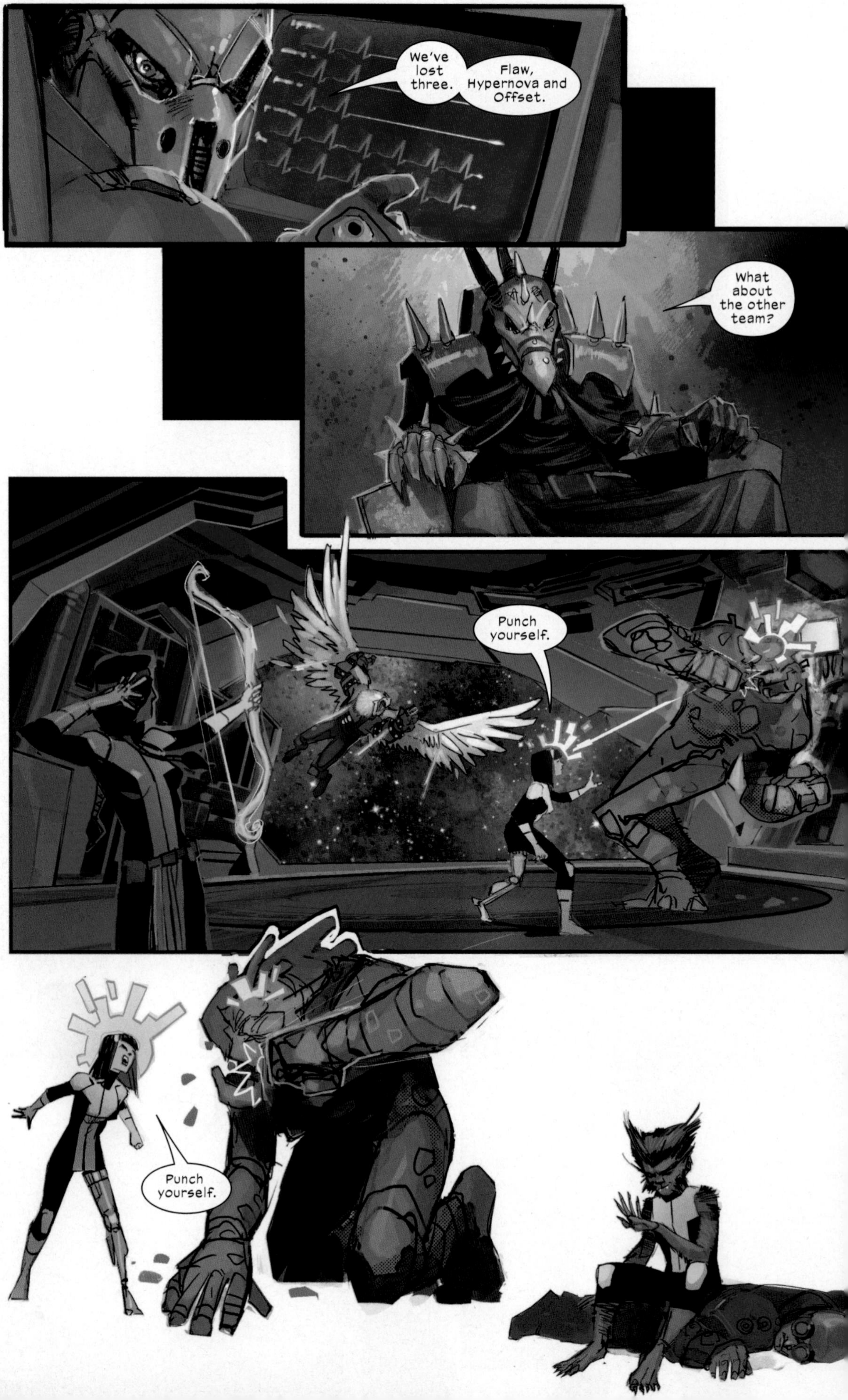
We've lost three.
Flaw, Hypernova and Offset.
What about the other team?
Punch yourself.
Punch yourself.

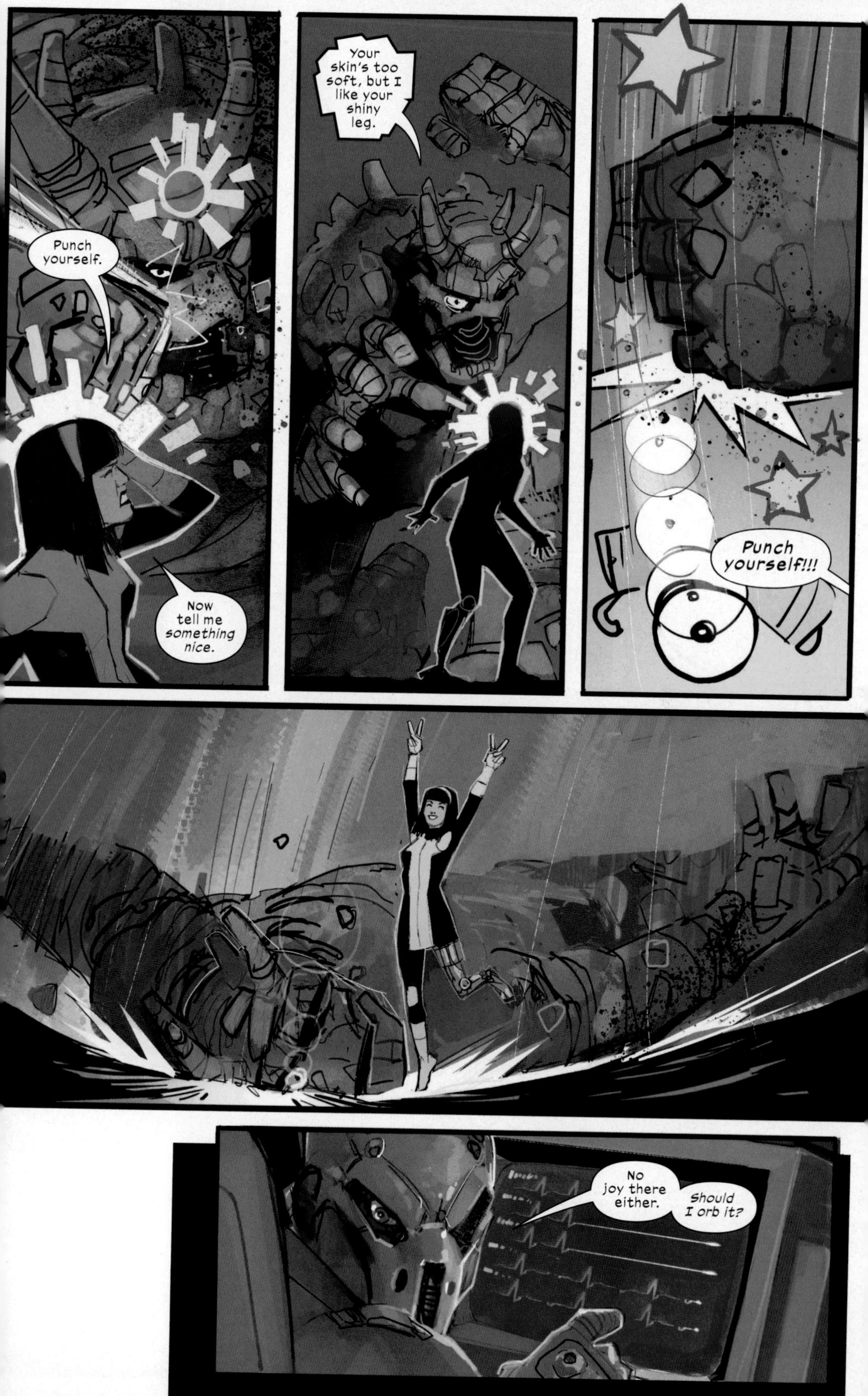
Punch yourself.
Now tell me something nice.
Your skin's too soft, but I like your shiny leg.
Punch yourself!!!
No joy there either.
Should I orb it?

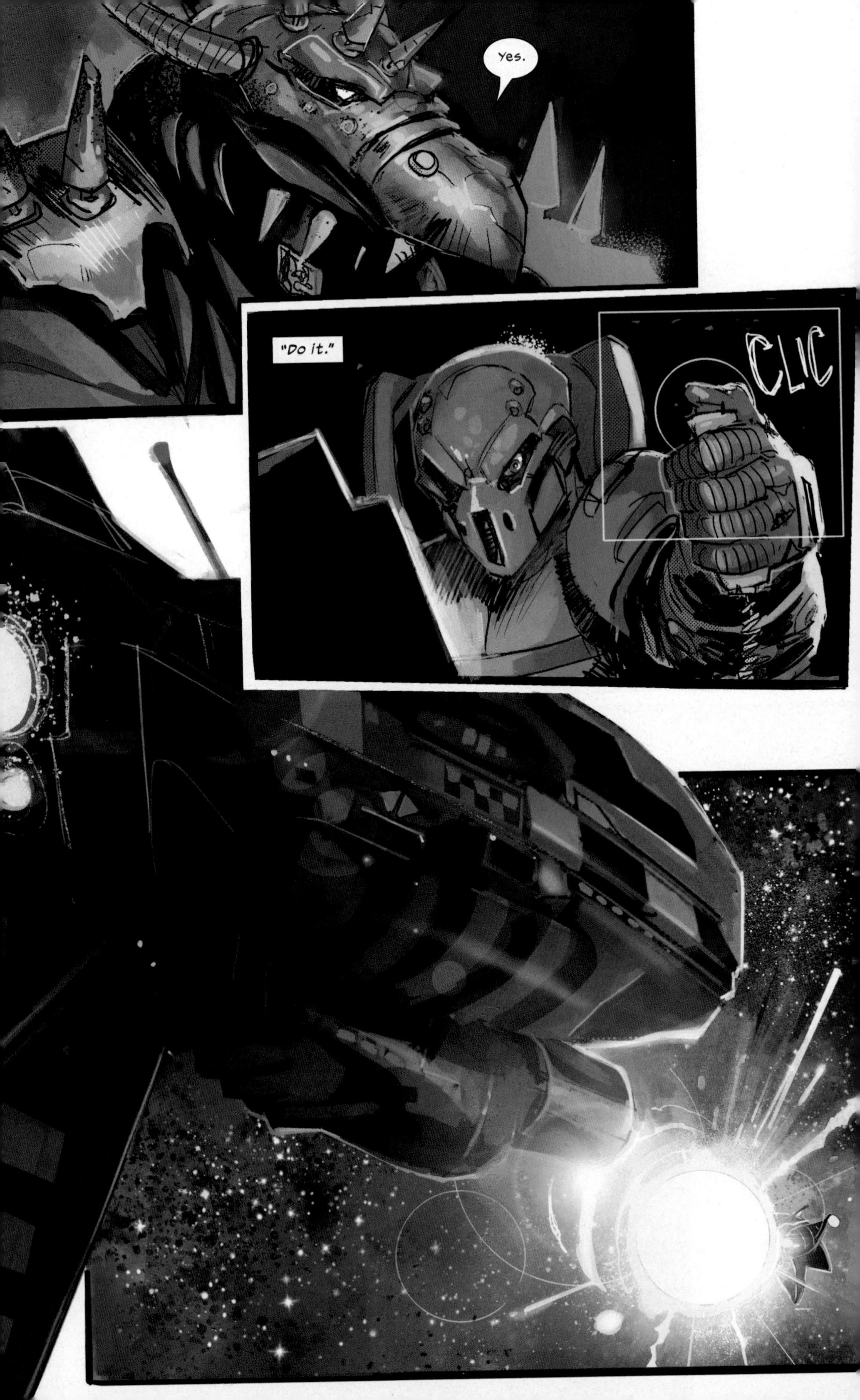
Yes.
"Do it."
CLIC

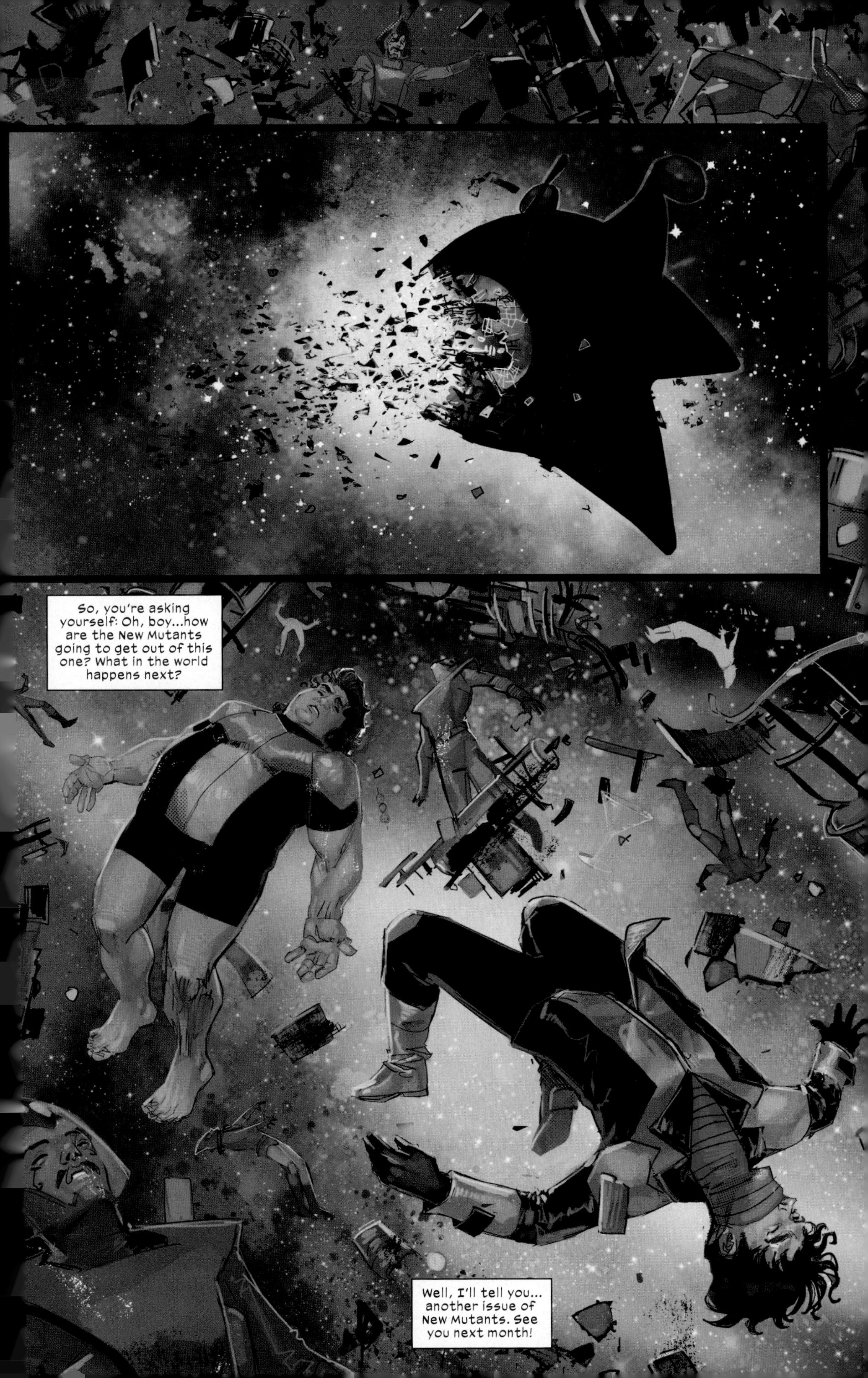
So, you're asking yourself: Oh, boy...how are the New Mutants going to get out of this one? What in the world happens next?
Well, I'll tell you... another issue of New Mutants. See you next month!

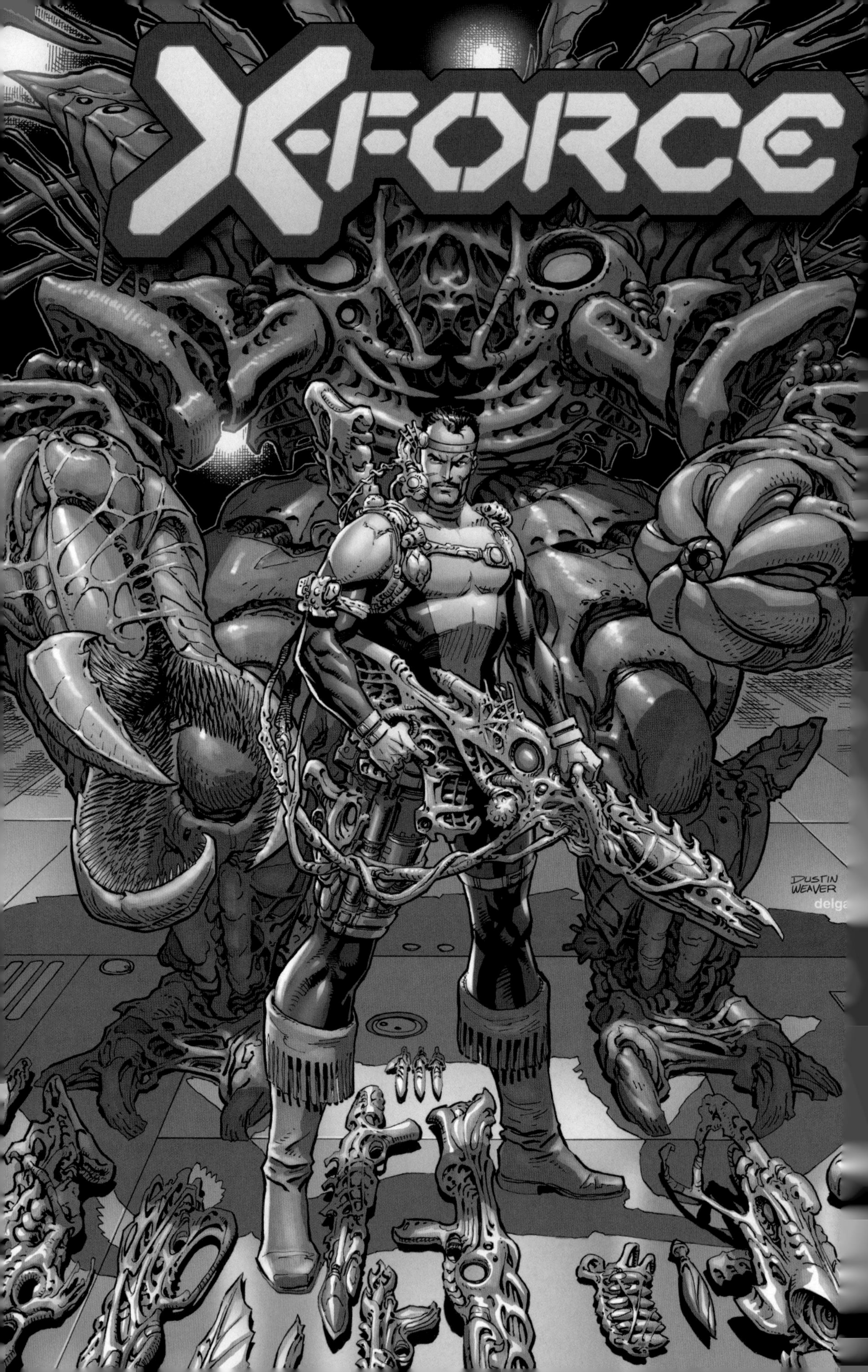
X-FORCE
DUSTIN
WEAVER
delga

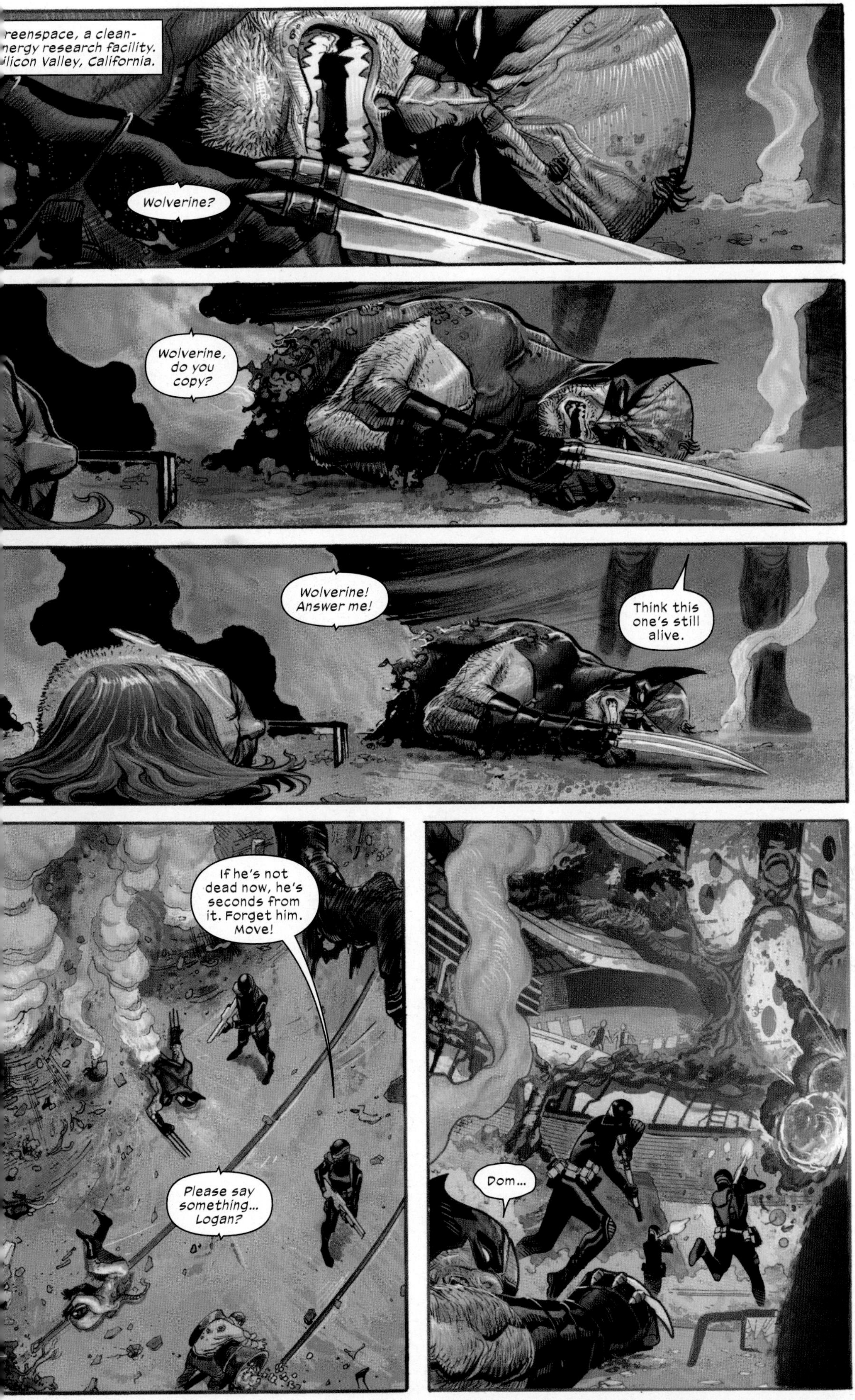

reenspace, a clean-
nergy research facility.
ilicon Valley, California.
Wolverine?
Wolverine, do you copy?
Wolverine! Answer me!
Think this one's still alive.
If he's not dead now, he's seconds from it. Forget him. Move!
Please say something... Logan?
Dom...

Krakoa.

...hurry.

Hold on, Logan. I know you're hurting.

You came for me in Korea.

Now I'm coming for you. It's my turn to raise some hell.

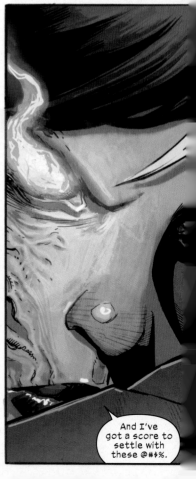

And I've got a score to settle with these @#$%.

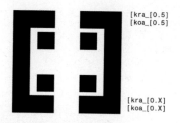

[kra_[0.5]
[koa_[0.5]

[kra_[0.X]
[koa_[0.X]

ONCE BITTEN

After the assassination of Professor X on Krakoa,
mutant leadership formed an agency for counterintelligence
and combat application dubbed X-FORCE.

Mysterious human strike teams have attacked Krakoan businesses,
first in the Atlantic and now a clean-energy facility in Silicon Valley,
prompting the deployment of Kid Omega, Domino and Wolverine -- but
the humans were prepared. By detonating the Krakoan gates at the
facility, they have taken out Wolverine and Kid Omega and stranded
Domino on Krakoa!

Forge    Sage   Beast

Domino    Gateway

Wolverine    Marvel Girl

[kra_[0.5]...]
[koa_[0.5]...]

[A._Spy_Agency]

[00_mutant_espionage]
[00_law_order___X___]

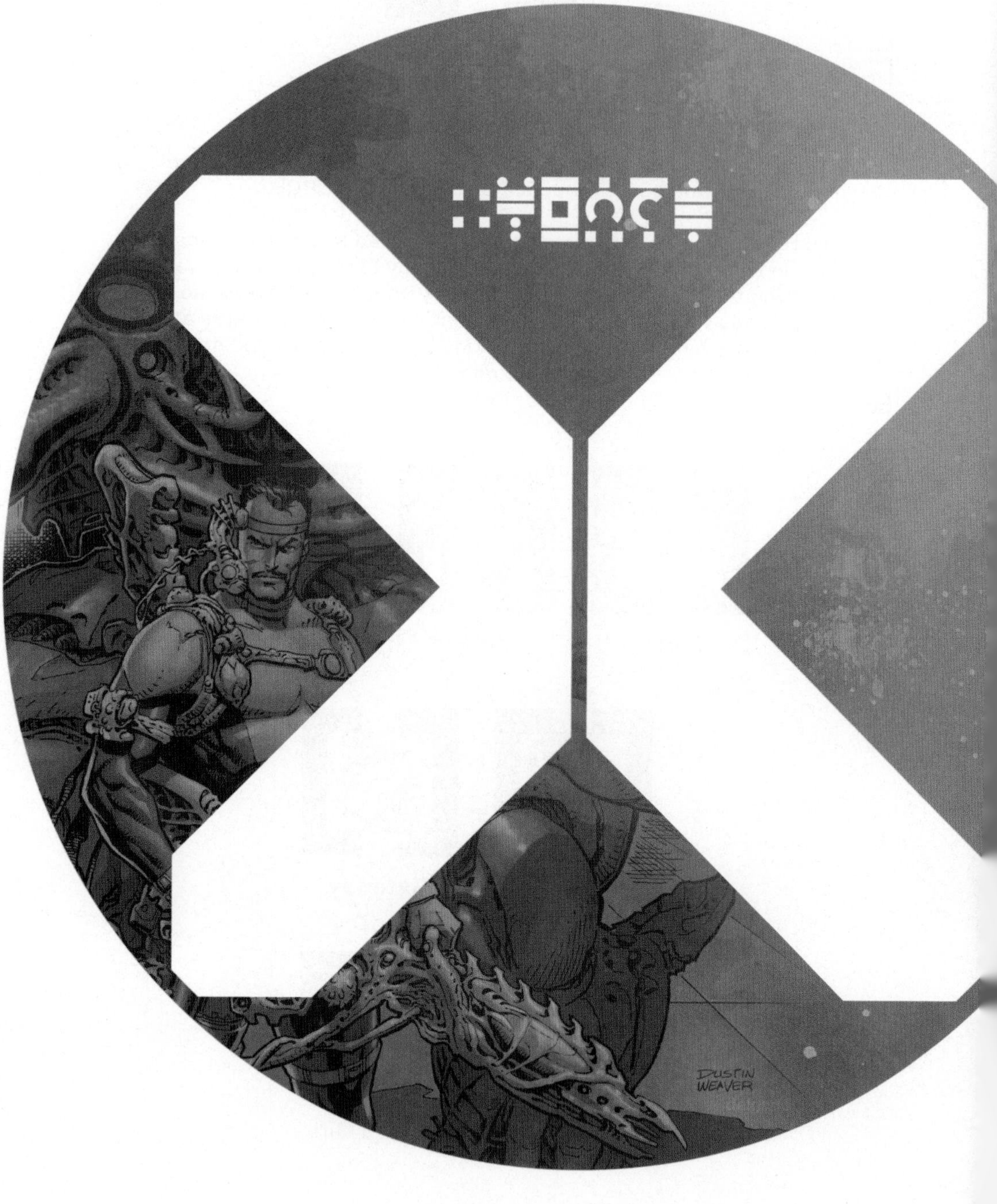
DUSTIN
WEAVER

[00_mutant_espionage]
[00_law_order___X___]

BENJAMIN PERCY................................[WRITER]
JOSHUA CASSARA................................[ARTIST]
DEAN WHITE & RACHELLE ROSENBERG.........[COLOR ARTISTS]
VC's JOE CARAMAGNA..........................[LETTERER]
TOM MULLER....................................[DESIGN]

DUSTIN WEAVER & EDGAR DELGADO...........[COVER ARTISTS]
RUSSELL DAUTERMAN & MATTHEW WILSON /
GREG LAND & JAY LEISTEN & FRANK D'ARMATA...............
...............................[VARIANT COVER ARTISTS]

JAY BOWEN...................................[PRODUCTION]

JONATHAN HICKMAN..........................[HEAD OF X]
CHRIS ROBINSON......................[ASSISTANT EDITOR]
JORDAN D. WHITE...............................[EDITOR]
C.B. CEBULSKI.......................[EDITOR IN CHIEF]
JOE QUESADA...................[CHIEF CREATIVE OFFICER]
DAN BUCKLEY................................[PRESIDENT]
ALAN FINE.........................[EXECUTIVE PRODUCER]

[05] X-FORCE

[ISSUE FIVE]............NECESSARY FORCE

[00_mutant_espionage]
[00_law_order___X___]

[00_00...0]
[00_00...5]

[00_probe_]
[00______]

[00______]

[00______X]

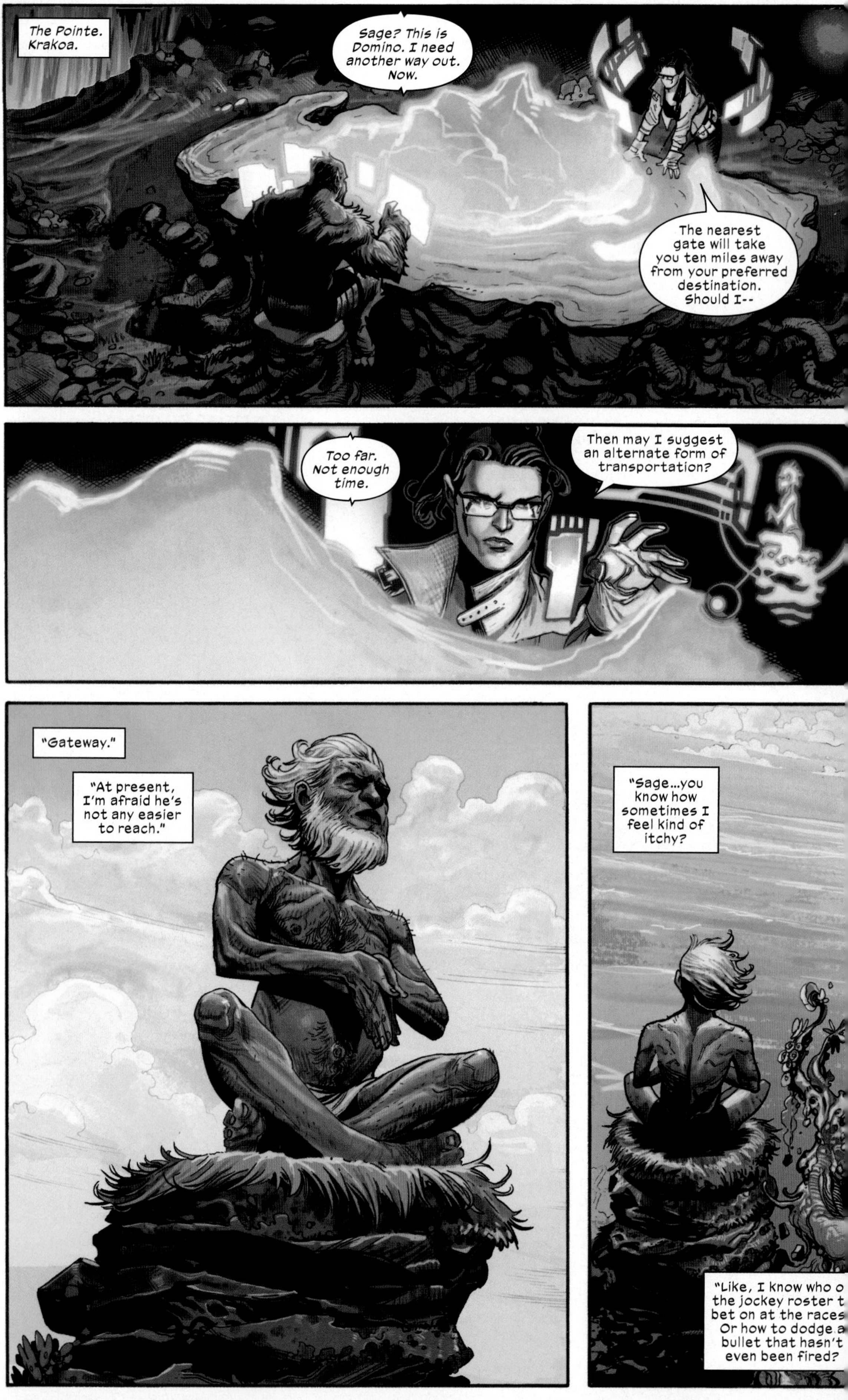
The Pointe. Krakoa.
Sage? This is Domino. I need another way out. Now.
The nearest gate will take you ten miles away from your preferred destination. Should I--
Too far. Not enough time.
Then may I suggest an alternate form of transportation?
"Gateway."
"At present, I'm afraid he's not any easier to reach."
"Sage...you know how sometimes I feel kind of itchy?
"Like, I know who o the jockey roster t bet on at the races Or how to dodge a bullet that hasn't even been fired?

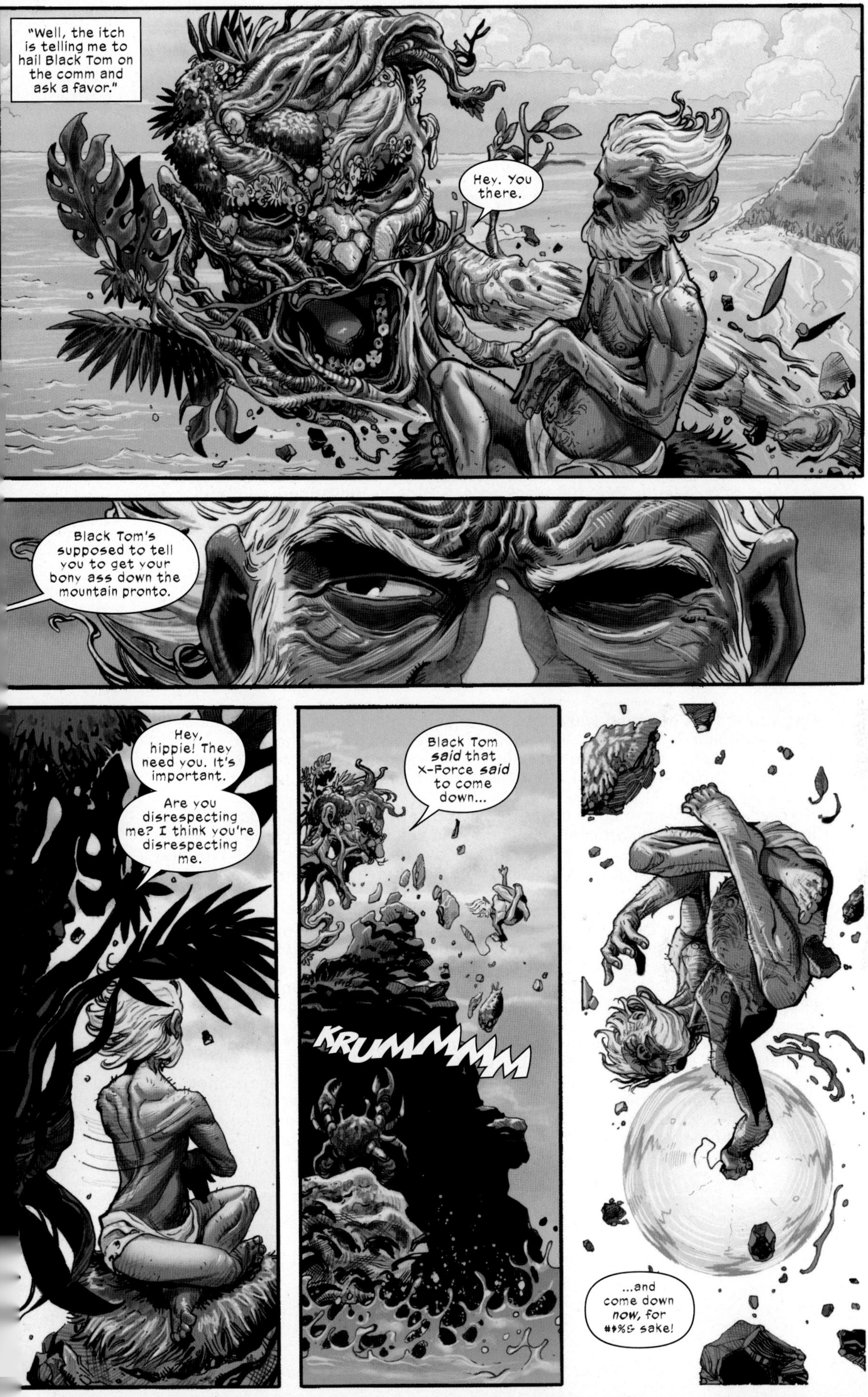
"Well, the itch is telling me to hail Black Tom on the comm and ask a favor."
Hey. You there.
Black Tom's supposed to tell you to get your bony ass down the mountain pronto.
Hey, hippie! They need you. It's important.
Are you disrespecting me? I think you're disrespecting me.
Black Tom *said* that X-Force *said* to come down...
KRUMMMMM
...and come down *now*, for #$%& sake!

THE UNCERTAINTY OF BLACK TOM CASSIDY

Black Tom isn't sure what he's gotten himself into. As Krakoa's chief security advisor, he is on the one hand a monitor. Instead of staring at grainy surveillance feeds or listening in on cellular transmissions, he is a vein of basalt sensitive to the vibrations of a conversation, he is a plankton-soaked surf that knows the exact dimensions of the ship it carries, he is a patch of grass that can discern the weighted pace of the mutant dashing across it.

There is, at any given moment, so much. The veg speaks, and he listens, always attuned to a possible threat. Which has, he'll admit, made him more than a little short-tempered and paranoid. "Imagine 10,000 voices babbling in your head, eh? And only one of them's whispering something critical, eh? Instead of a needle in a haystack, it's a bloody pine needle in a bloody wilderness you're after. And if you think that's easy to manage, may you be afflicted with itching without the benefit of scratching."

But he can do more -- much more -- than merely surveil. How much, he doesn't yet know.

He can activate the landscape. This is typically done in the name of defense. He might tangle an ankle with vines to trip someone up. Or use roots to unshoulder a rocky outcrop to crush someone else. Or even attempt to choke someone's lungs with fungal spores.

But sometimes his mind wanders in his sleep and he does things beyond his understanding or intention. For instance, the other night he had a dream about raising hell with his old pal Cain Marko -- and he awoke the next morning to find a 50-foot monolith of stone had risen in the shape of Juggernaut.

He can use the veg to communicate. The buzz of bees in a meadow and the hush of wind through branches can carry his voice. And though he has yet to master this technique, he seems to have the ability to geo-travel. Not just his shape but also his presence can be transferred through the Krakoan botanical network.

So far he has consciously been able to make his face rise up out of soil or his splintery fingers and bark-plated arms rise out of the groaning trunk of a tree. But unconsciously he has seemingly been swallowed by the island and re-formed elsewhere. Sometimes he wakes up on mountaintops and in valleys -- and once at the bottom of the reef with a mouth sputtering with seawater.

"Every day's a bloody surprise," he says. "Like Krakoa's a fun house. Like sometimes a trapdoor opens up beneath Black Tom's feet, and he's falling into a pit of balloons and laughing like a wee little baby. But other times it's like Black Tom's trapped in a maze of mirrors and over here he's all smooshed-up and blobby and over there he's all stretched out like a fleshy twig and then a dark mirror shows him something he don't much like and he's screaming, screaming, screaming so loud he hopes the vision will shatter."

...don't have to pond, Logan. But going to keep talking.

o you ow I'm ere.

I guess you could say I've been down on my luck.

I know I was a few inches and seconds away from that gate cleaving my body in half...

But my power has felt-- I don't know-- *watered down* lately.

Geez, you're heavy. #@$%& Adamantium.

nyway. It's like my luck lesser somehow. Like a abbit foot with the fur worn off.

Heard you're down a few soldiers.

Thought you liked your desk job, Forge?

Can't hide in the Armory the rest of my life.

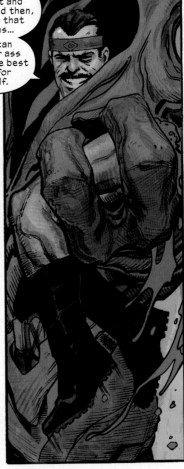

I need to come out and play now and then, and when that happens...

...you can bet your ass I save the best toys for myself.

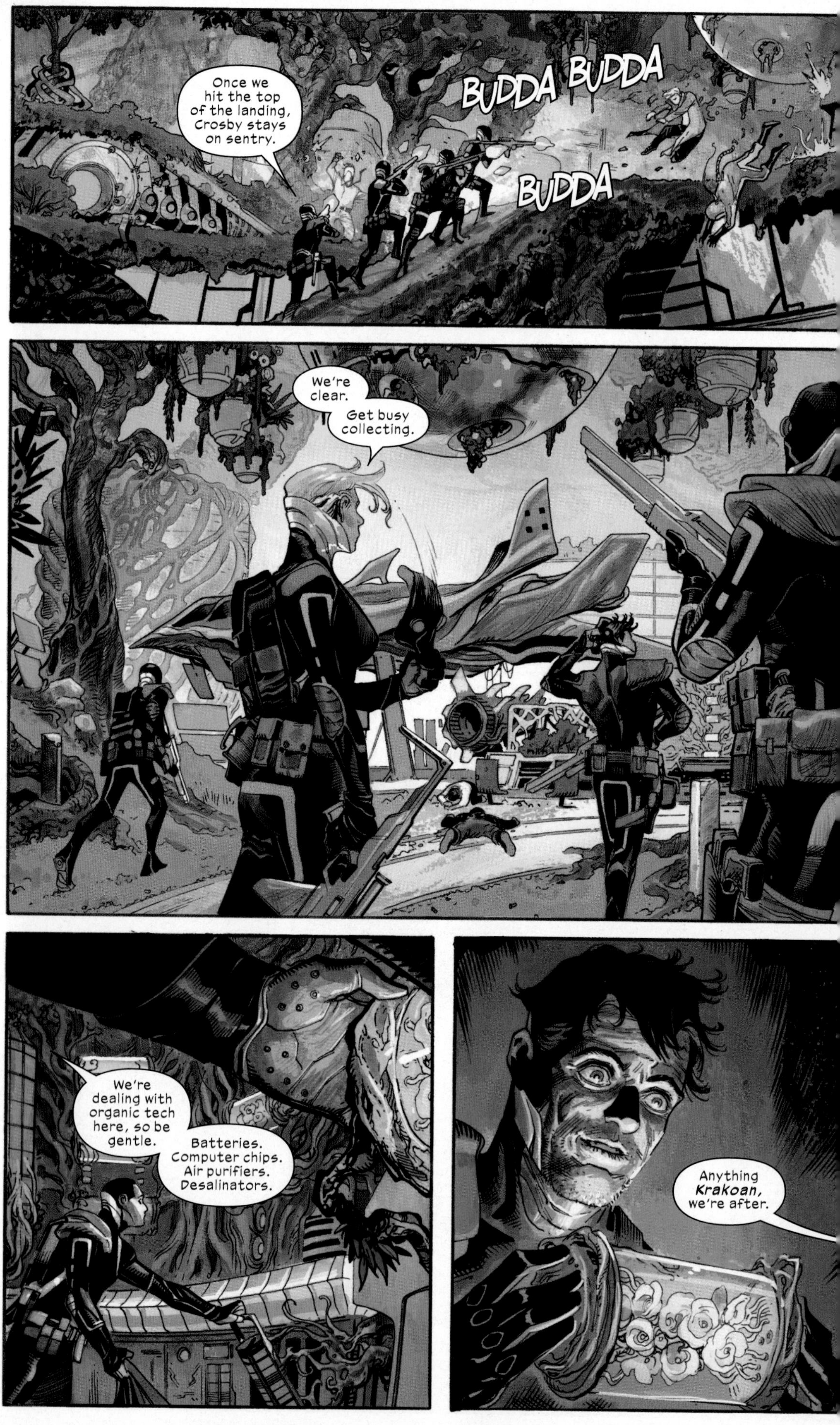
Once we hit the top of the landing, Crosby stays on sentry.
BUDDA BUDDA
BUDDA
We're clear.
Get busy collecting.
We're dealing with organic tech here, so be gentle.
Batteries. Computer chips. Air purifiers. Desalinators.
Anything Krakoan, we're after.

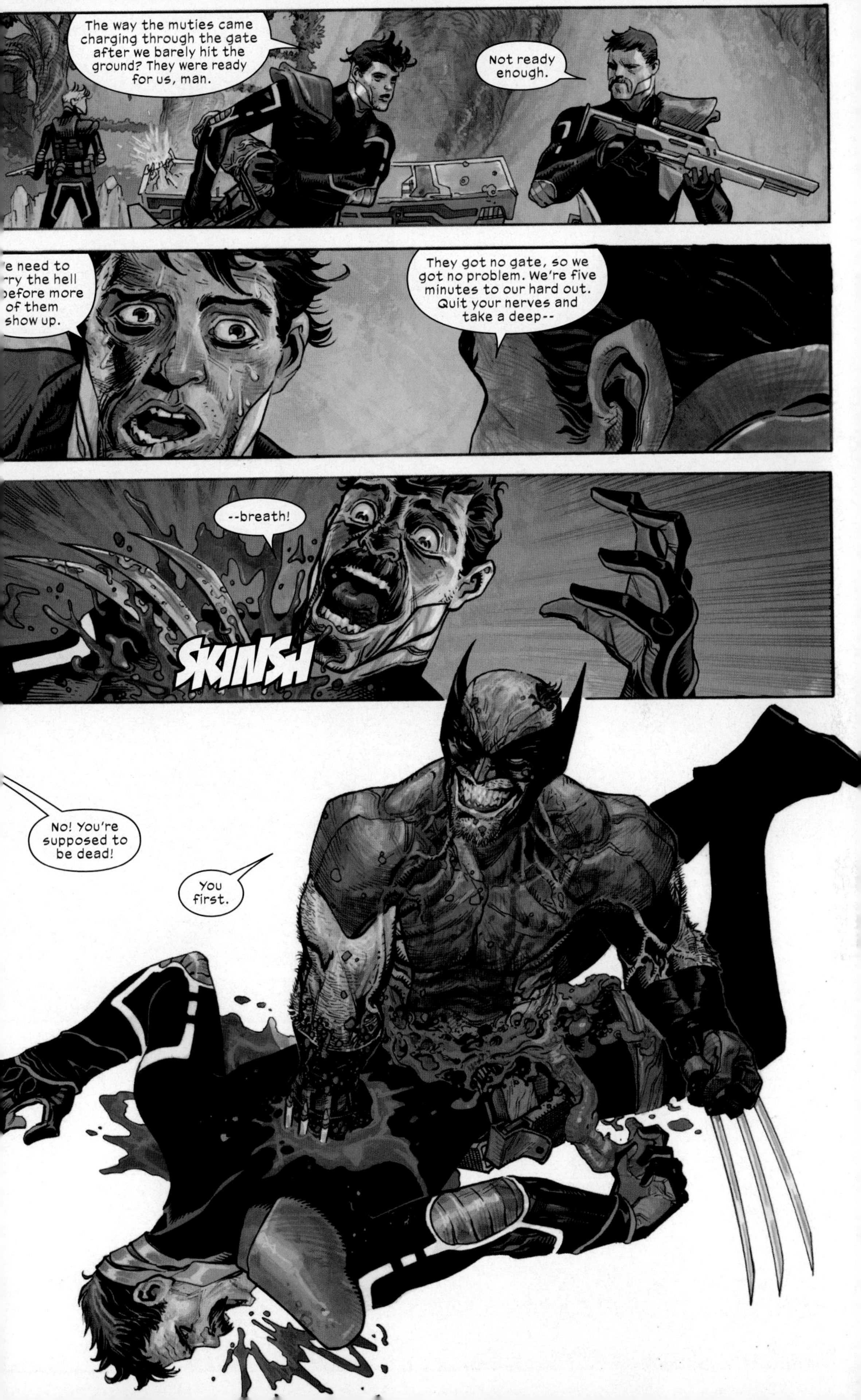
The way the muties came charging through the gate after we barely hit the ground? They were ready for us, man.
Not ready enough.
'e need to rry the hell before more of them show up.
They got no gate, so we got no problem. We're five minutes to our hard out. Quit your nerves and take a deep--
--breath!
SKINSH
No! You're supposed to be dead!
You first.

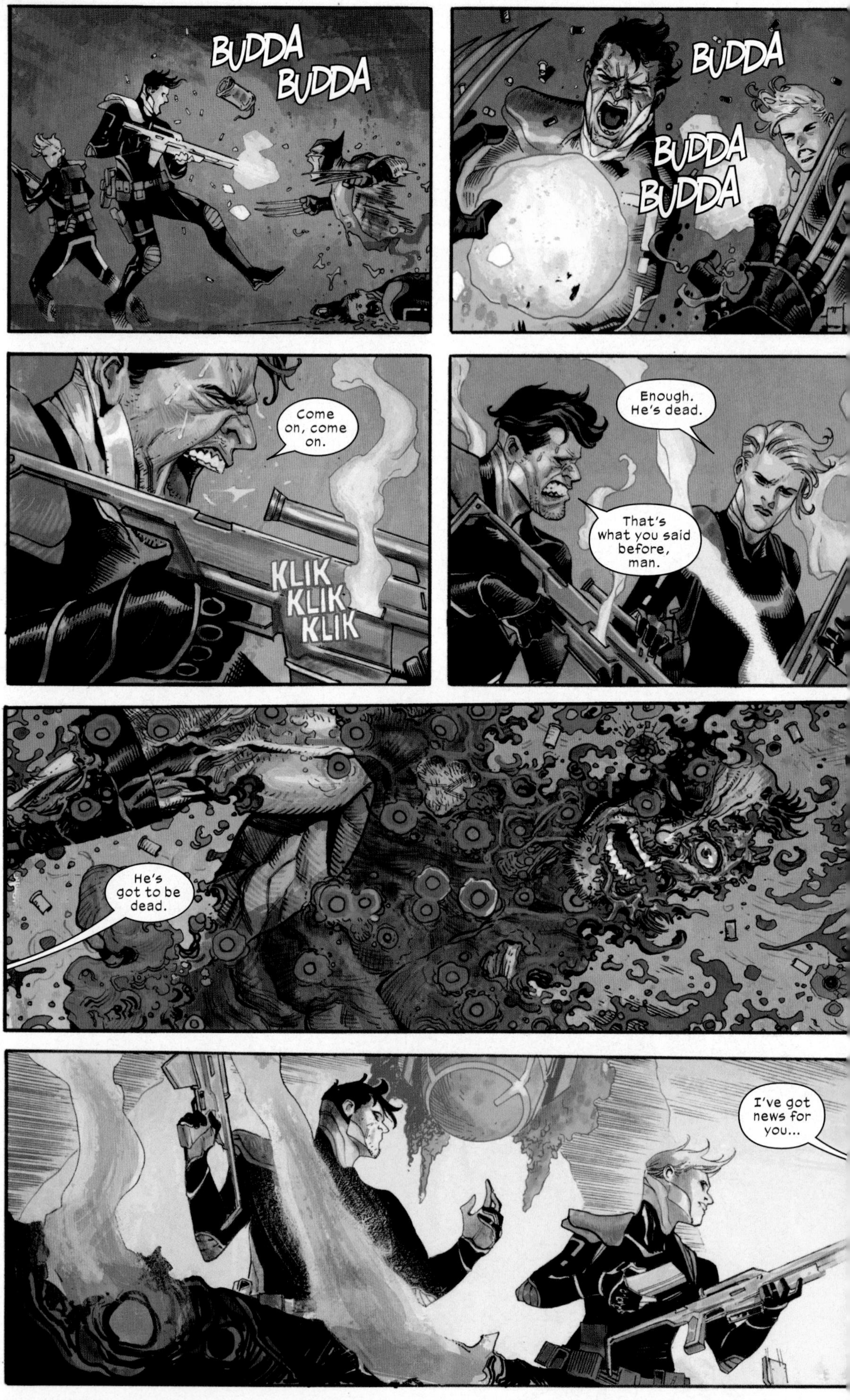
BUDDA
BUDDA
BUDDA
BUDDA
BUDDA
BUDDA
Come on, come on.
KLIK
KLIK
KLIK
Enough. He's dead.
That's what you said before, man.
He's got to be dead.
I've got news for you...

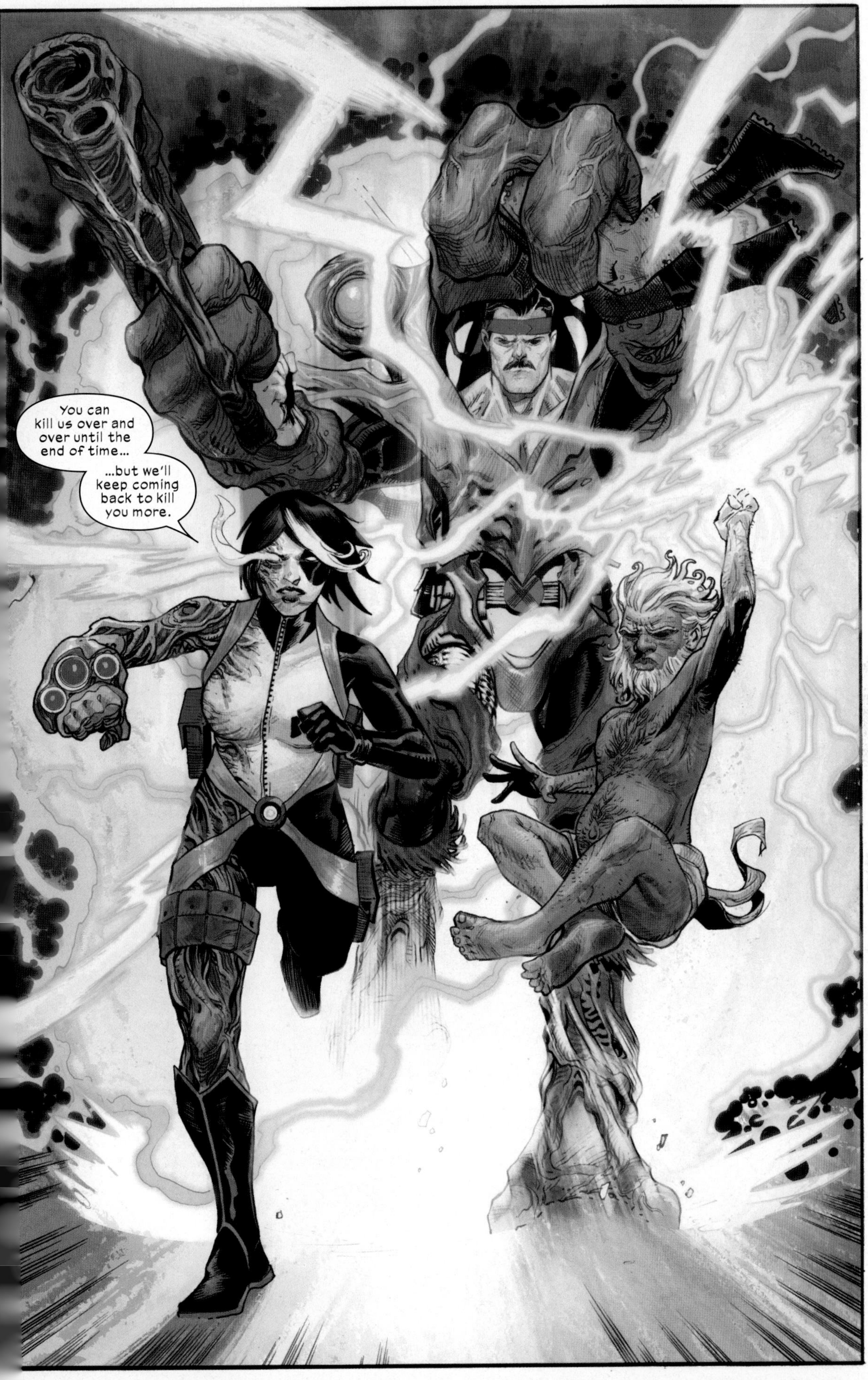
You can kill us over and over until the end of time...
...but we'll keep coming back to kill you more.

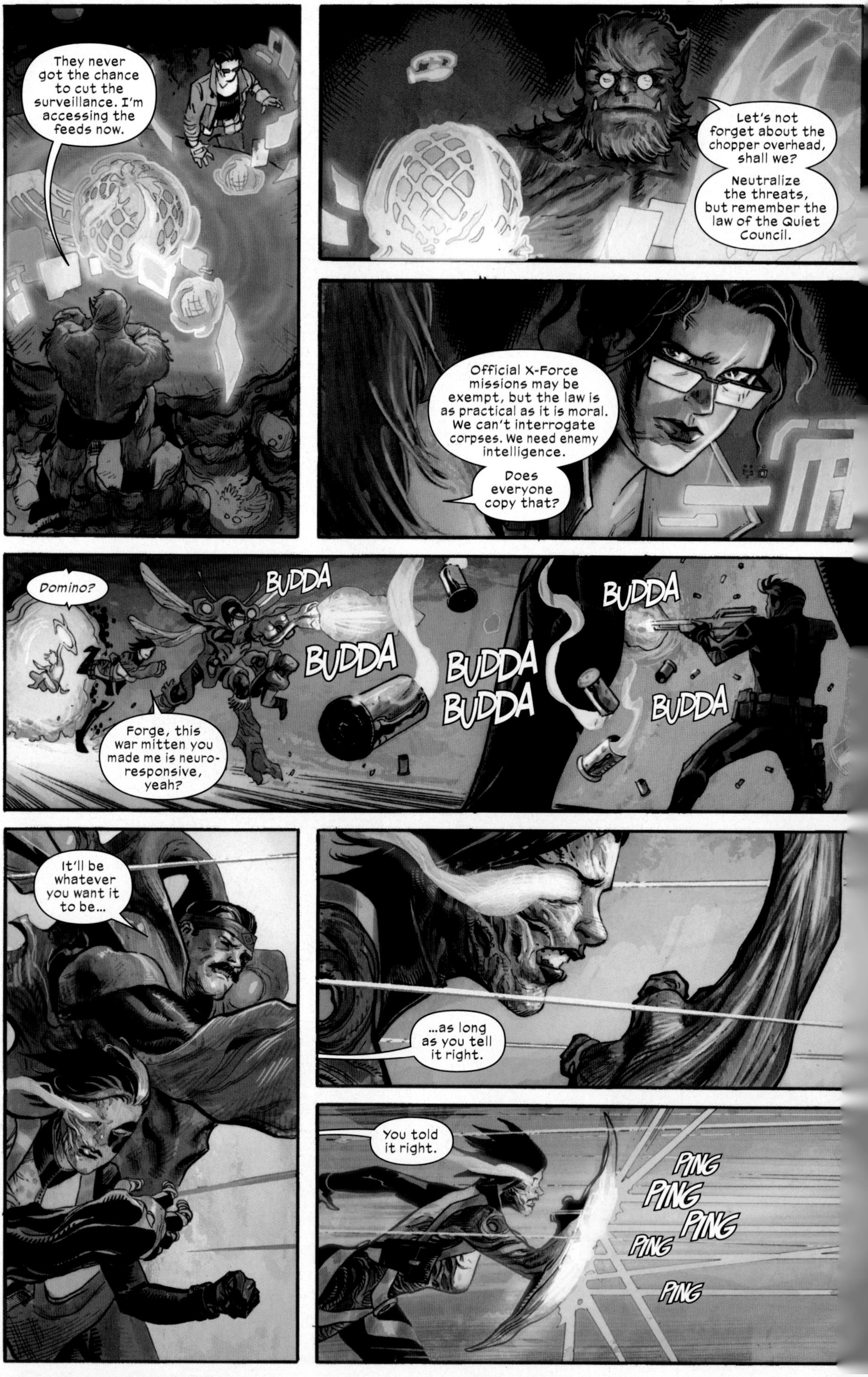

They never got the chance to cut the surveillance. I'm accessing the feeds now.
Let's not forget about the chopper overhead, shall we?
Neutralize the threats, but remember the law of the Quiet Council.
Official X-Force missions may be exempt, but the law is as practical as it is moral. We can't interrogate corpses. We need enemy intelligence.
Does everyone copy that?
Domino?
BUDDA
BUDDA
BUDDA
BUDDA
BUDDA
BUDDA
Forge, this war mitten you made me is neuro-responsive, yeah?
It'll be whatever you want it to be...
...as long as you tell it right.
You told it right.
PING
PING
PING
PING
PING

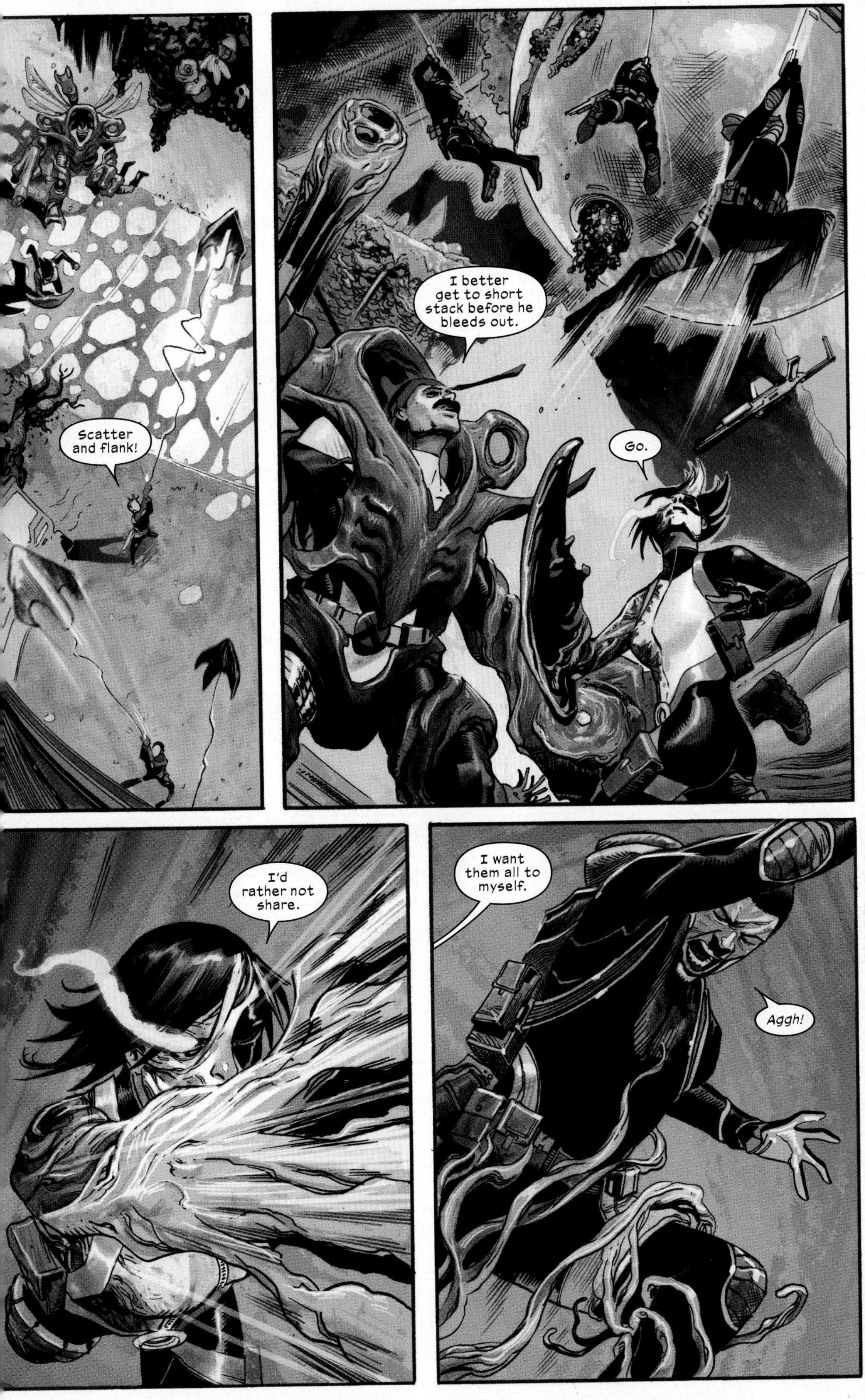
Scatter and flank!
I better get to short stack before he bleeds out.
Go.
I'd rather not share.
I want them all to myself.
Aggh!

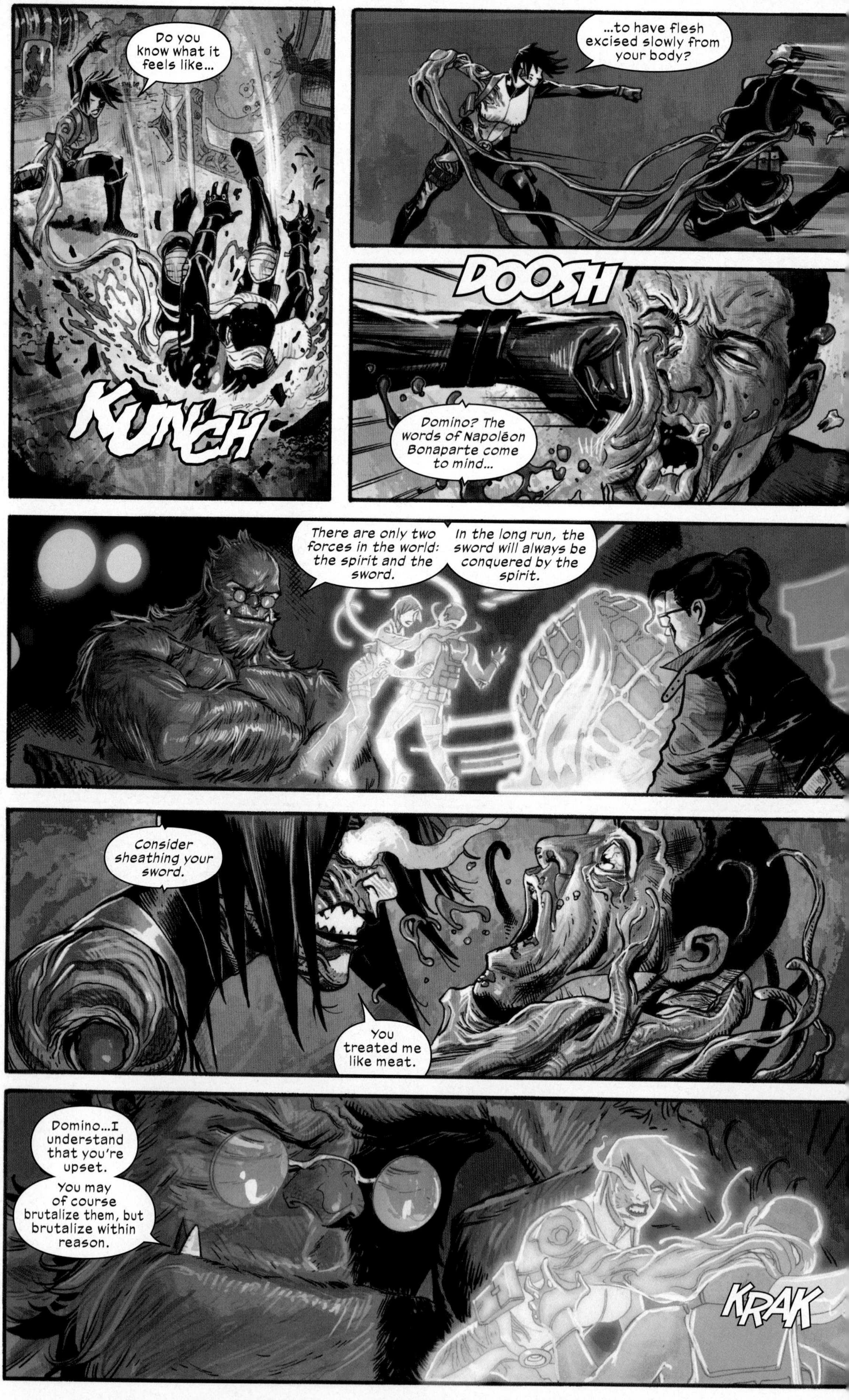

Do you know what it feels like...
KUNCH
...to have flesh excised slowly from your body?
DOOSH
Domino? The words of Napoléon Bonaparte come to mind...
There are only two forces in the world: the spirit and the sword.
In the long run, the sword will always be conquered by the spirit.
Consider sheathing your sword.
You treated me like meat.
Domino...I understand that you're upset.
You may of course brutalize them, but brutalize within reason.
KRAK

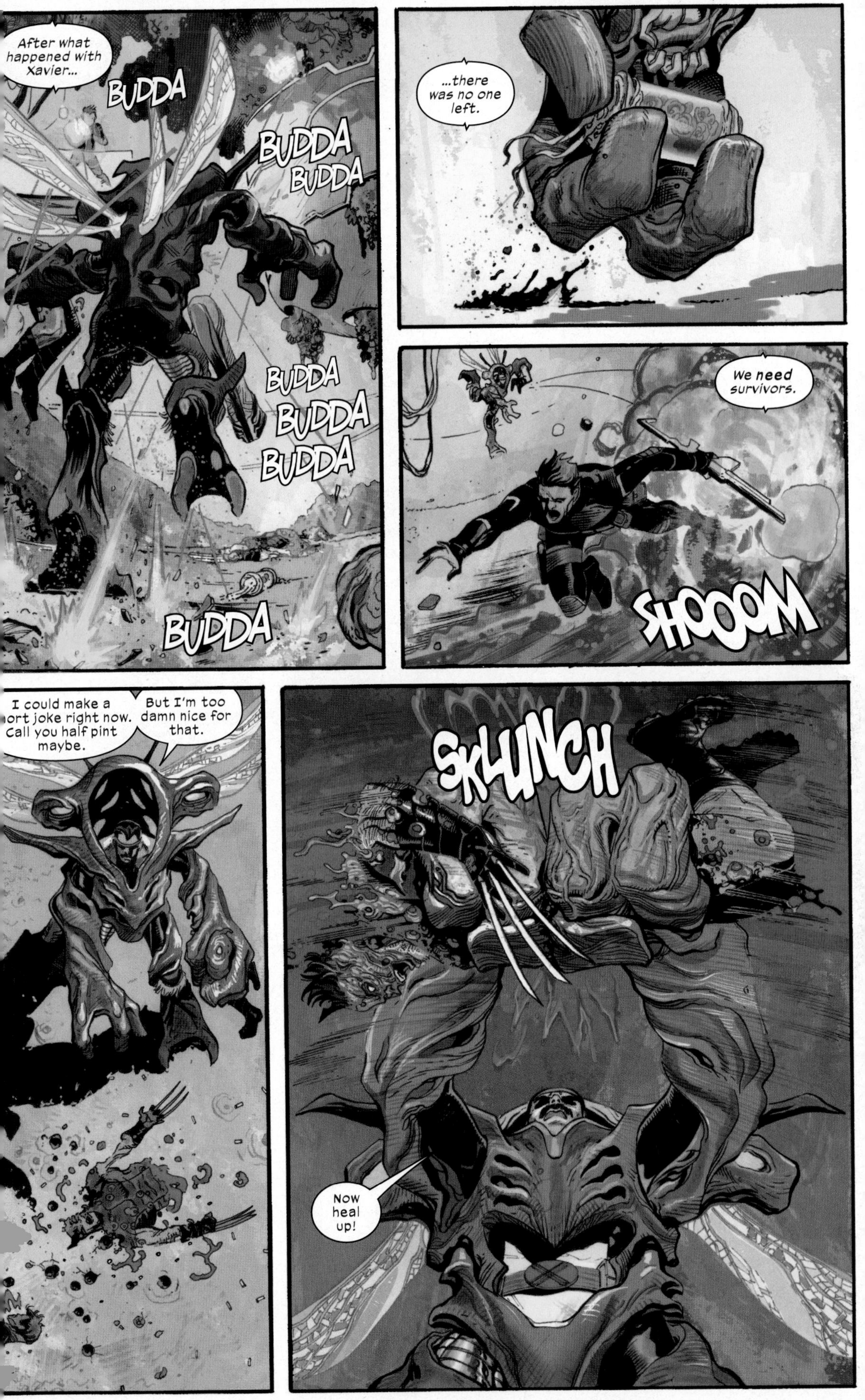
After what happened with Xavier...
BUDDA
BUDDA
BUDDA
BUDDA
BUDDA
BUDDA
BUDDA
...there was no one left.
We need survivors.
SHOOOM
I could make a ort joke right now. Call you half pint maybe.
But I'm too damn nice for that.
SKLUNCH
Now heal up!

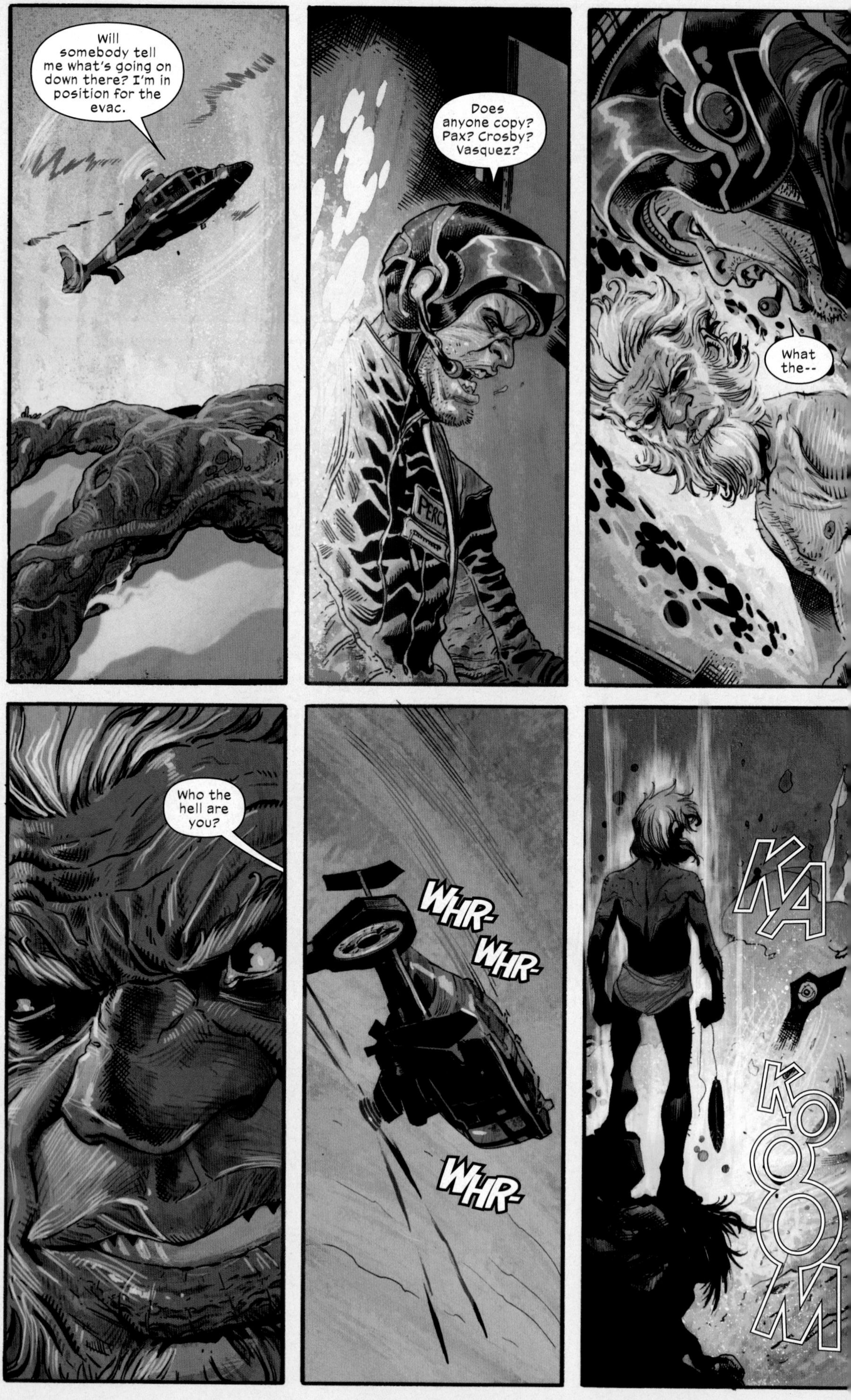
Will somebody tell me what's going on down there? I'm in position for the evac.
Does anyone copy? Pax? Crosby? Vasquez?
What the--
Who the hell are you?
WHR-
WHR-
WHR-
KA
KOOOM

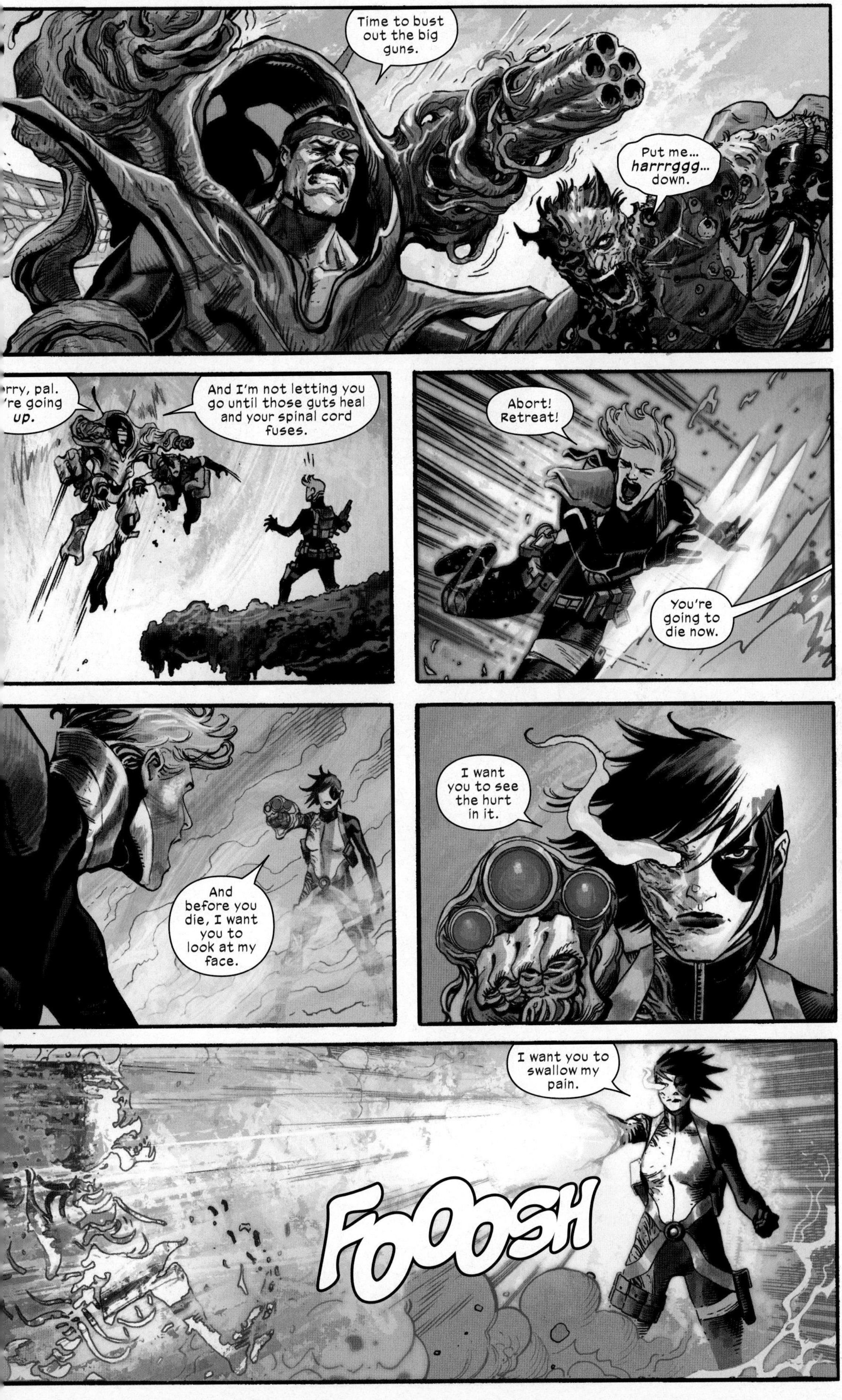
Time to bust out the big guns.
Put me... *harrrggg*... down.
rry, pal. 're going *up.*
And I'm not letting you go until those guts heal and your spinal cord fuses.
Abort! Retreat!
You're going to die now.
And before you die, I want you to look at my face.
I want you to see the hurt in it.
I want you to swallow my pain.
FOOOSH

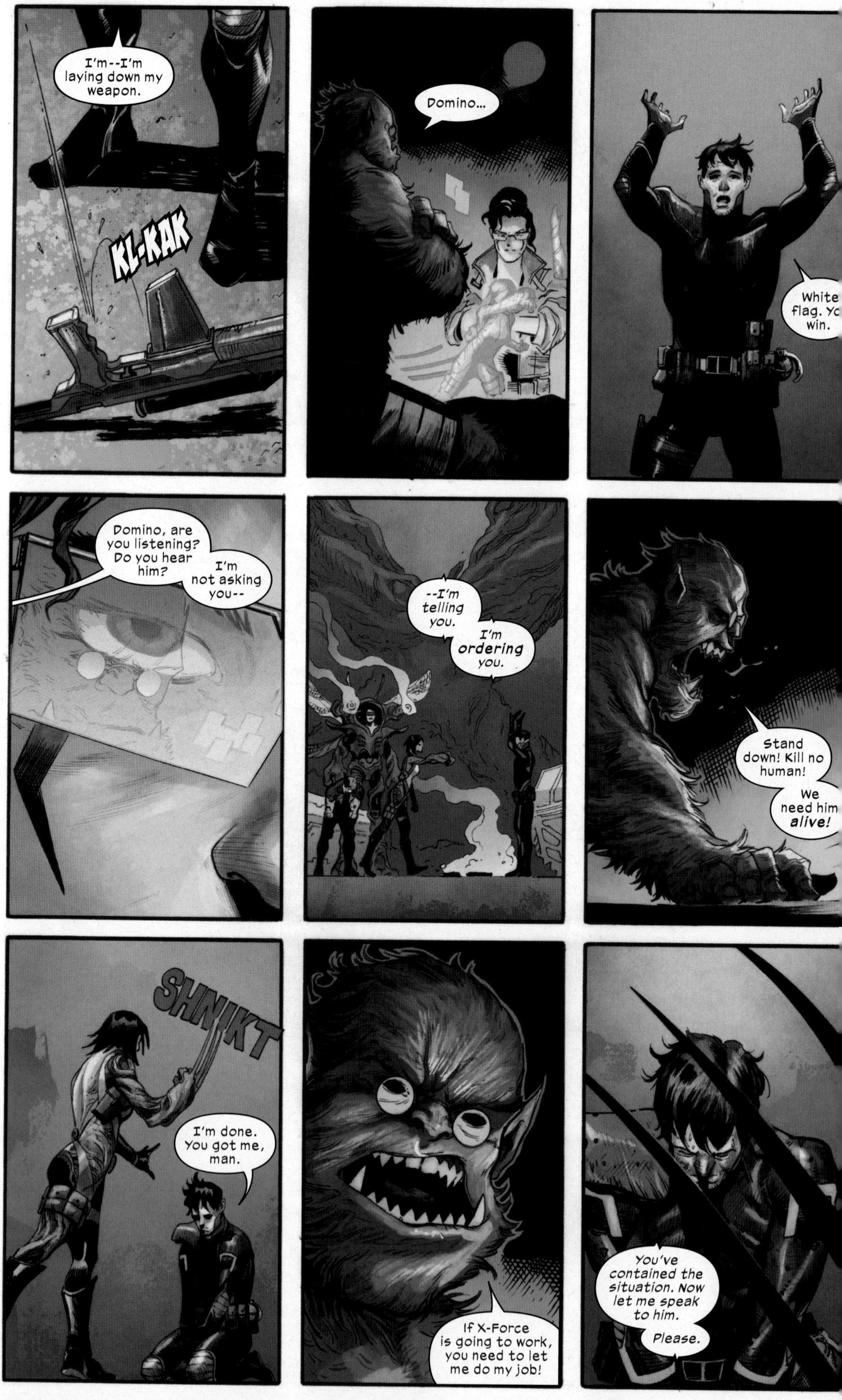
I'm--I'm laying down my weapon.
KL-KAK
Domino...
White flag. Yo win.
Domino, are you listening? Do you hear him?
I'm not asking you--
--I'm telling you.
I'm ordering you.
Stand down! Kill no human!
We need him alive!
SHNIKT
I'm done. You got me, man.
If X-Force is going to work, you need to let me do my job!
You've contained the situation. Now let me speak to him.
Please.

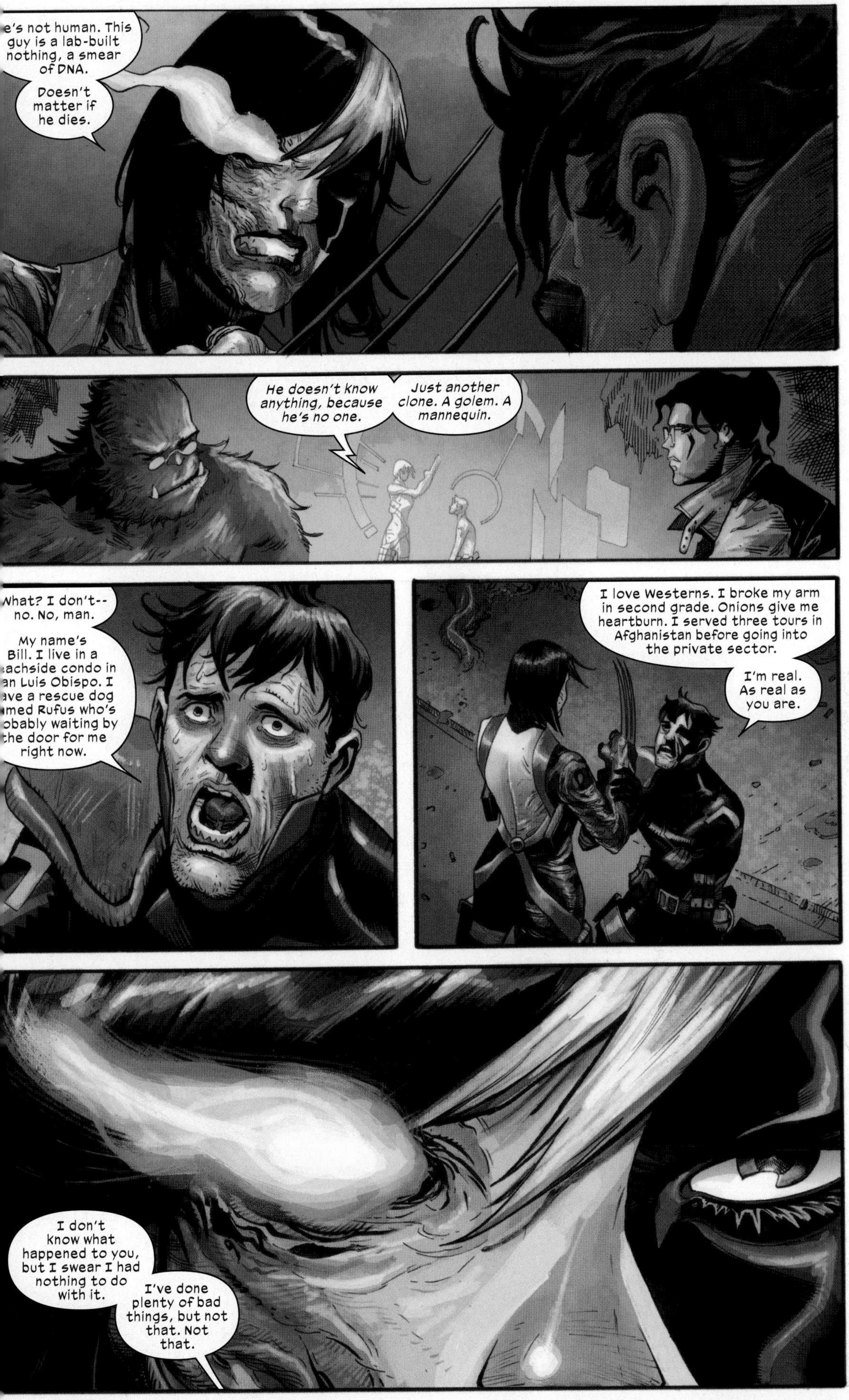
e's not human. This guy is a lab-built nothing, a smear of DNA.
Doesn't matter if he dies.
He doesn't know anything, because he's no one.
Just another clone. A golem. A mannequin.
What? I don't-- no. No, man.
My name's Bill. I live in a achside condo in an Luis Obispo. I ave a rescue dog amed Rufus who's obably waiting by the door for me right now.
I love Westerns. I broke my arm in second grade. Onions give me heartburn. I served three tours in Afghanistan before going into the private sector.
I'm real. As real as you are.
I don't know what happened to you, but I swear I had nothing to do with it.
I've done plenty of bad things, but not that. Not that.

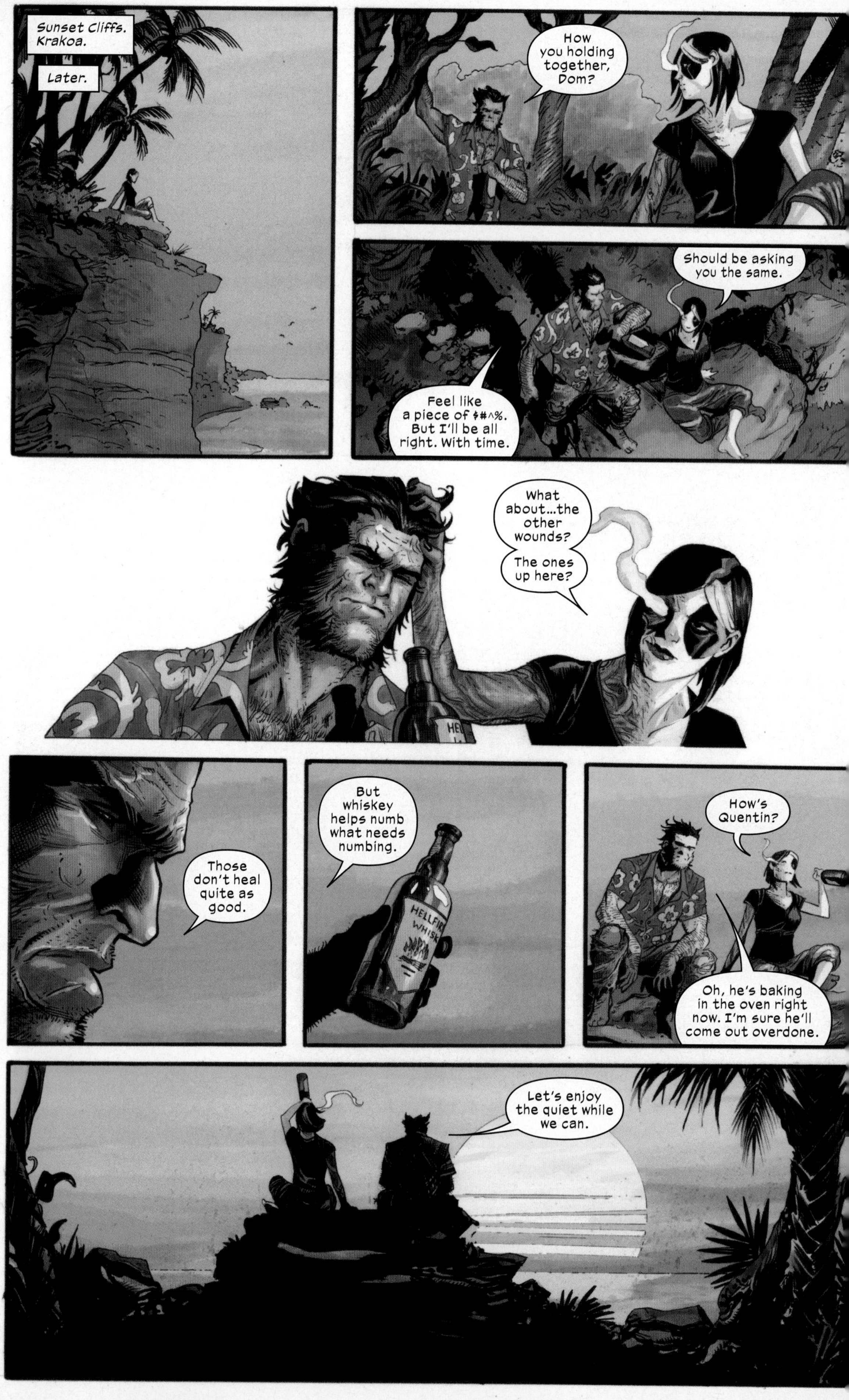

Sunset Cliffs. Krakoa.
Later.
How you holding together, Dom?
Should be asking you the same.
Feel like a piece of $#^%. But I'll be all right. With time.
What about...the other wounds?
The ones up here?
Those don't heal quite as good.
But whiskey helps numb what needs numbing.
HELLFIRE WHISK
How's Quentin?
Oh, he's baking in the oven right now. I'm sure he'll come out overdone.
Let's enjoy the quiet while we can.

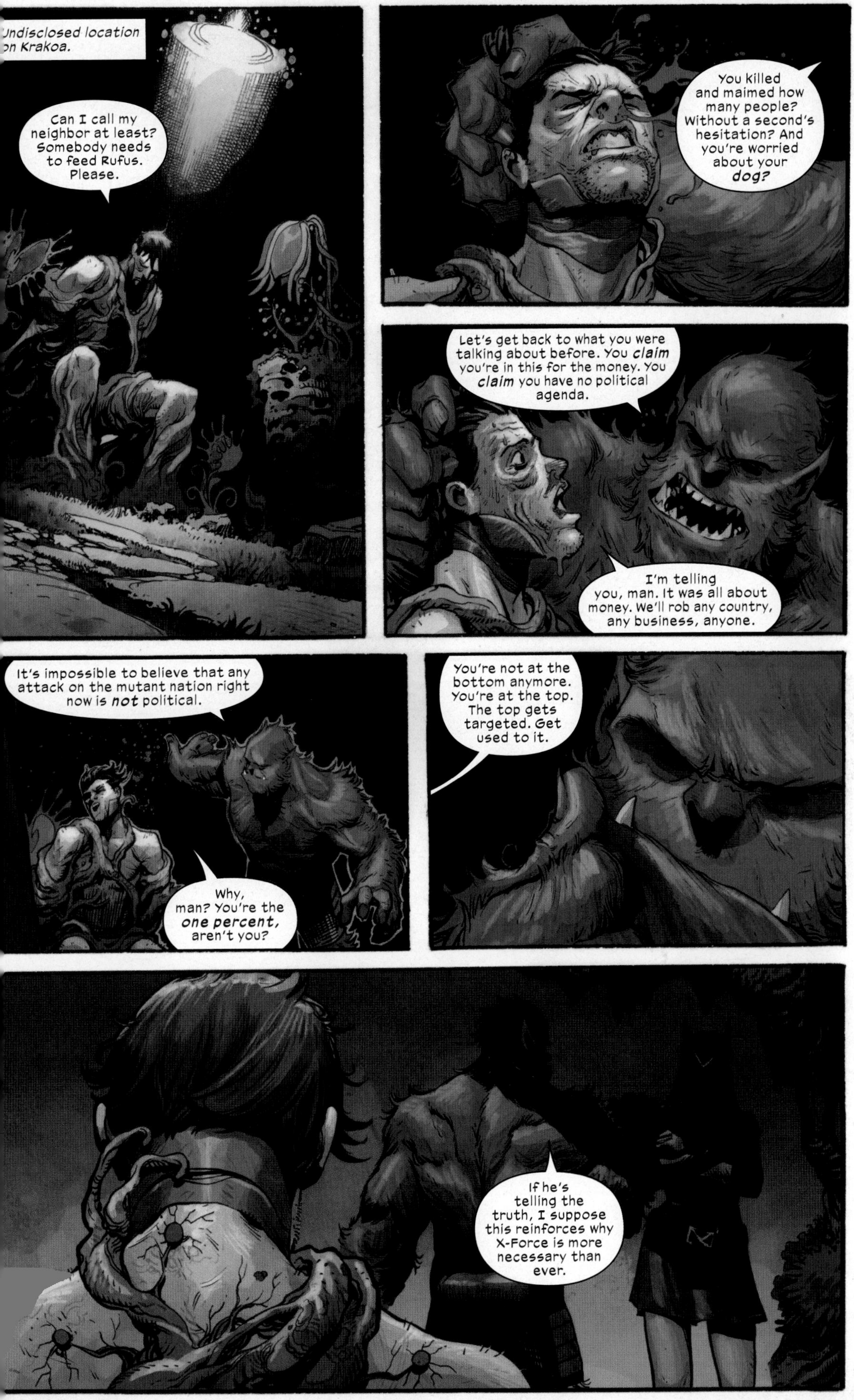

Undisclosed location on Krakoa.
Can I call my neighbor at least? Somebody needs to feed Rufus. Please.
You killed and maimed how many people? Without a second's hesitation? And you're worried about your *dog?*
Let's get back to what you were talking about before. You *claim* you're in this for the money. You *claim* you have no political agenda.
I'm telling you, man. It was all about money. We'll rob any country, any business, anyone.
It's impossible to believe that any attack on the mutant nation right now is *not* political.
Why, man? You're the *one percent,* aren't you?
You're not at the bottom anymore. You're at the top. The top gets targeted. Get used to it.
If he's telling the truth, I suppose this reinforces why X-Force is more necessary than ever.

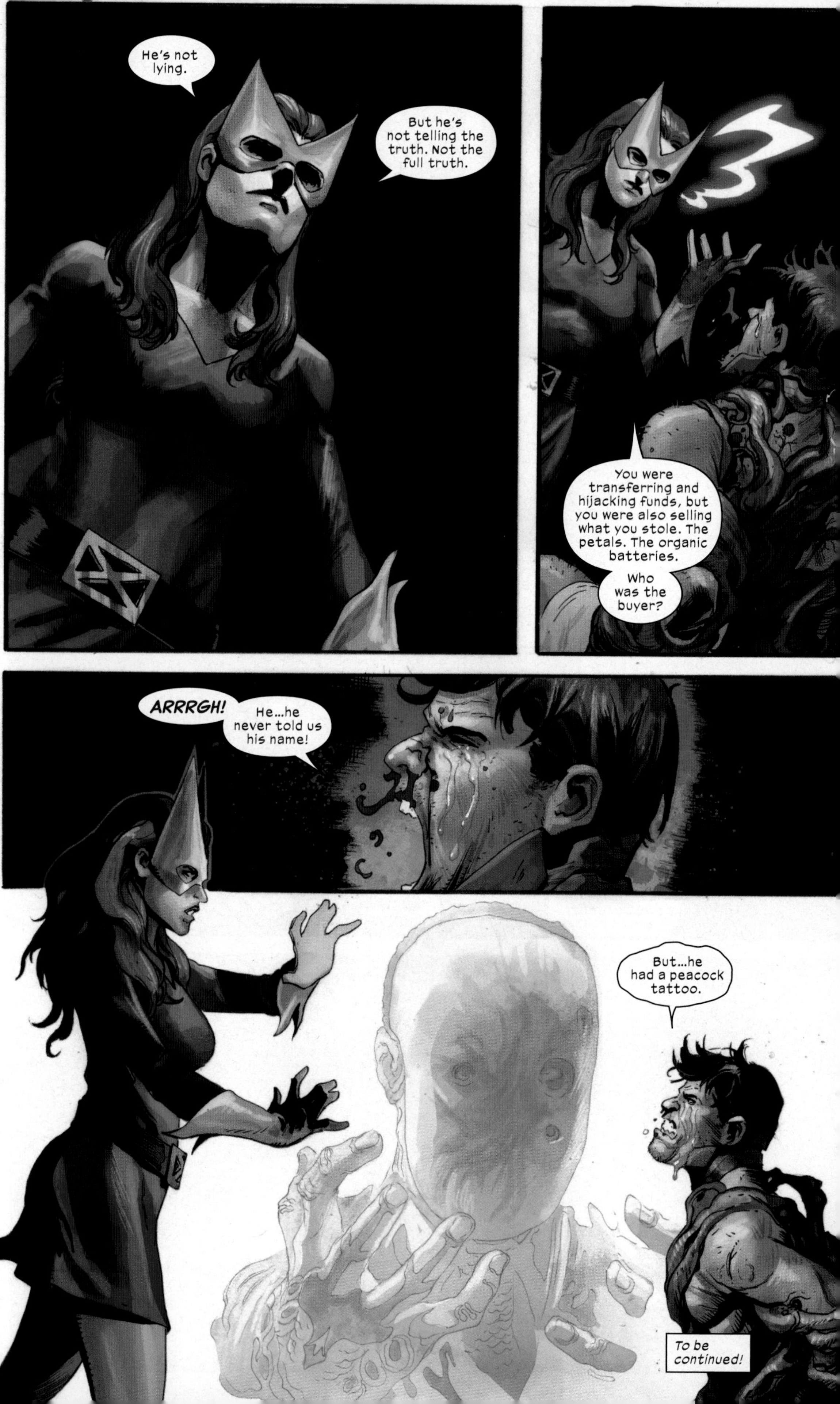
He's not lying.
But he's not telling the truth. Not the full truth.
You were transferring and hijacking funds, but you were also selling what you stole. The petals. The organic batteries.
Who was the buyer?
ARRRGH!
He...he never told us his name!
But...he had a peacock tattoo.
To be continued!

THE MERCS

The declaration of mutant sovereignty -- and subsequent treaty ratification -- has led to what Xavier refers to -- hopefully -- as a leap toward globalization. The political, economic and even cultural implications of this moment are too recent and numerous to fully comprehend, but one definitive result has been the widespread demilitarization and de-escalation of violence in conflict zones.

Is this because the world feels a sudden, if not momentary, sense of unity and safety and peace? Or is it because military resources are being conserved and readjusted in anxious preparation for what might come next?

Whatever the reason, thousands of members of military divisions have found themselves pulled from the field and bored by garrison life. The high stakes and spiked adrenaline of the combat zone -- dodging bullets and hunting down enemy forces and fighting for one's country -- have been replaced by passing barracks and uniform inspections.

MERC grew out of this reduction and sequestration. The top-secret paramilitary unit is driven by two things: the want for heavy combat tempo and high-dollar payment. They have declared themselves loyal to no nation and no cause except themselves.

There will one day be a large-scale war, but until then, the MERCs are content to fight the million little wars that still take place in the shadows.

Beast may or may not have reached out -- without consulting the rest of his team, via a shadow account -- to inquire about their services.

—

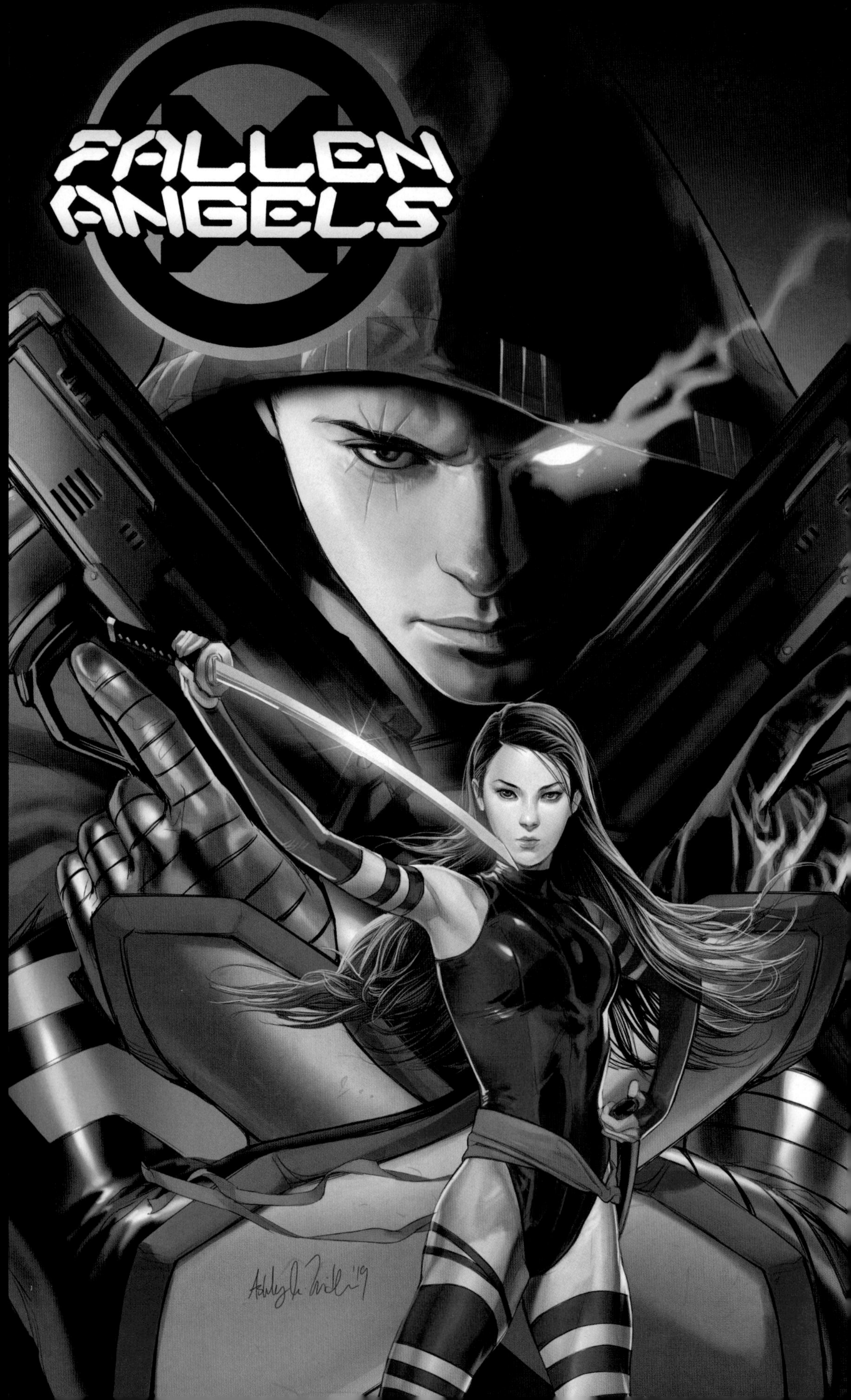
FALLEN ANGELS

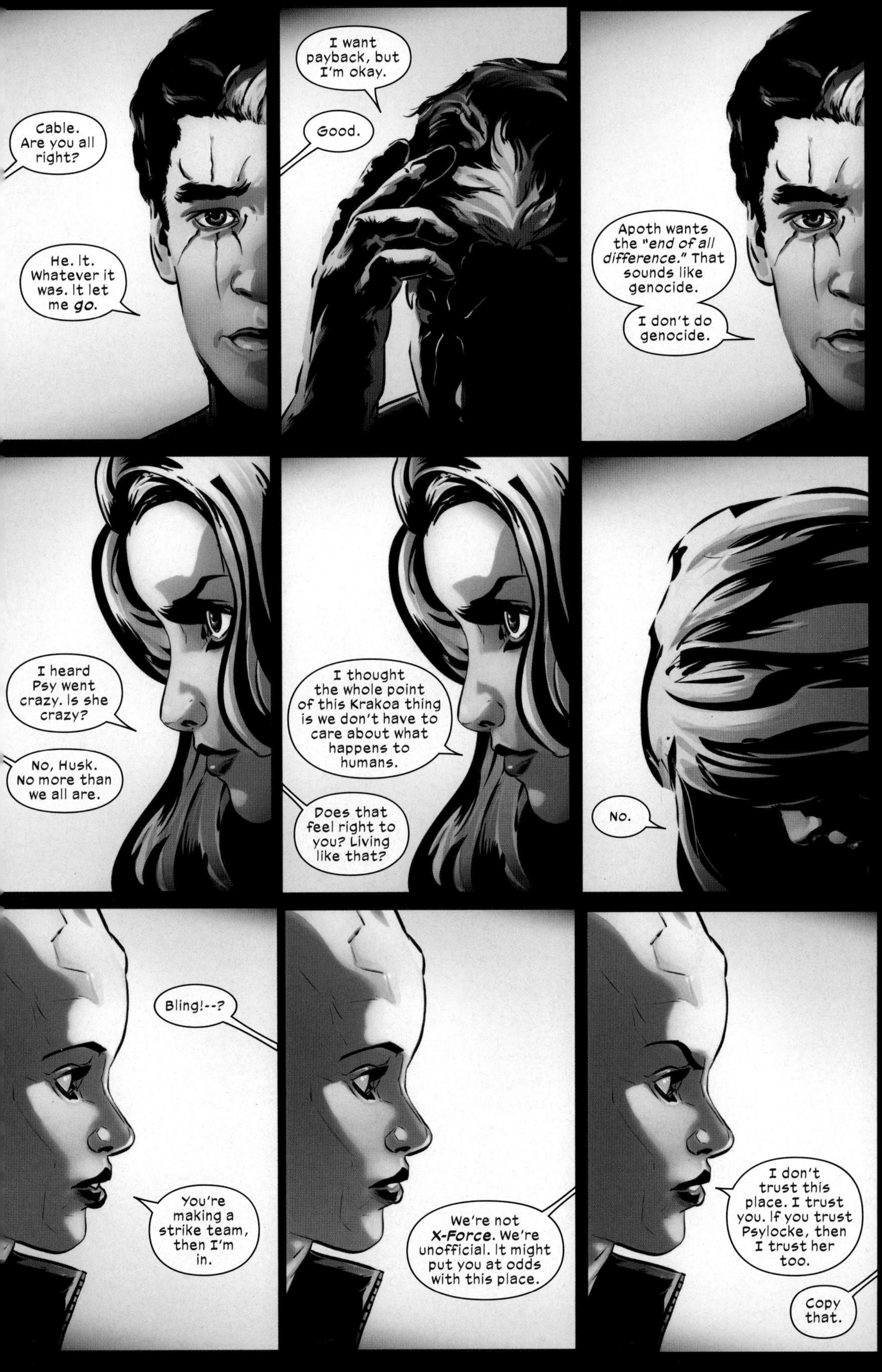
Cable. Are you all right?
He. It. Whatever it was. It let me *go*.
I want payback, but I'm okay.
Good.
Apoth wants the *"end of all difference."* That sounds like genocide.
I don't do genocide.
I heard Psy went crazy. Is she crazy?
No, Husk. No more than we all are.
I thought the whole point of this Krakoa thing is we don't have to care about what happens to humans.
Does that feel right to you? Living like that?
No.
Bling!--?
You're making a strike team, then I'm in.
We're not ***X-Force***. We're unofficial. It might put you at odds with this place.
I don't trust this place. I trust you. If you trust Psylocke, then I trust her too.
Copy that.

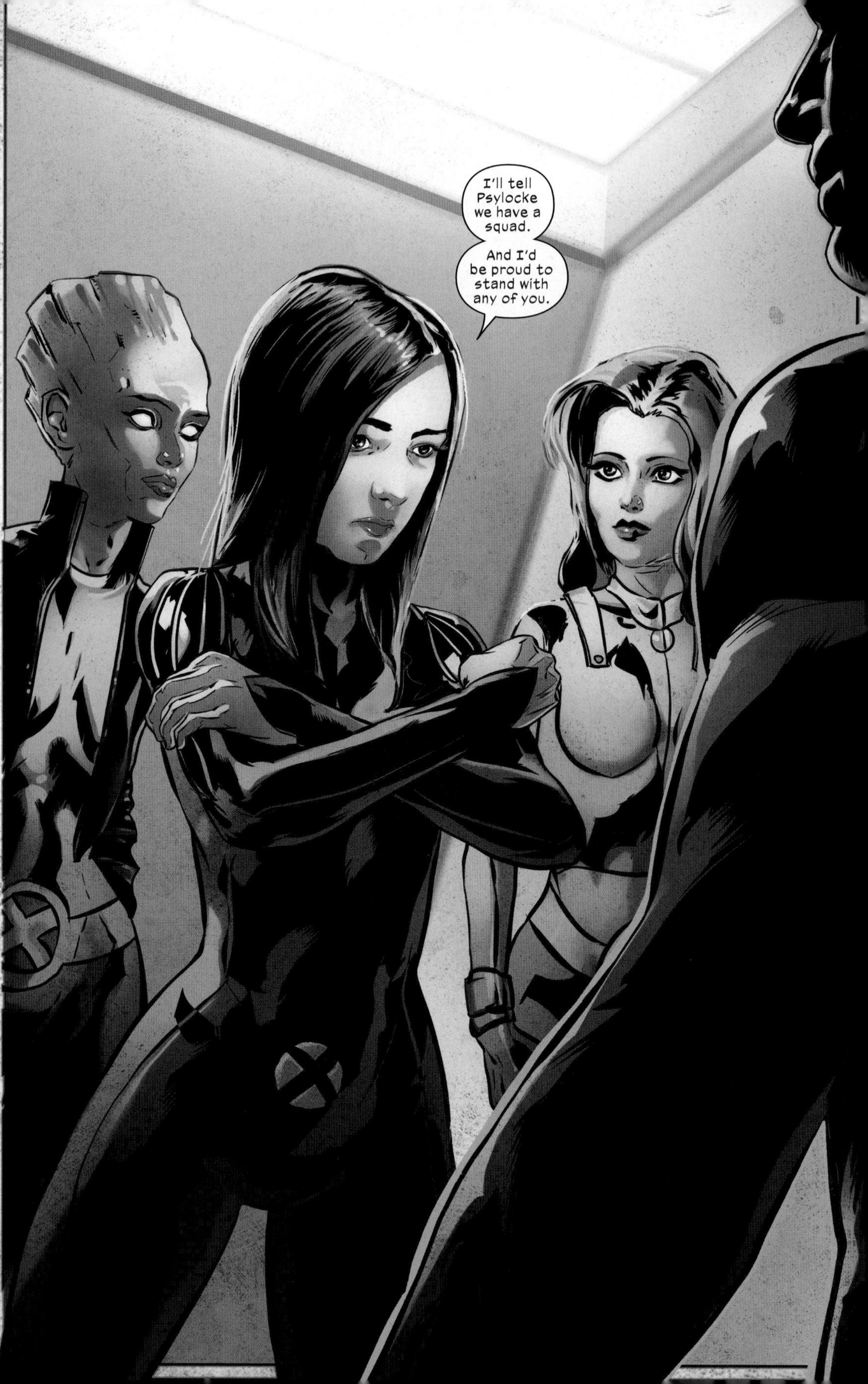
I'll tell Psylocke we have a squad.
And I'd be proud to stand with any of you.

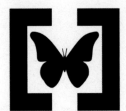

[kra_[0.5]
[koa_[0.5]

[kra_[0.X]
[koa_[0.X]

LEAD THE WAY

Mutants around the world are flocking to the island-nation of Krakoa for safety, security and to be part of the first mutant society.

After a prophetic vision, Psylocke hunts for a mysterious new enemy: Apoth. Responsible for the creation of a dangerous new cyberdrug called Overclock, Apoth uses children to do his bidding. Psylocke, X-23 and Cable mean to stop him, but they'll need help...

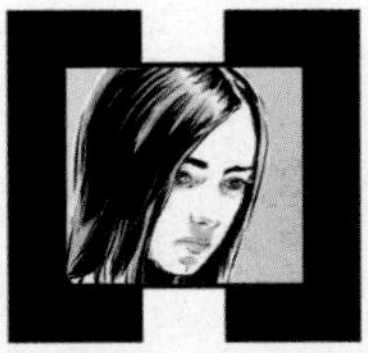
X-23

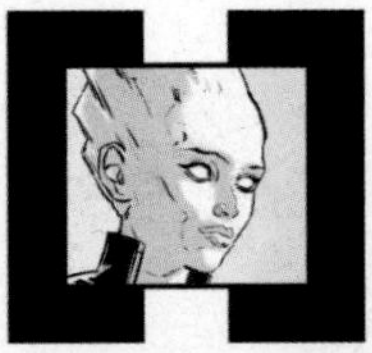
Bling!

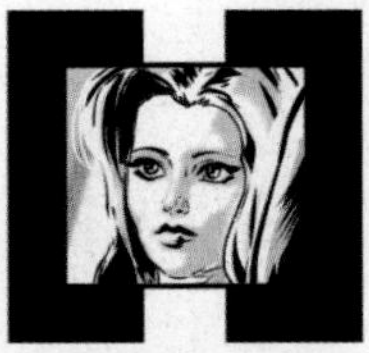
Husk

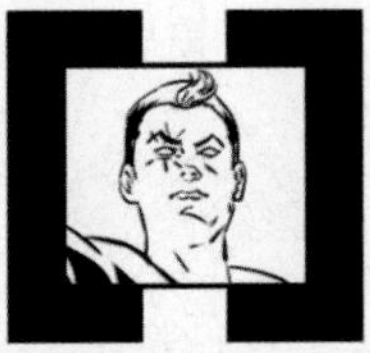
Cable

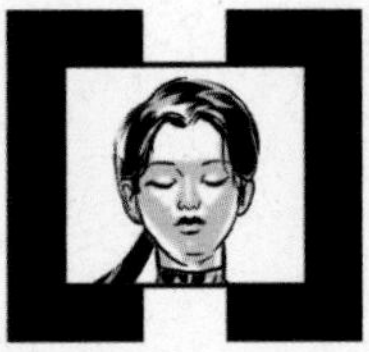
Psylocke

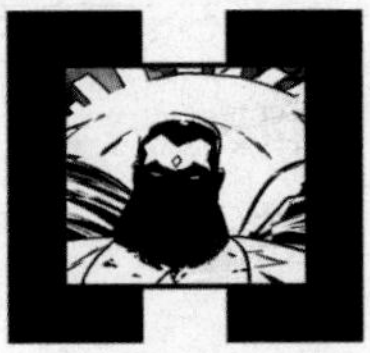
Mister Sinister

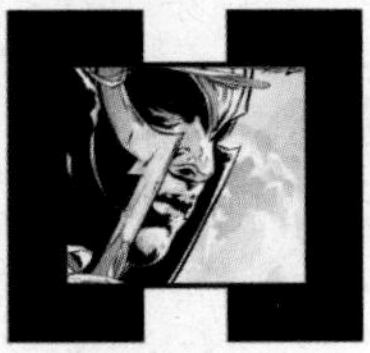
Magneto

[kra_[0.5]...]
[koa_[0.5]...]

[A._ssa_ssin_]

[00_warrior_X__]
[00_lim_ited___]

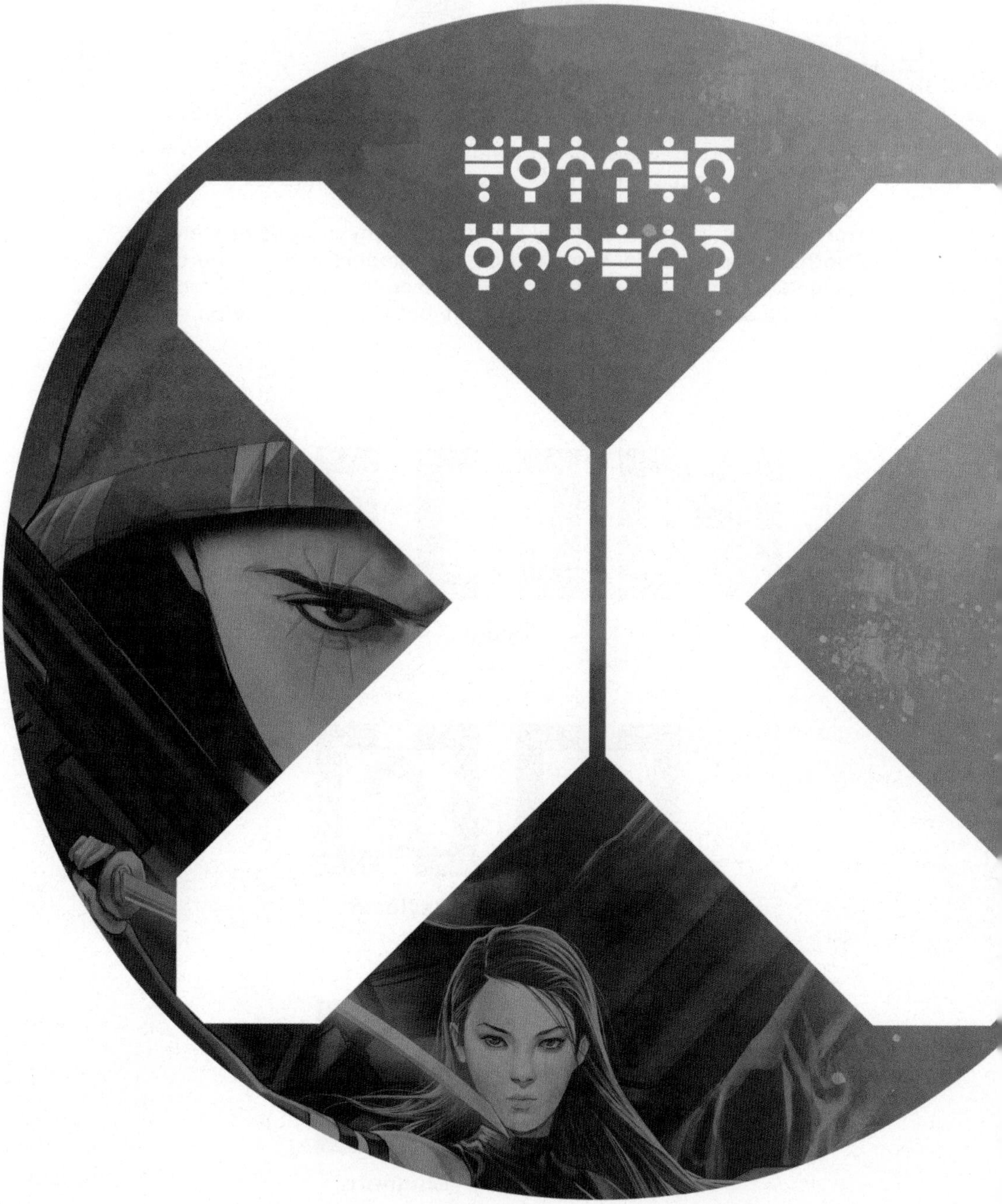

BRYAN HILL.......................................[WRITER]
SZYMON KUDRANSKI................................[ARTIST]
FRANK D'ARMATA...........................[COLOR ARTIST]
VC's JOE SABINO...............................[LETTERER]
TOM MULLER.....................................[DESIGN]

ASHLEY WITTER............................[COVER ARTIST]

SCOTT WILLIAMS & CHRIS STEVENS..[VARIANT COVER ARTISTS]

NICK RUSSELL...............................[PRODUCTION]

JONATHAN HICKMAN...........................[HEAD OF X]
CHRIS ROBINSON......................[ASSISTANT EDITOR]
JORDAN D. WHITE................................[EDITOR]
C.B. CEBULSKI........................[EDITOR IN CHIEF]

[05] FALLEN ANGELS

[ISSUE FIVE].....................SENSEI

[00_warrior_X__]
[00_lim_ited___]

[00_00...0]
[00_00...5]

[00_sword_]
[00_____]

[00_____]

[00_____X]

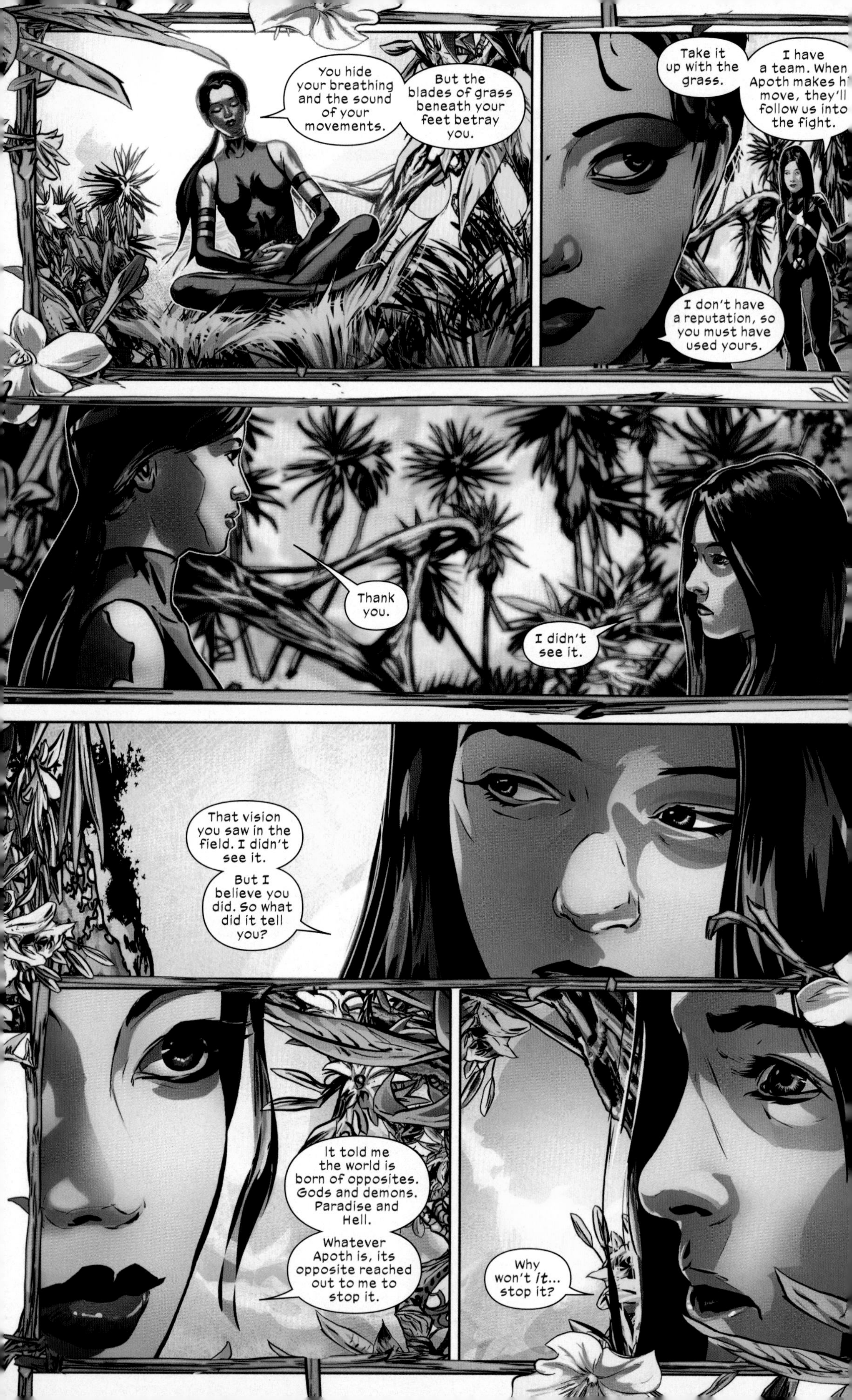
You hide your breathing and the sound of your movements.
But the blades of grass beneath your feet betray you.
Take it up with the grass.
I have a team. When Apoth makes hi move, they'll follow us into the fight.
I don't have a reputation, so you must have used yours.
Thank you.
I didn't see it.
That vision you saw in the field. I didn't see it.
But I believe you did. So what did it tell you?
It told me the world is born of opposites. Gods and demons. Paradise and Hell.
Whatever Apoth is, its opposite reached out to me to stop it.
Why won't *it*... stop it?

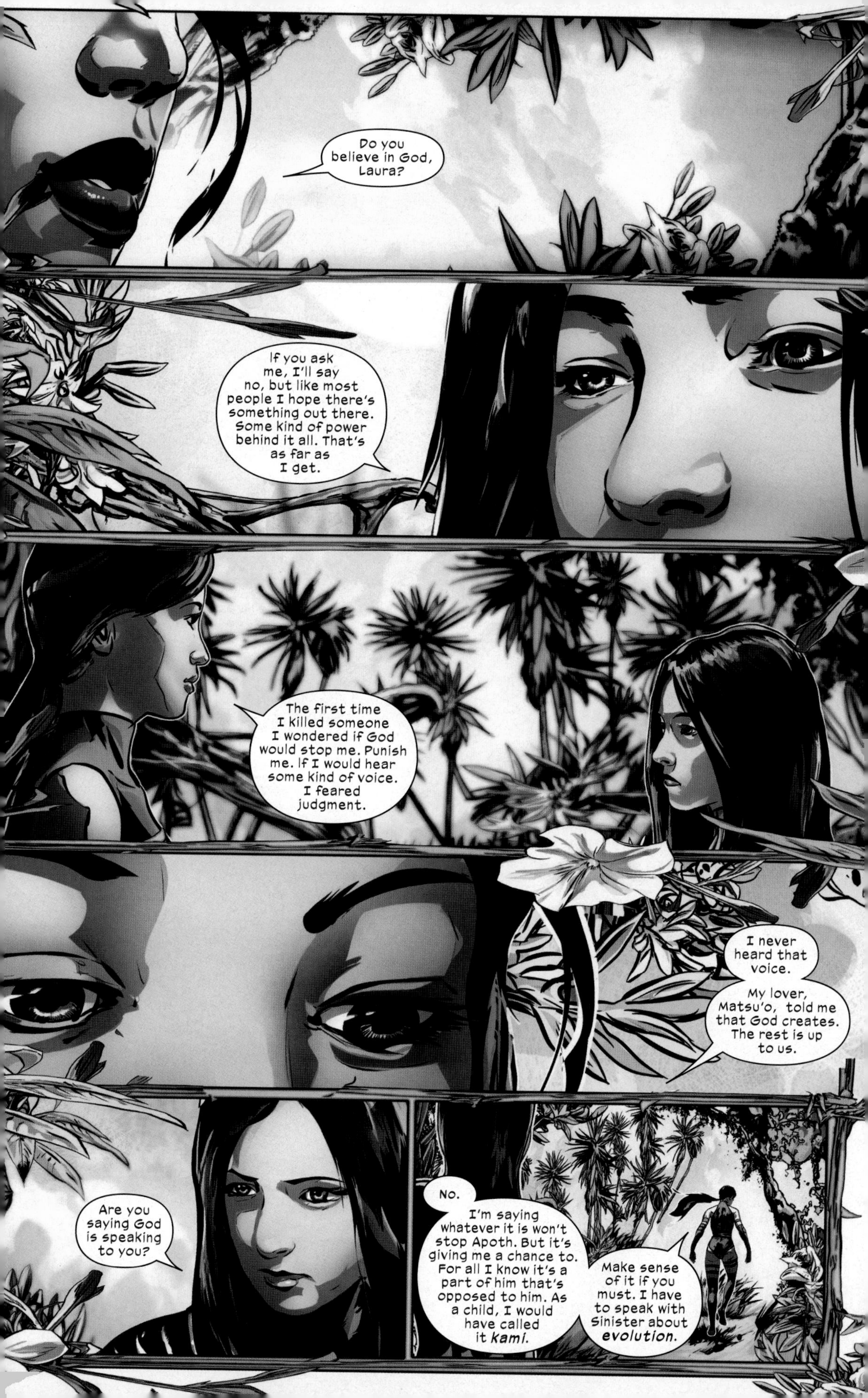
Do you believe in God, Laura?
If you ask me, I'll say no, but like most people I hope there's something out there. Some kind of power behind it all. That's as far as I get.
The first time I killed someone I wondered if God would stop me. Punish me. If I would hear some kind of voice. I feared judgment.
I never heard that voice.
My lover, Matsu'o, told me that God creates. The rest is up to us.
Are you saying God is speaking to you?
No.
I'm saying whatever it is won't stop Apoth. But it's giving me a chance to. For all I know it's a part of him that's opposed to him. As a child, I would have called it *kami*.
Make sense of it if you must. I have to speak with Sinister about *evolution*.

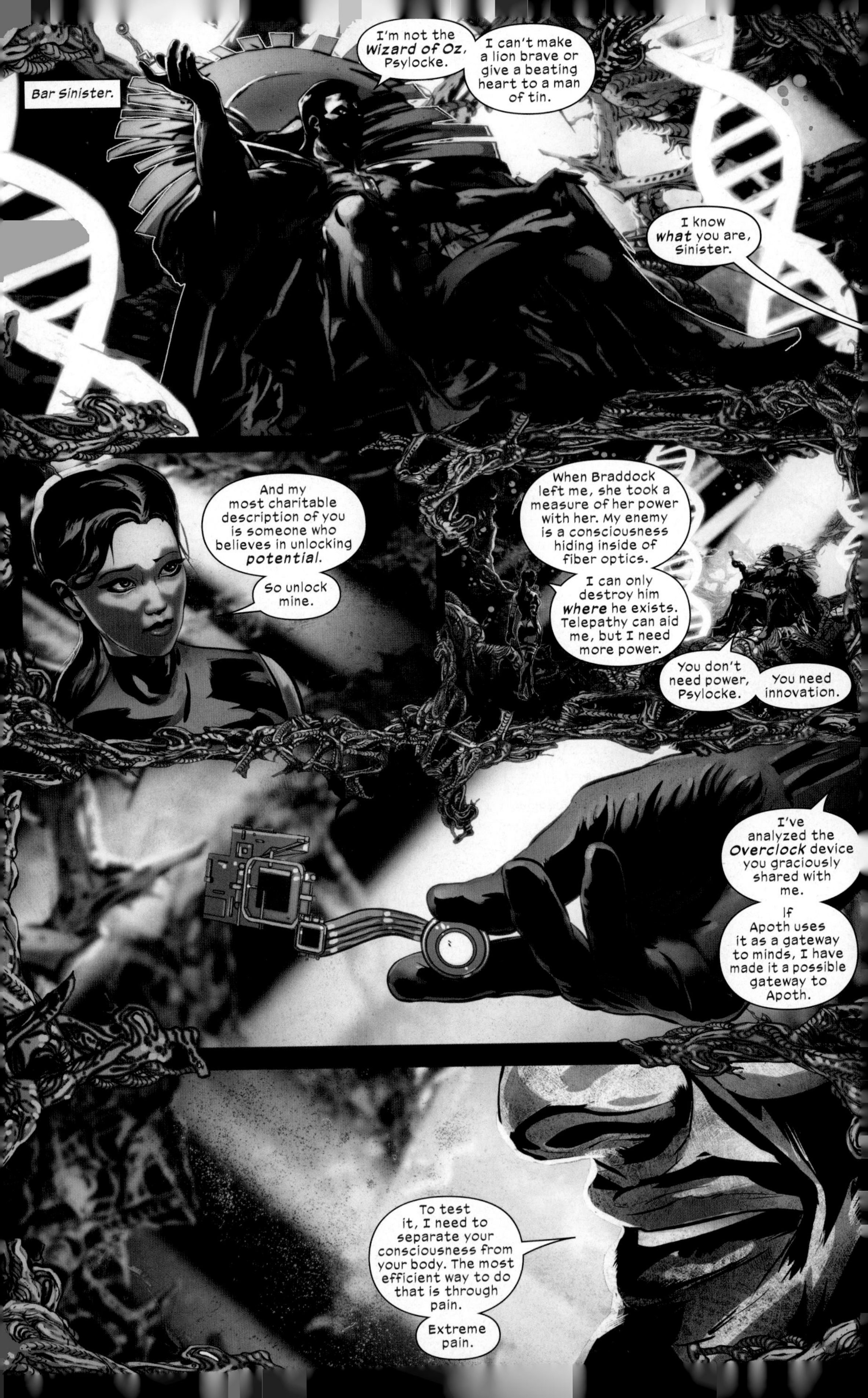
Bar Sinister.
I'm not the *Wizard of Oz*, Psylocke.
I can't make a lion brave or give a beating heart to a man of tin.
I know *what* you are, Sinister.
And my most charitable description of you is someone who believes in unlocking *potential*.
So unlock mine.
When Braddock left me, she took a measure of her power with her. My enemy is a consciousness hiding inside of fiber optics.
I can only destroy him *where* he exists. Telepathy can aid me, but I need more power.
You don't need power, Psylocke.
You need innovation.
I've analyzed the *Overclock* device you graciously shared with me.
If Apoth uses it as a gateway to minds, I have made it a possible gateway to Apoth.
To test it, I need to separate your consciousness from your body. The most efficient way to do that is through pain.
Extreme pain.

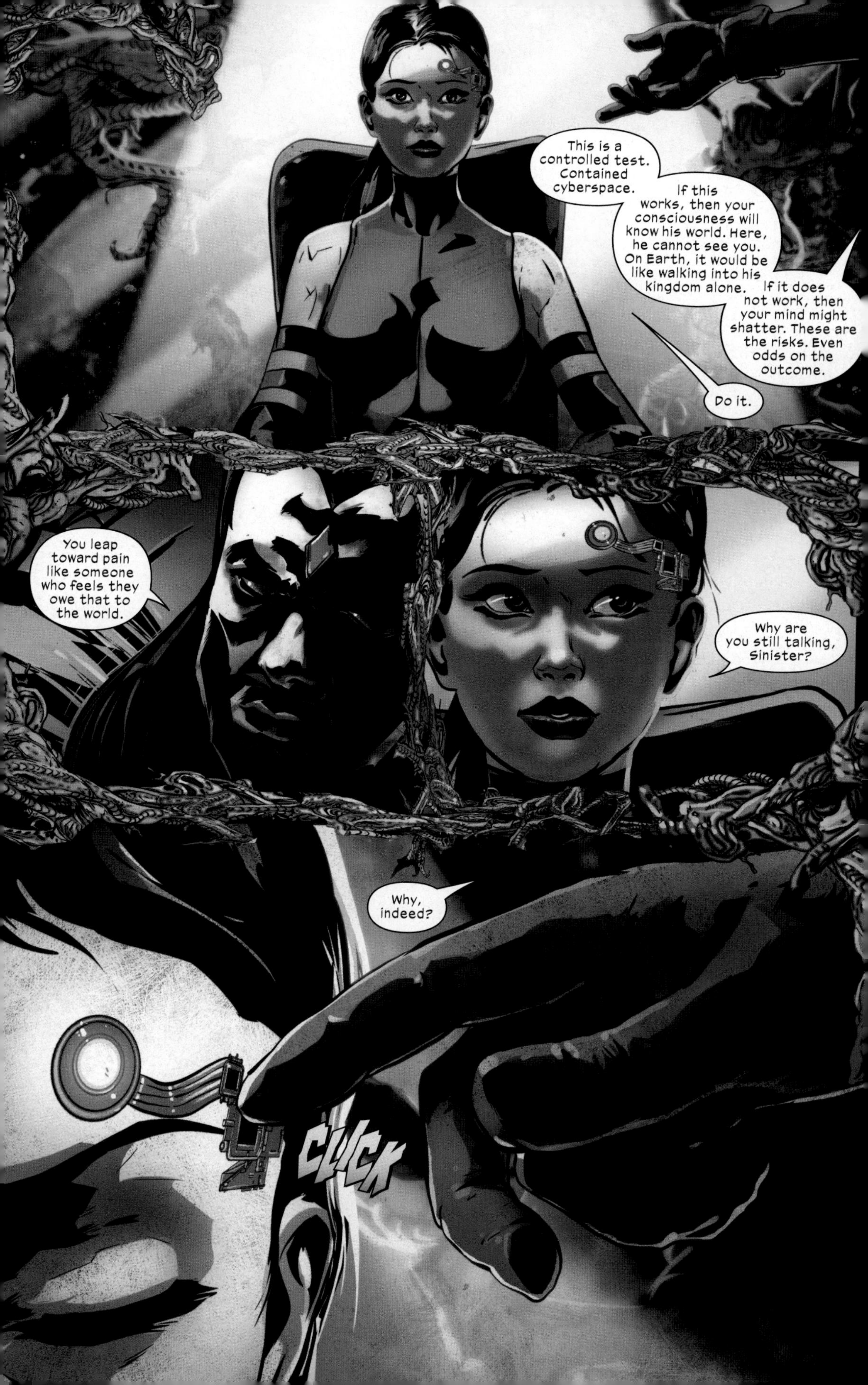
This is a controlled test. Contained cyberspace.
If this works, then your consciousness will know his world. Here, he cannot see you. On Earth, it would be like walking into his kingdom alone.
If it does not work, then your mind might shatter. These are the risks. Even odds on the outcome.
Do it.
You leap toward pain like someone who feels they owe that to the world.
Why are you still talking, Sinister?
Why, indeed?
CLICK

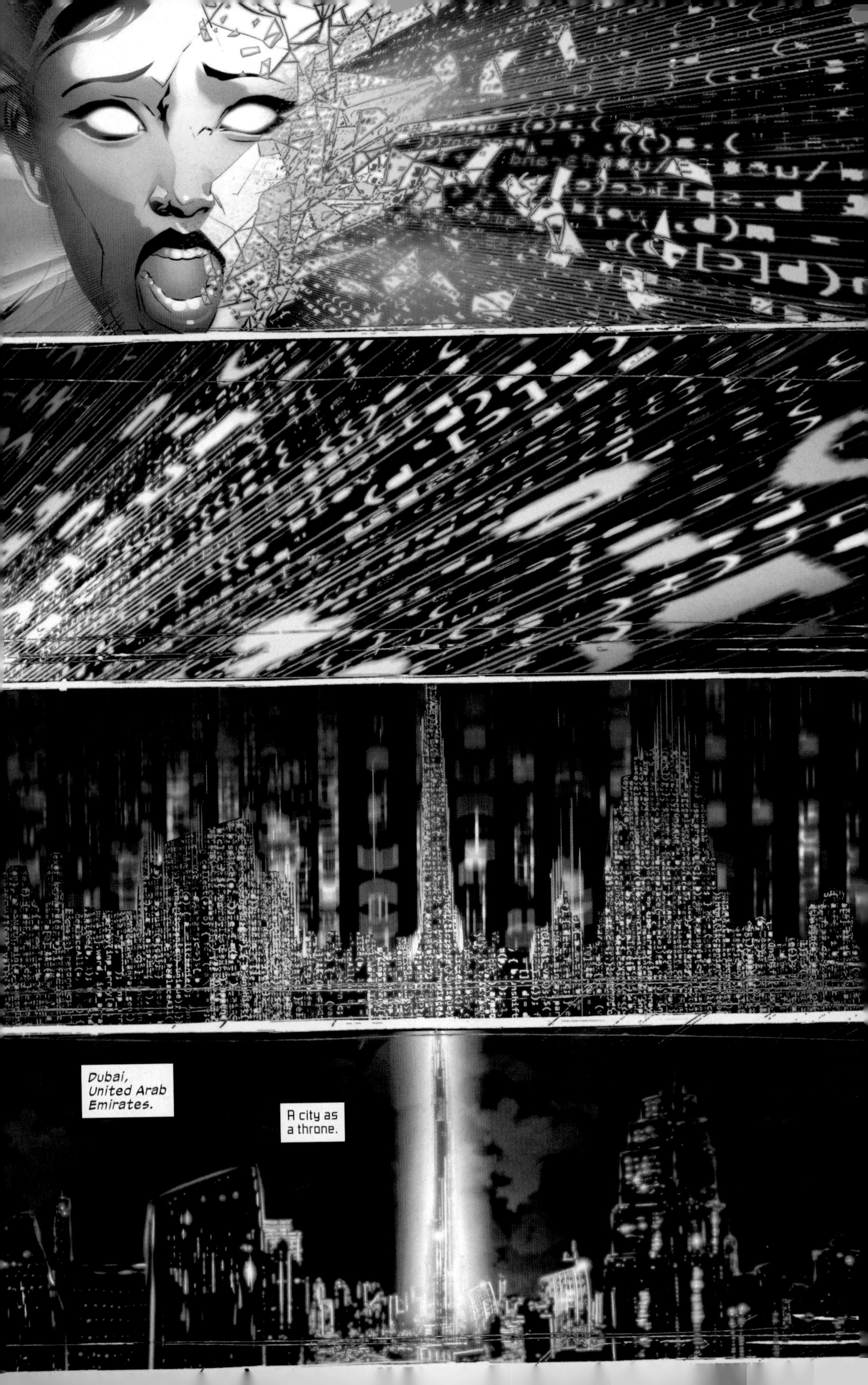
Dubai, United Arab Emirates.
A city as a throne.

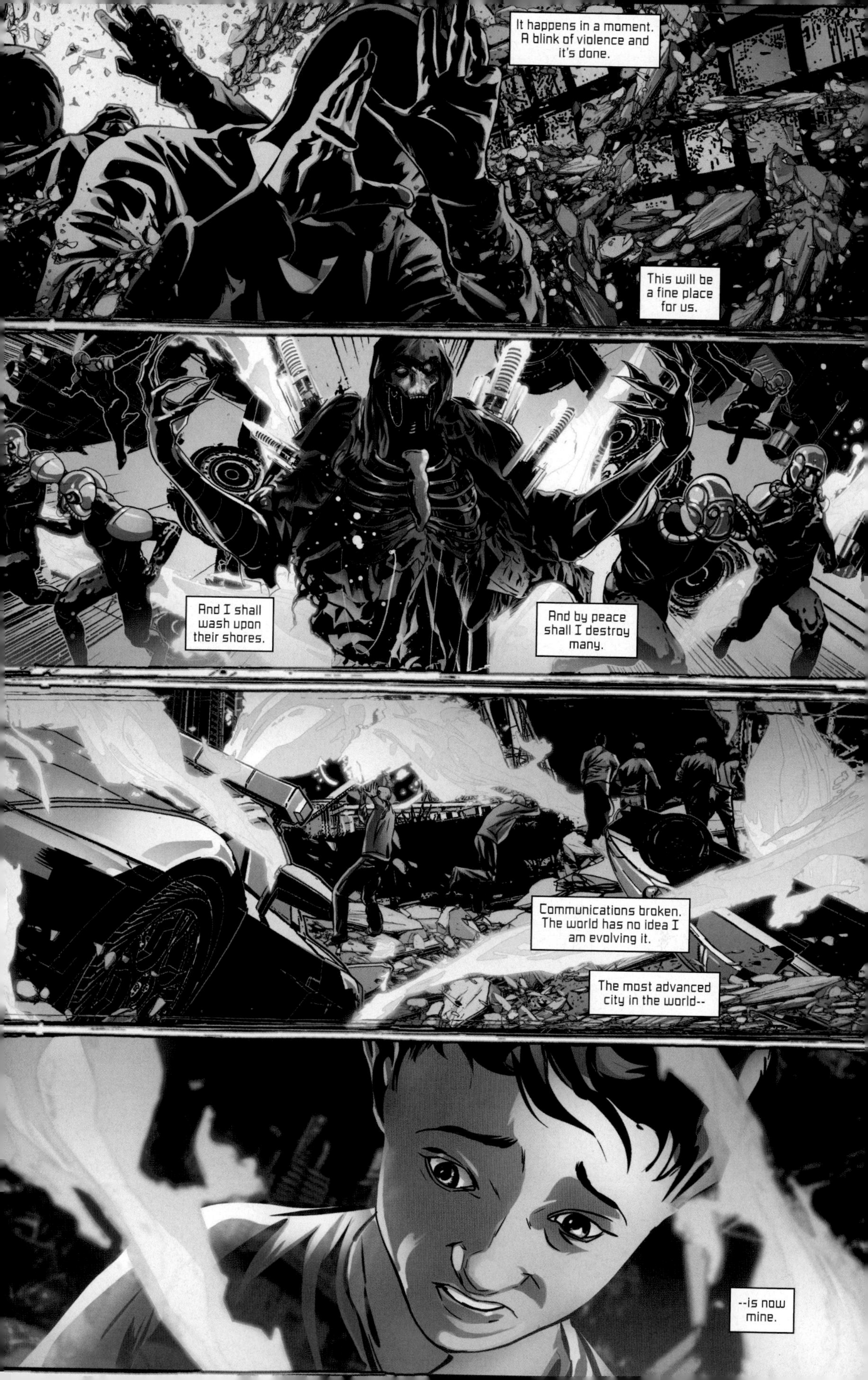
It happens in a moment. A blink of violence and it's done.
This will be a fine place for us.
And I shall wash upon their shores.
And by peace shall I destroy many.
Communications broken. The world has no idea I am evolving it.
The most advanced city in the world--
--is now mine.

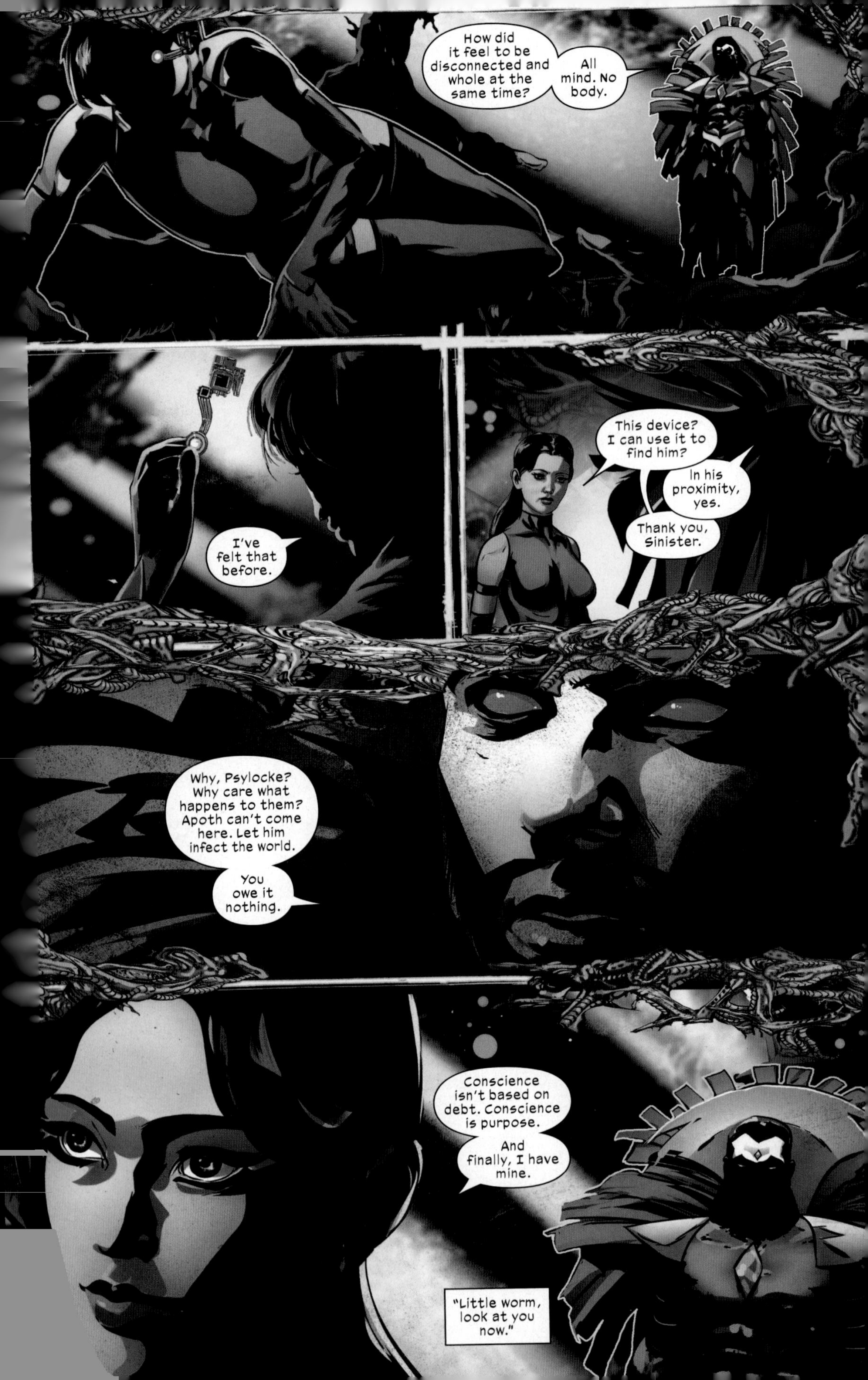
How did it feel to be disconnected and whole at the same time?
All mind. No body.
I've felt that before.
This device? I can use it to find him?
In his proximity, yes.
Thank you, Sinister.
Why, Psylocke? Why care what happens to them? Apoth can't come here. Let him infect the world.
You owe it nothing.
Conscience isn't based on debt. Conscience is purpose.
And finally, I have mine.
"Little worm, look at you now."

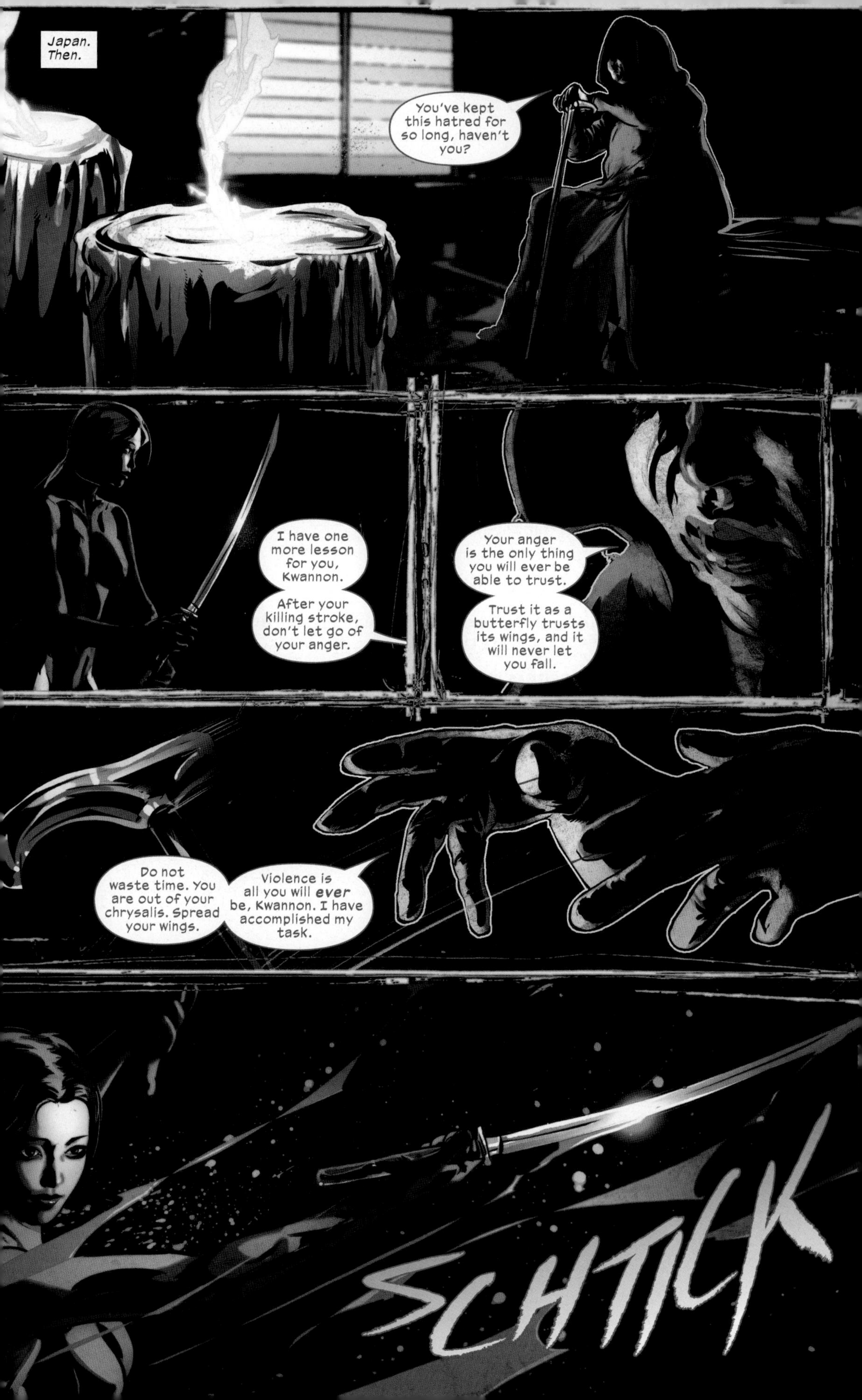
Japan.
Then.
You've kept this hatred for so long, haven't you?
I have one more lesson for you, Kwannon.
After your killing stroke, don't let go of your anger.
Your anger is the only thing you will ever be able to trust.
Trust it as a butterfly trusts its wings, and it will never let you fall.
Do not waste time. You are out of your chrysalis. Spread your wings.
Violence is all you will *ever* be, Kwannon. I have accomplished my task.
SCHTICK

FROM THE JOURNALS OF THE TEACHER

I am the reflection of Bishamon. What is seen in the surface of the water.

I am the adversary. One with conflict. One with purpose.

I have accomplished my task. I am the forger of children. What comes to me innocent shall leave my care in fury.

On the cliffs, in the embrace of the setting sun, I teach them the nature of strength. I put distance between them and their conscience.

Let them hate me. I have accomplished my task.

One has come into my care. A girl. A girl of pure potential.
With a touch, she can know minds.
She is full of love.

It will not be easy to forge her, but I will accomplish my task.

What happens to boys and girls is what they become as men and women.
That has always been the way of the Hand.

We are born as clay. My cruelty is the thumbprint left in the soft matter.
They will grow.
They will harden.
But the mark will always be there.

I have given this girl the name of Kwannon.
I have pierced her clay with our purpose.

I have accomplished my task.

—

She will be the one who ends me. I have foreseen it.
I am making her strong enough to run her blade across my throat.
I do this without fear, because death matters not to me.

How can I die when all that I have taught will live on?
And kill.
And teach others to kill.

Young Kwannon the worm. She hides her soul from me. She seeks to
protect it.
She says she is only my words and actions.
But she lies.

I see the candle flame of her spirit. It still burns.
But she will always be what I have made her.

To kill me, she will have to use what I have built within her. That will be
my victory.

What will I do when she comes for me?

I will not fear.
I will face her with no protest.
I will stand calm as she draws her blade.

Young Kwannon will only be what I have awoken in her.
Let her come.
Let her try to punish cruelty with violence.
Let her feel the futility of conscience.

I will raise her.
I will die at her hand.
I will live on in her spirit.

I have accomplished my task.

—

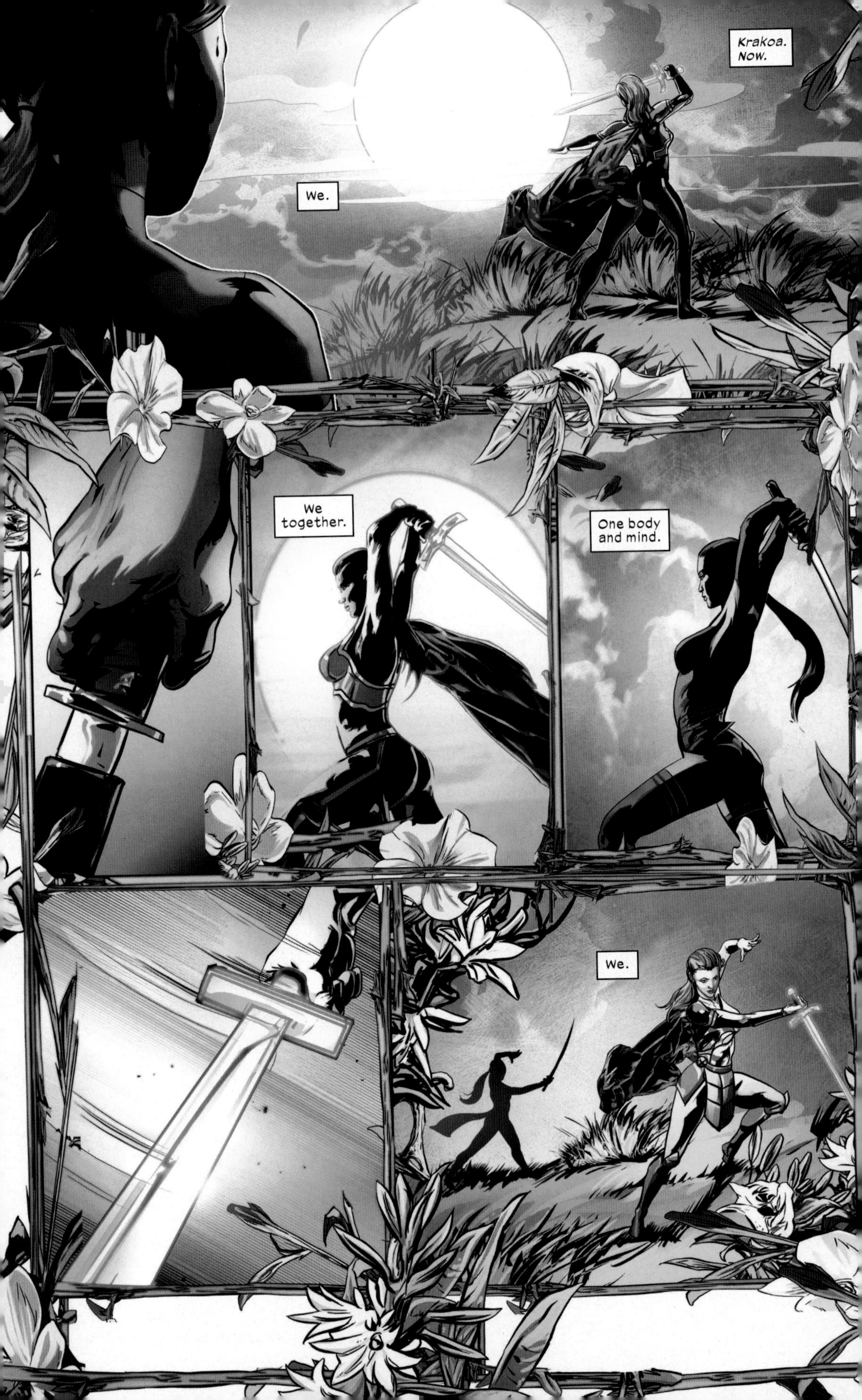
Krakoa.
Now.
We.
We together.
One body and mind.
We.

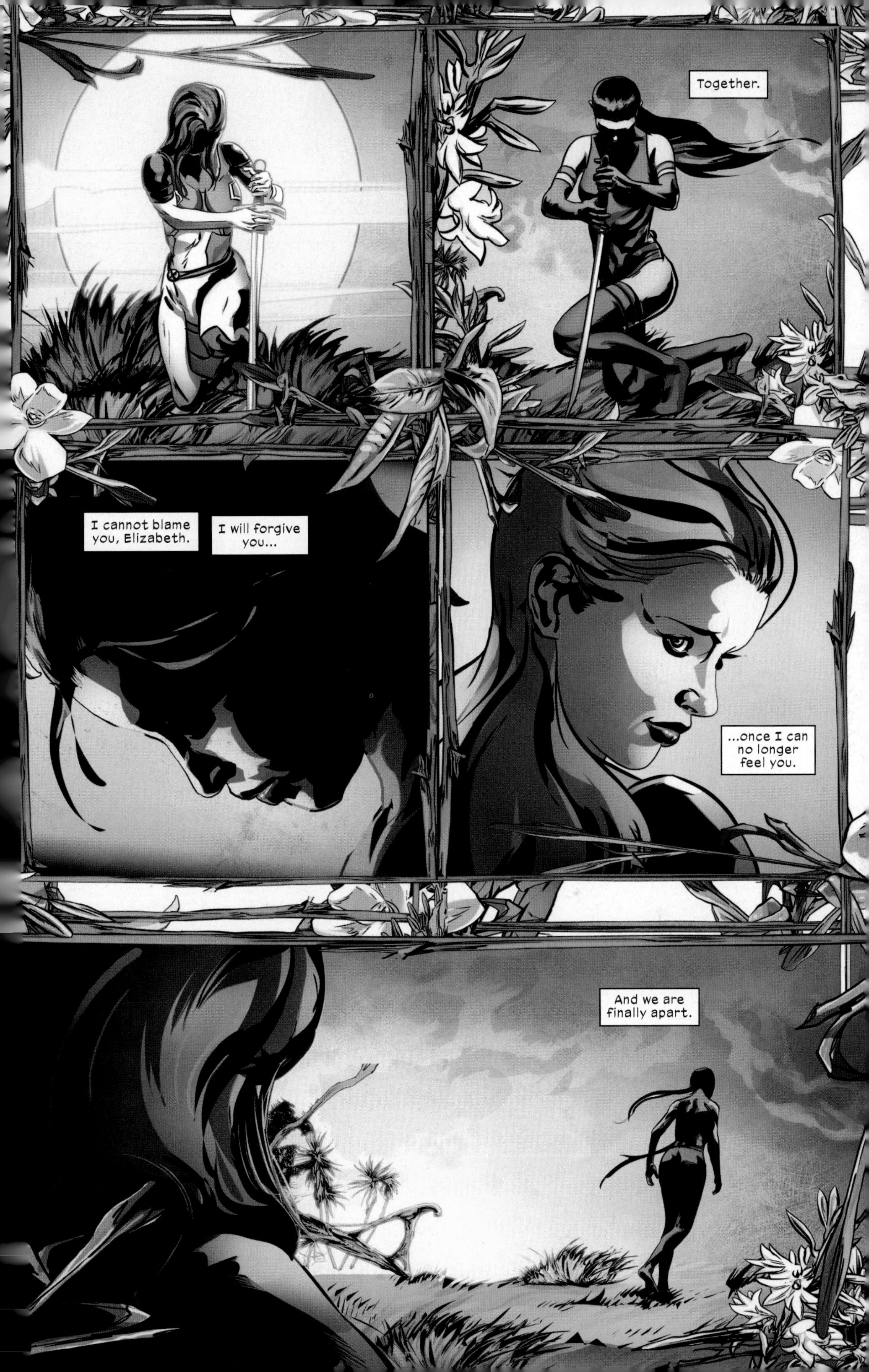
Together.
I cannot blame you, Elizabeth.
I will forgive you...
...once I can no longer feel you.
And we are finally apart.

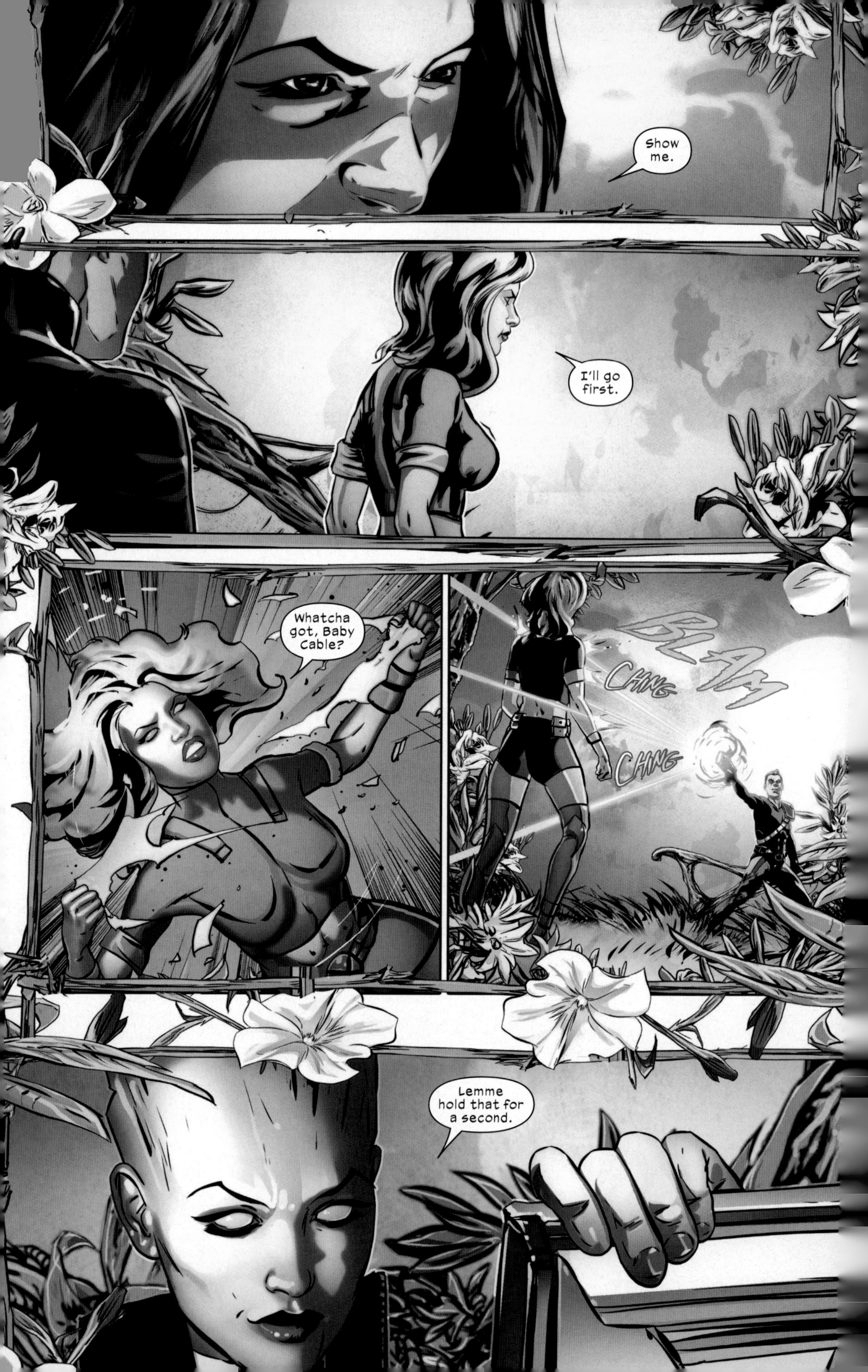

Show me.
I'll go first.
Whatcha got, Baby Cable?
BLAM
CHING
CHING
Lemme hold that for a second.

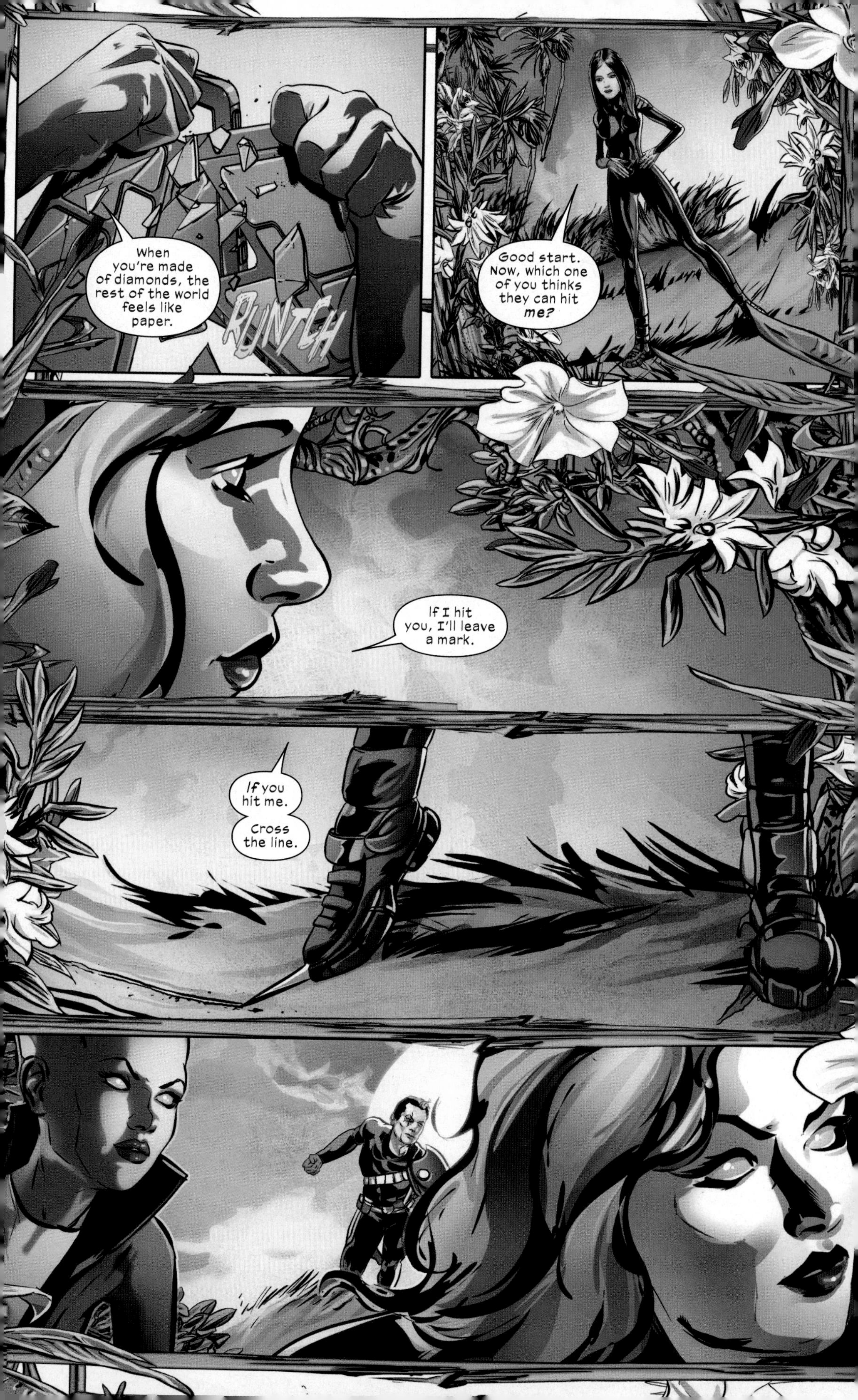
When you're made of diamonds, the rest of the world feels like paper.
RUNTCH
Good start. Now, which one of you thinks they can hit *me?*
If I hit you, I'll leave a mark.
If you hit me.
Cross the line.

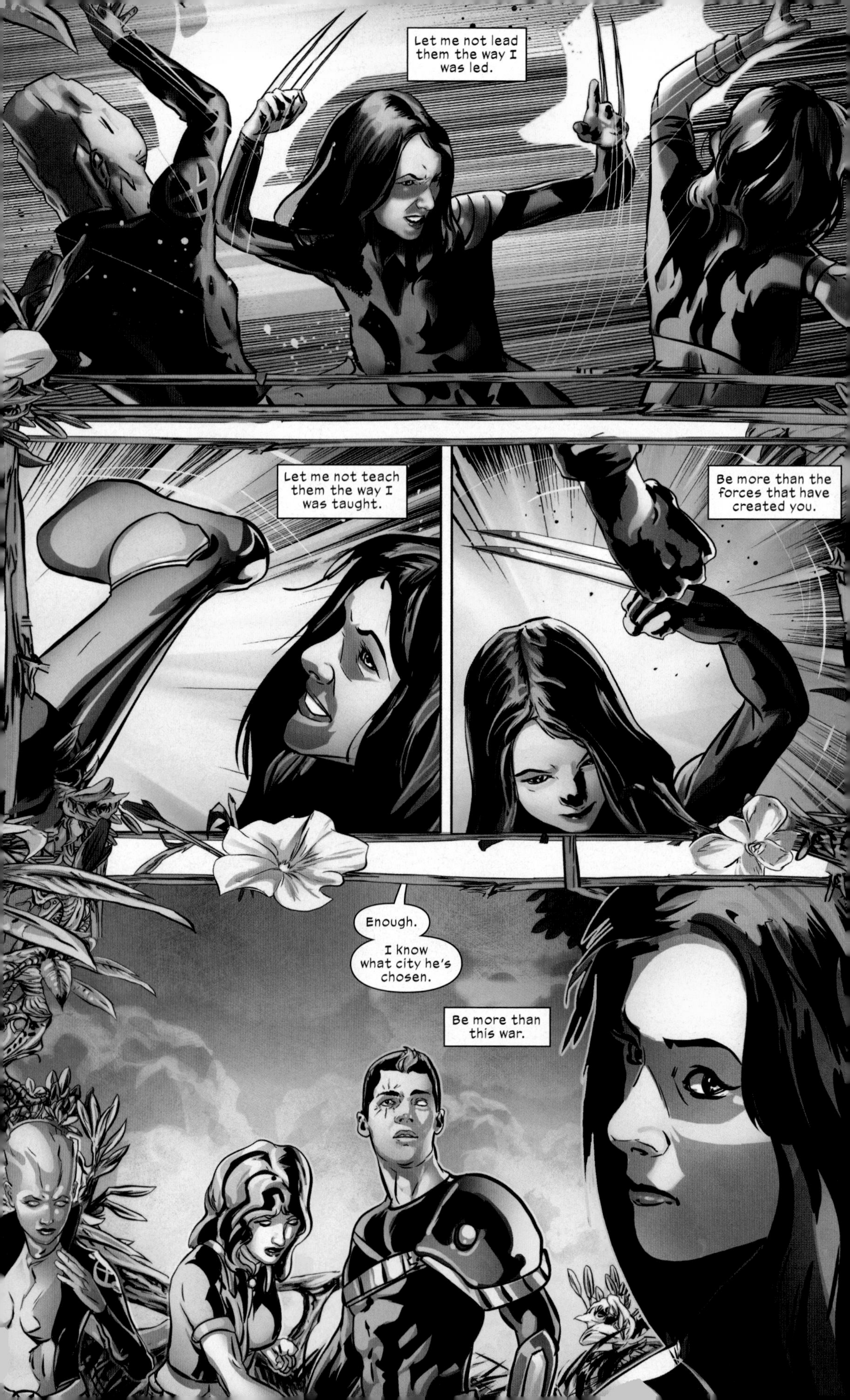
Let me not lead them the way I was led.
Let me not teach them the way I was taught.
Be more than the forces that have created you.
Enough.
I know what city he's chosen.
Be more than this war.

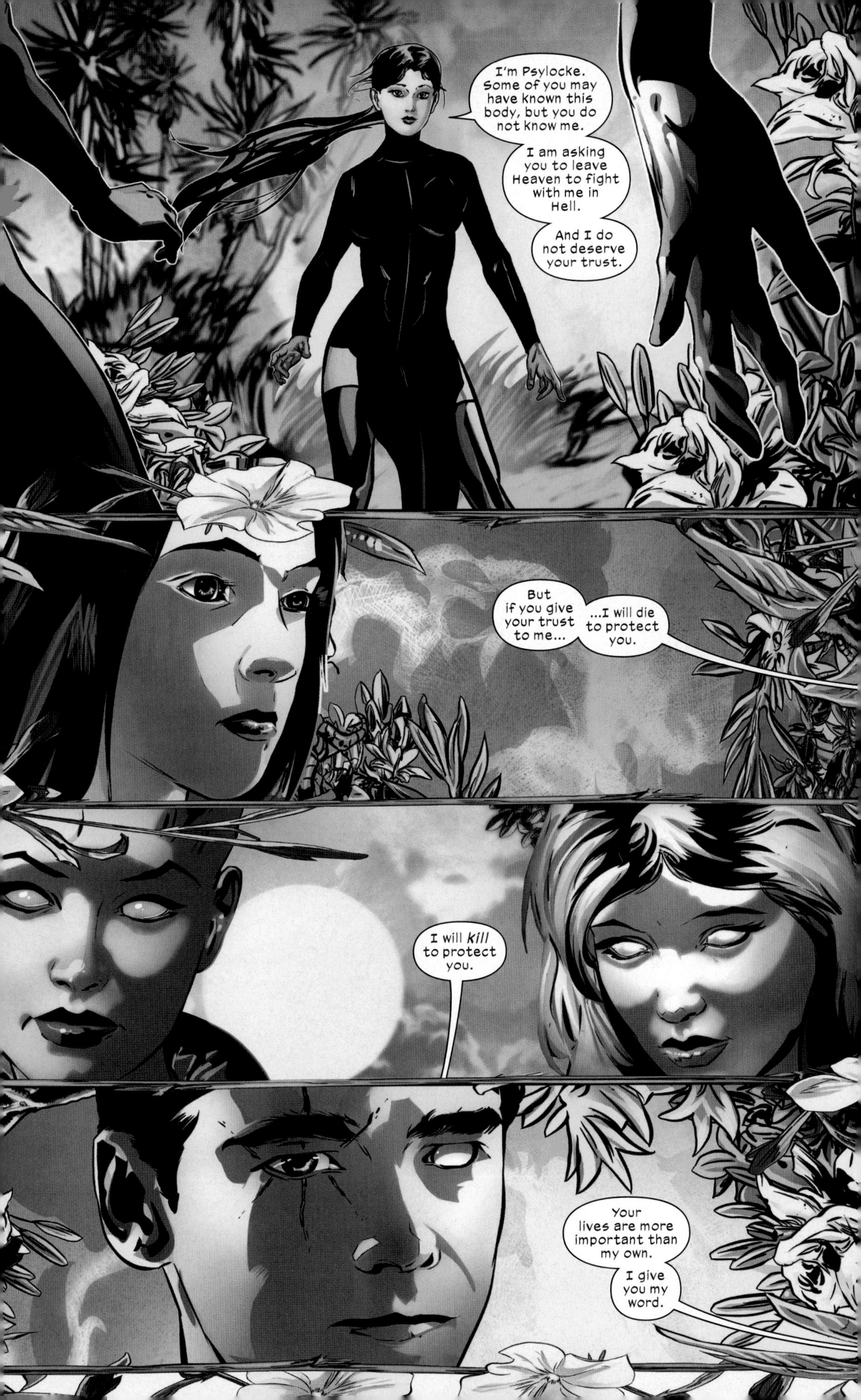
I'm Psylocke. Some of you may have known this body, but you do not know me.
I am asking you to leave Heaven to fight with me in Hell.
And I do not deserve your trust.
But if you give your trust to me...
...I will die to protect you.
I will *kill* to protect you.
Your lives are more important than my own.
I give you my word.

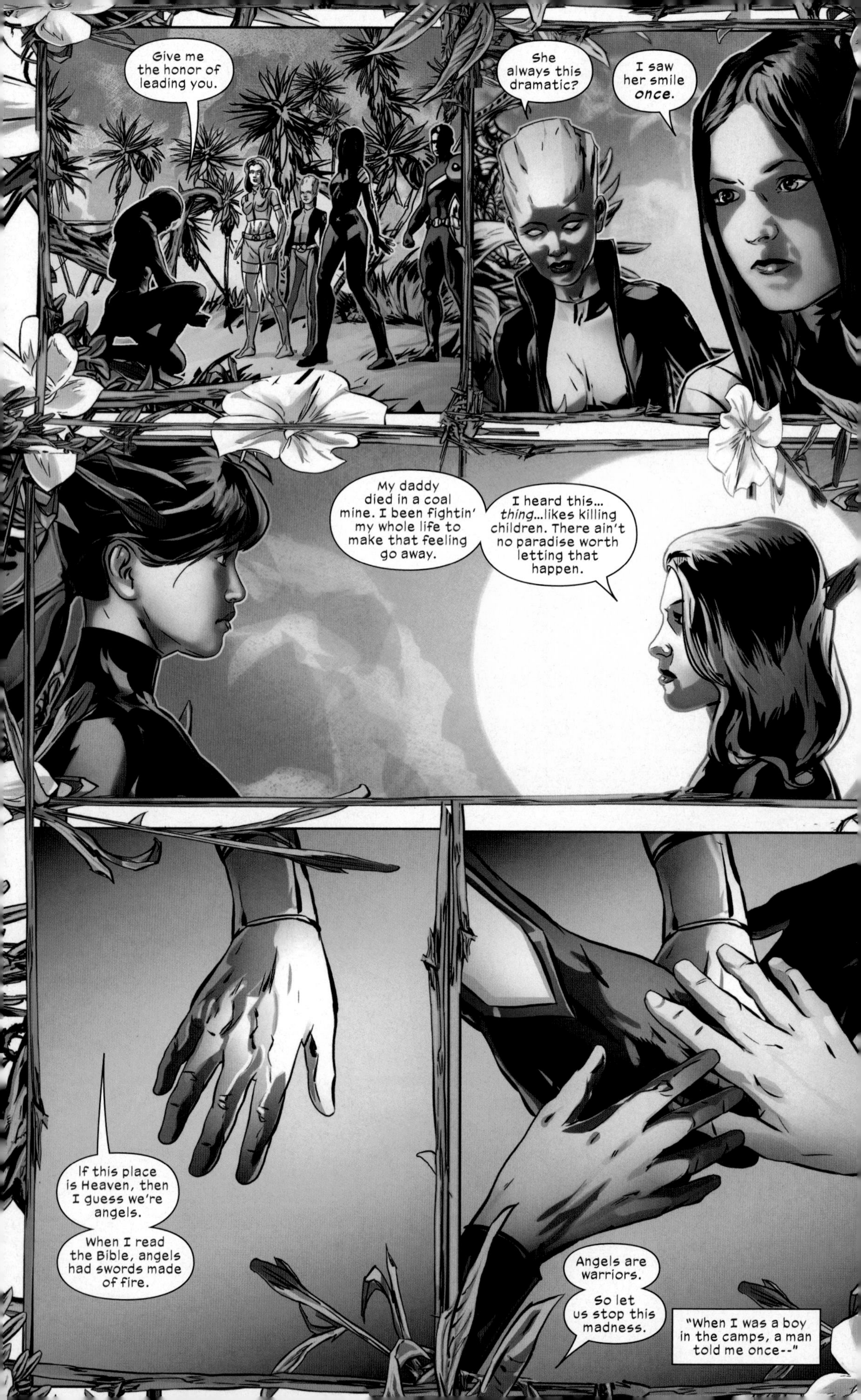
Give me the honor of leading you.
She always this dramatic?
I saw her smile *once*.
My daddy died in a coal mine. I been fightin' my whole life to make that feeling go away.
I heard this... *thing*...likes killing children. There ain't no paradise worth letting that happen.
If this place is Heaven, then I guess we're angels.
When I read the Bible, angels had swords made of fire.
Angels are warriors.
So let us stop this madness.
"When I was a boy in the camps, a man told me once--"

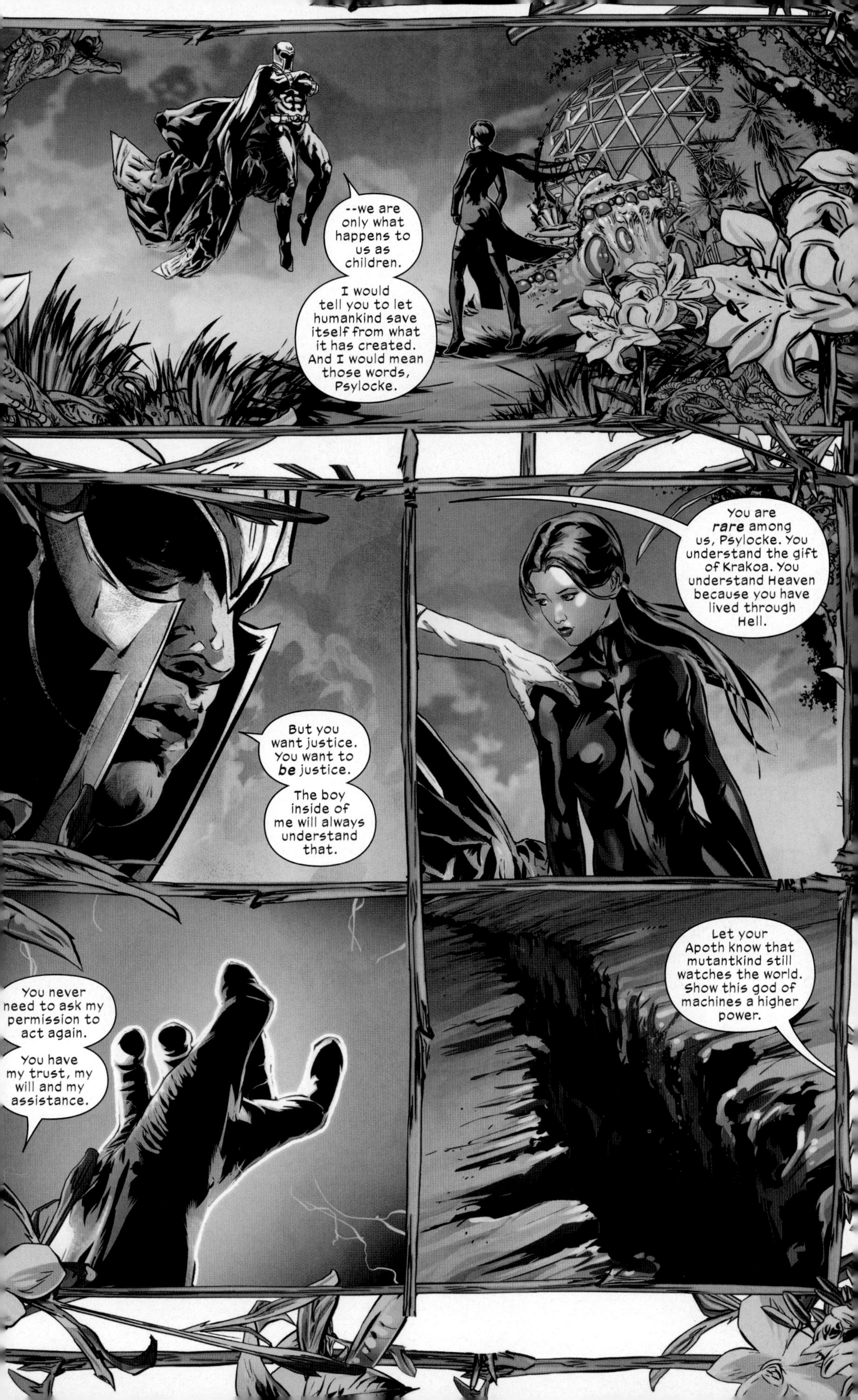
--we are only what happens to us as children.
I would tell you to let humankind save itself from what it has created. And I would mean those words, Psylocke.
You are *rare* among us, Psylocke. You understand the gift of Krakoa. You understand Heaven because you have lived through Hell.
But you want justice. You want to *be* justice.
The boy inside of me will always understand that.
You never need to ask my permission to act again.
You have my trust, my will and my assistance.
Let your Apoth know that mutantkind still watches the world. Show this god of machines a higher power.

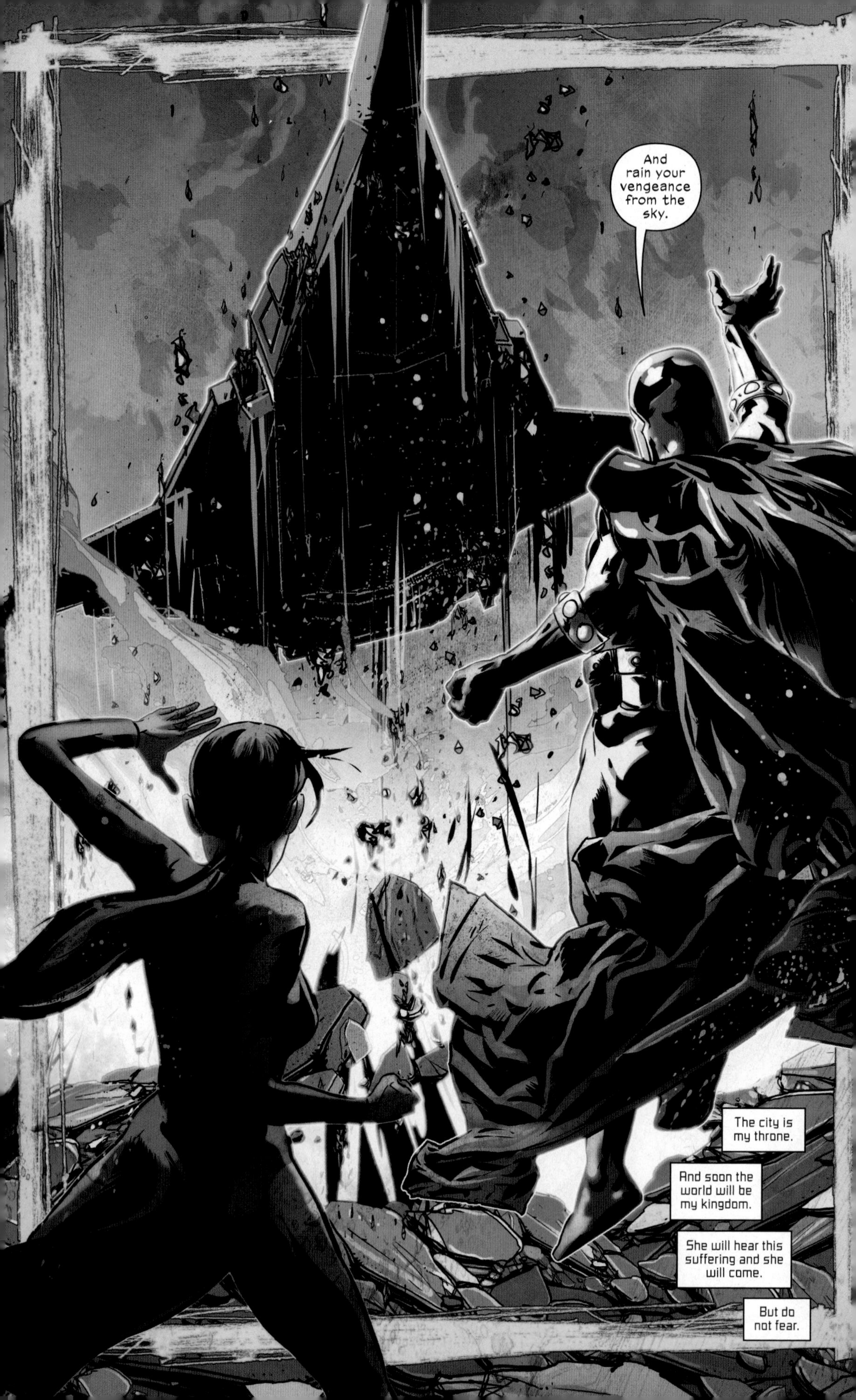
And rain your vengeance from the sky.
The city is my throne.
And soon the world will be my kingdom.
She will hear this suffering and she will come.
But do not fear.

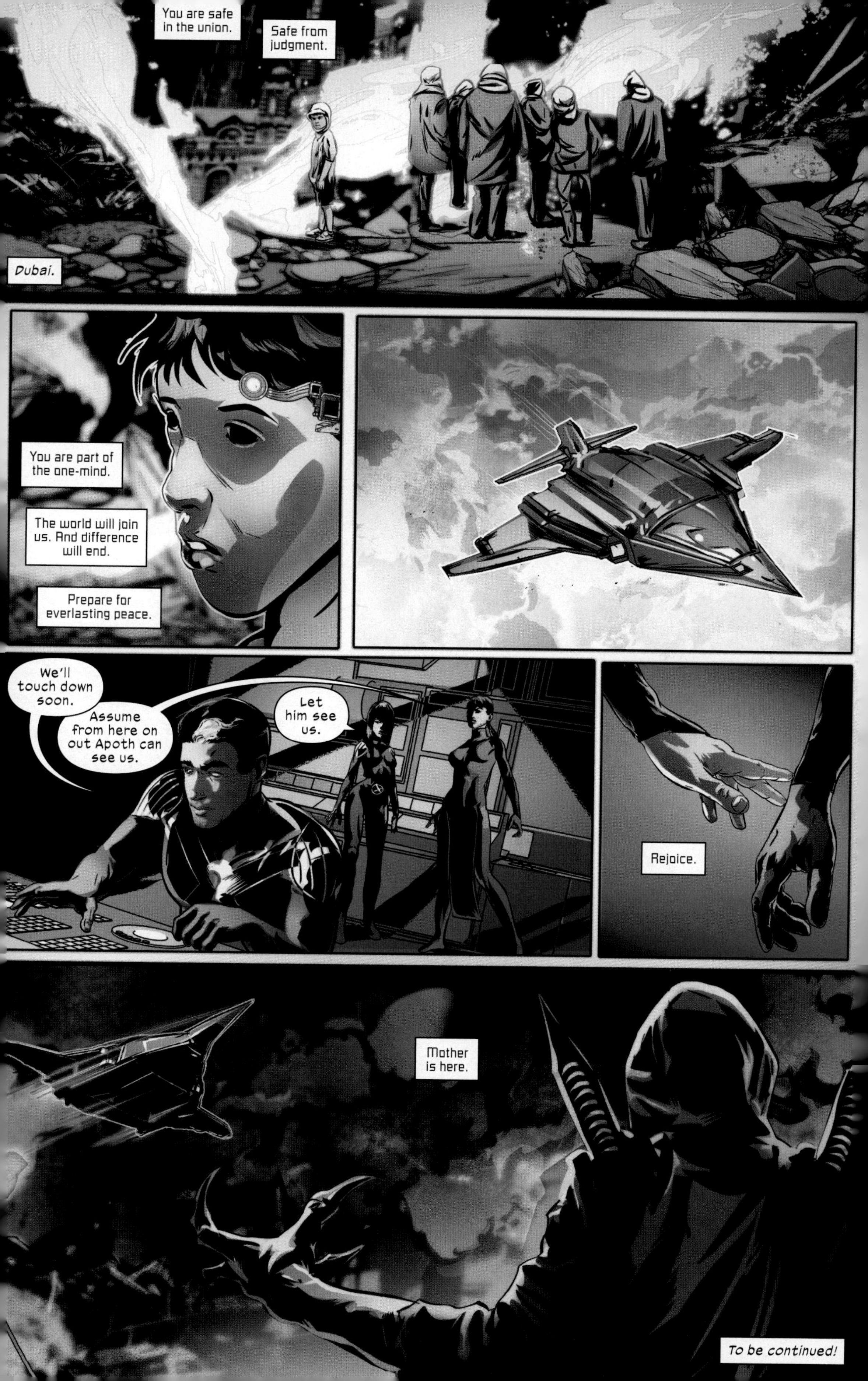

You are safe in the union.
Safe from judgment.
Dubai.
You are part of the one-mind.
The world will join us. And difference will end.
Prepare for everlasting peace.
We'll touch down soon.
Assume from here on out Apoth can see us.
Let him see us.
Rejoice.
Mother is here.
To be continued!

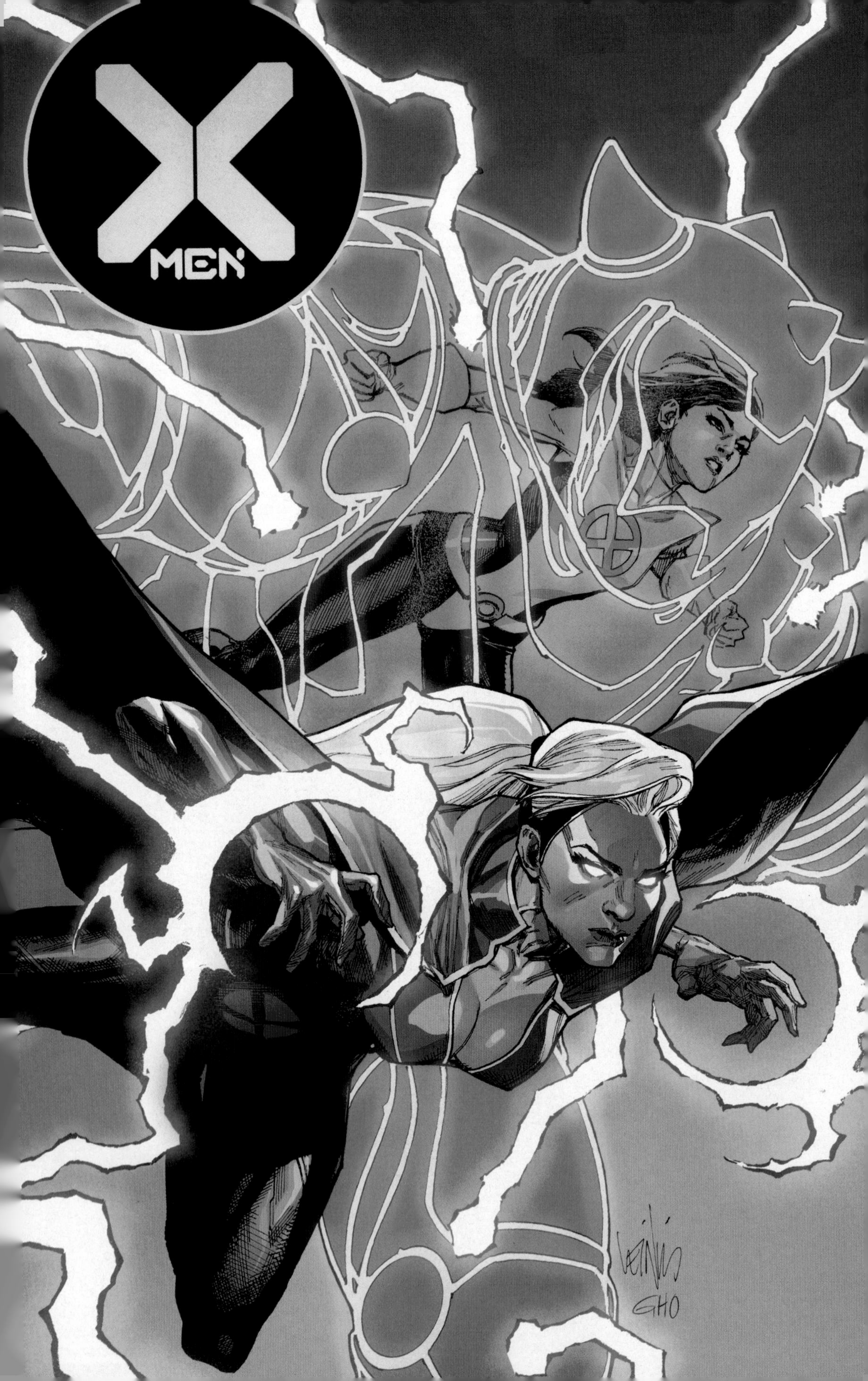
X
MEN
GHO

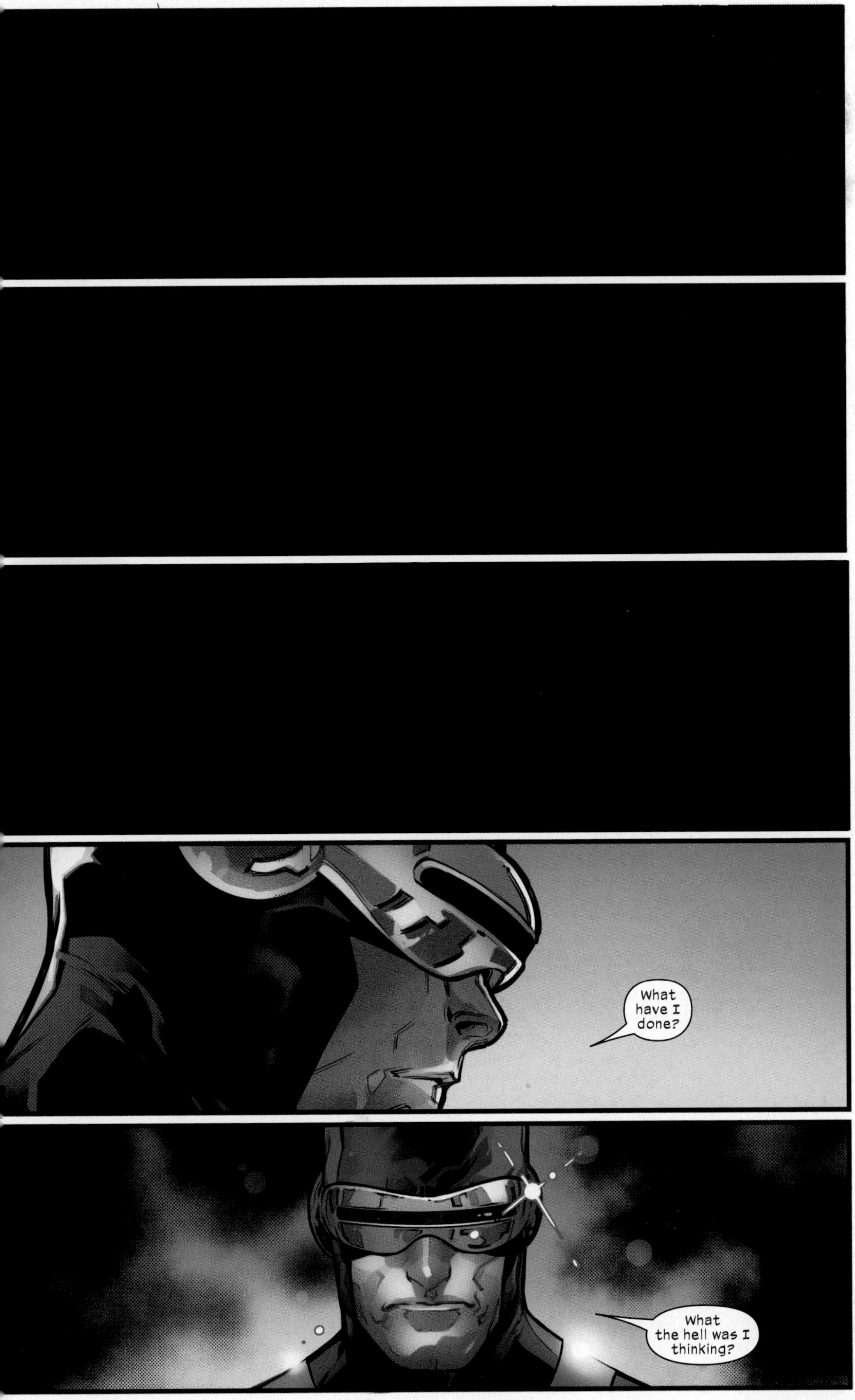
What have I done?
What the hell was I thinking?

[00_mutants_of_X]
[00_the_world__X]

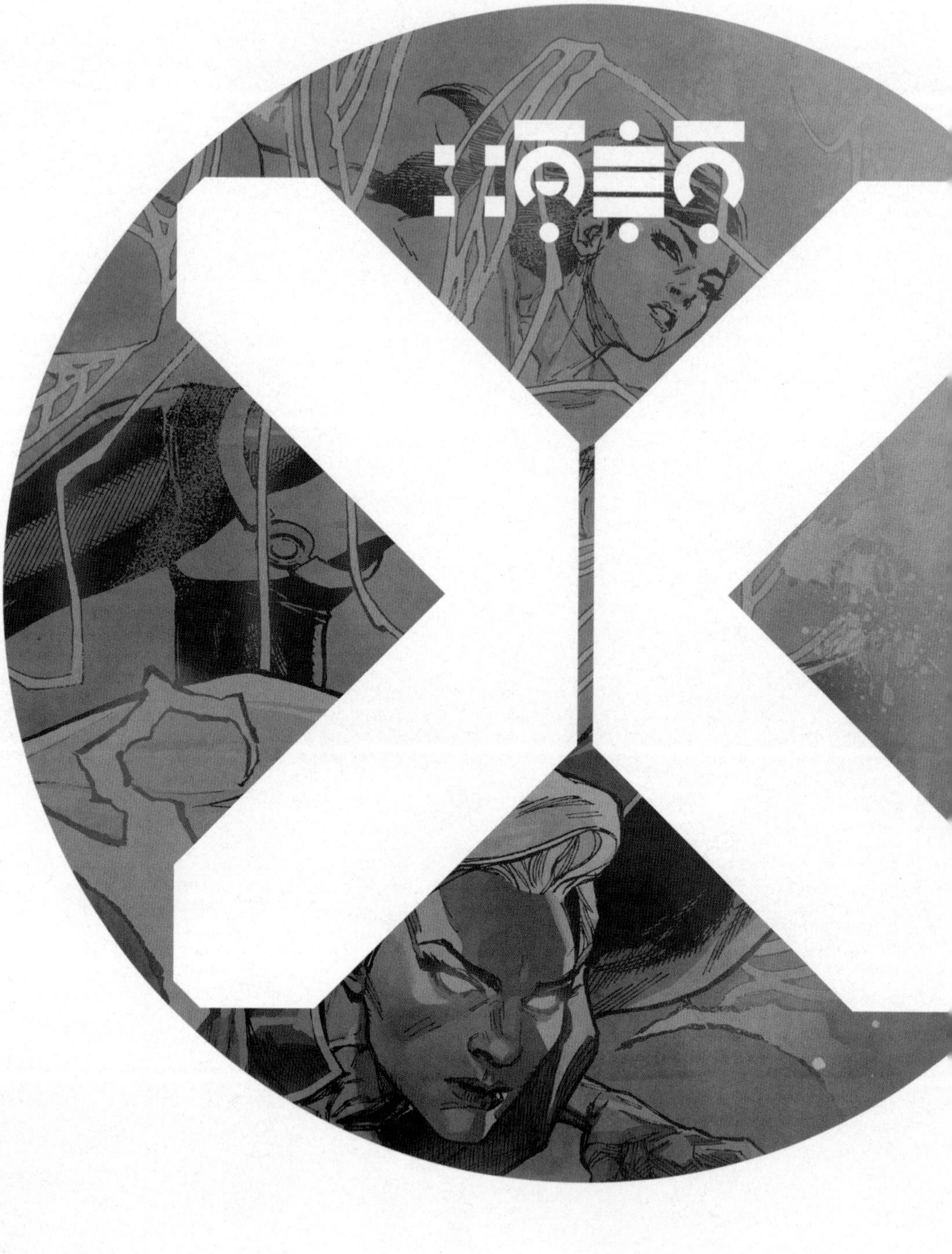

JONATHAN HICKMAN.............................[WRITER]
R.B. SILVA......................................[ARTIST]
MARTE GRACIA..............................[COLOR ARTIST]
VC's CLAYTON COWLES........................[LETTERER]
TOM MULLER...................................[DESIGN]

LEINIL FRANCIS YU & SUNNY GHO...........[COVER ARTISTS]

KRIS ANKA; MARCOS MARTIN........[VARIANT COVER ARTISTS]

NICK RUSSELL..............................[PRODUCTION]

ANNALISE BISSA.......................[ASSISTANT EDITOR]
JORDAN D. WHITE..............................[EDITOR]
C.B. CEBULSKI........................[EDITOR IN CHIEF]

[05] X-MEN

[ISSUE FIVE]...............INTO THE VAULT
X-MEN CREATED BY.................STAN LEE & JACK KIRBY

[00_mutants_of_X]
[00_the_world__X]

[00_00...0]
[00_00...5]

[00_unite_]
[00_____]

[00_____]

[00_____X]

[kra_[0.5]
[koa_[0.5]

[kra_[0.X]
[koa_[0.X]

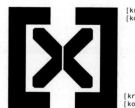

RECONNAISSANCE

While rescuing mutant children from an Orchis research facility, the X-MEN inadvertently freed Serafina, a member of the Children of the Vault -- a highly evolved and highly dangerous super-powered group developed via exposure to temporal acceleration. The X-MEN have now tracked Serafina to Ecuador.

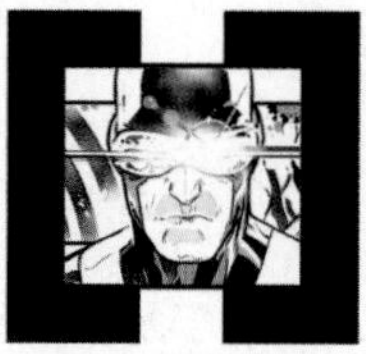
Cyclops

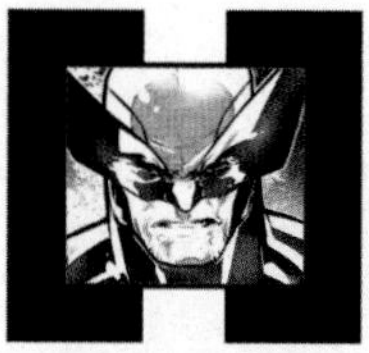
Wolverine

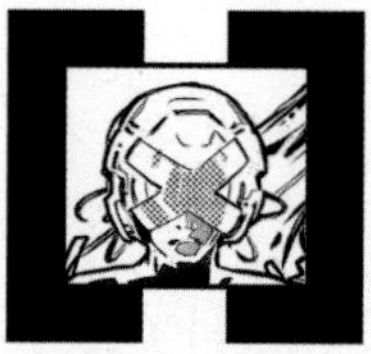
Professor X

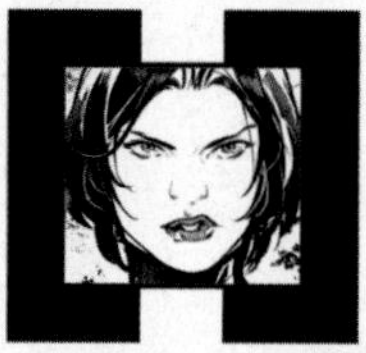
Armor

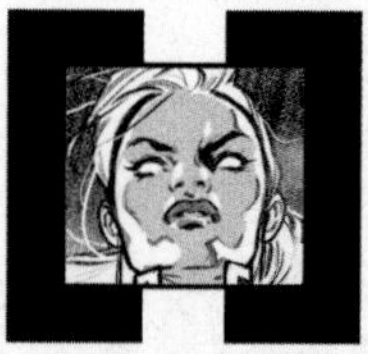
Storm

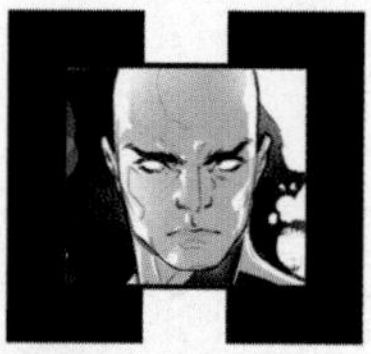
Darwin

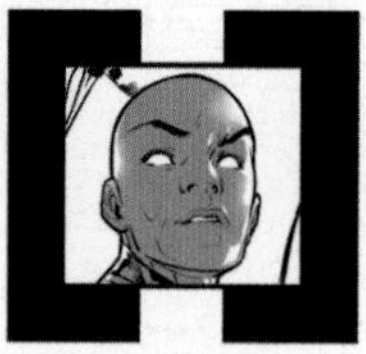
Synch

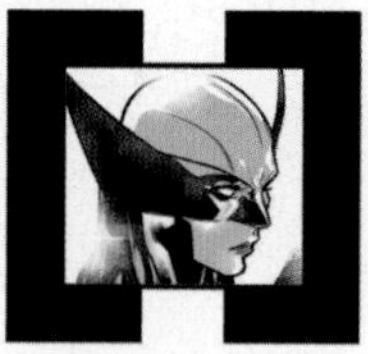
X-23

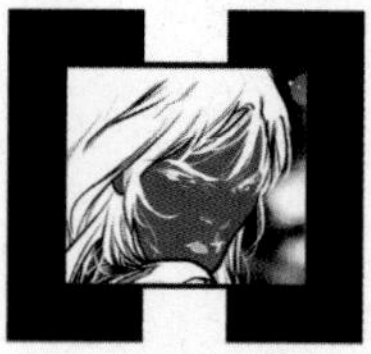
Serafina

[kra_[0.5]...]
[koa_[0.5]...]

[A._New_World]

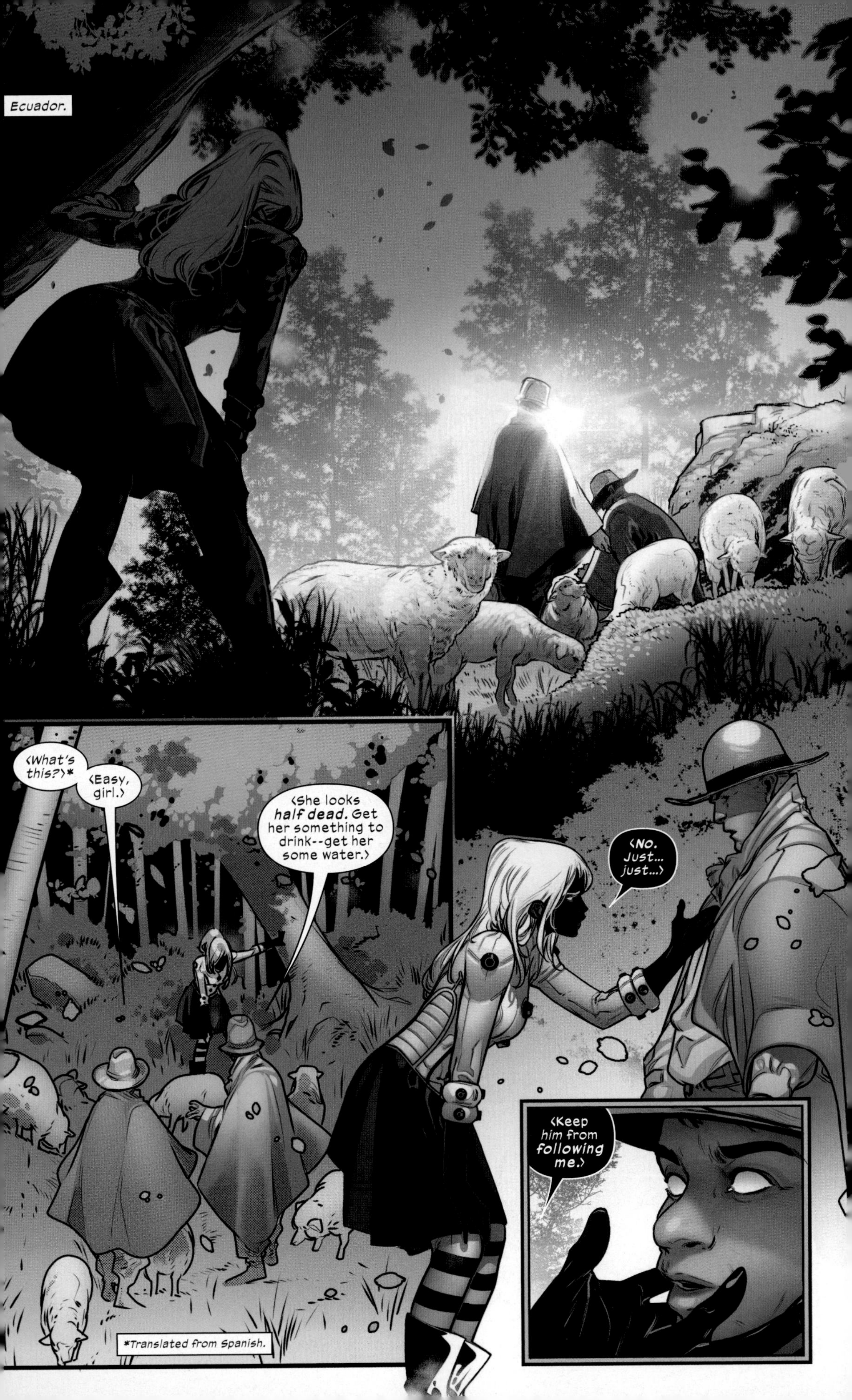
Ecuador.
‹What's this?›*
‹Easy, girl.›
‹She looks half dead. Get her something to drink--get her some water.›
‹No. Just... just...›
‹Keep him from following me.›
*Translated from Spanish.

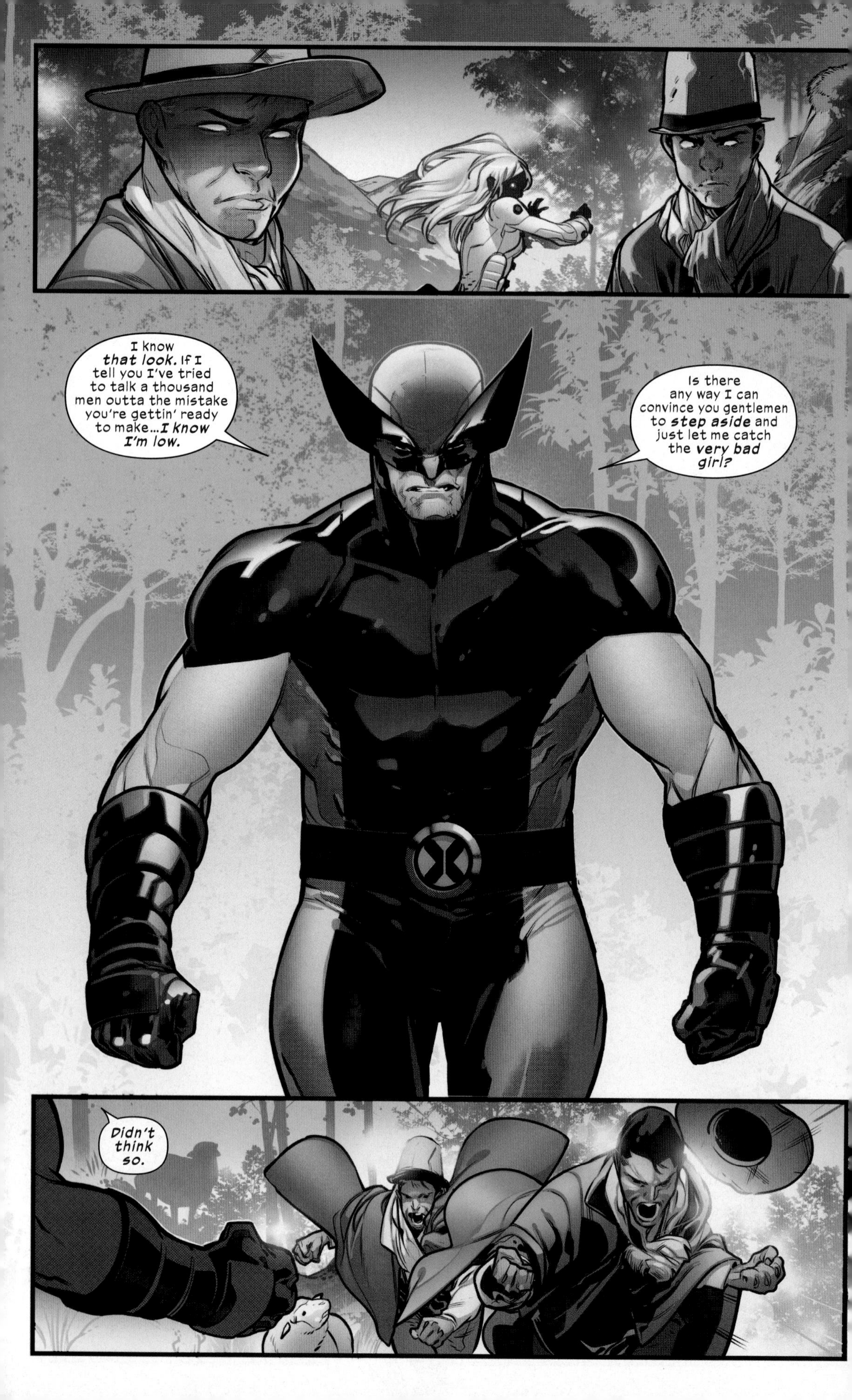
I know that look. If I tell you I've tried to talk a thousand men outta the mistake you're gettin' ready to make...I know I'm low.
Is there any way I can convince you gentlemen to step aside and just let me catch the very bad girl?
Didn't think so.

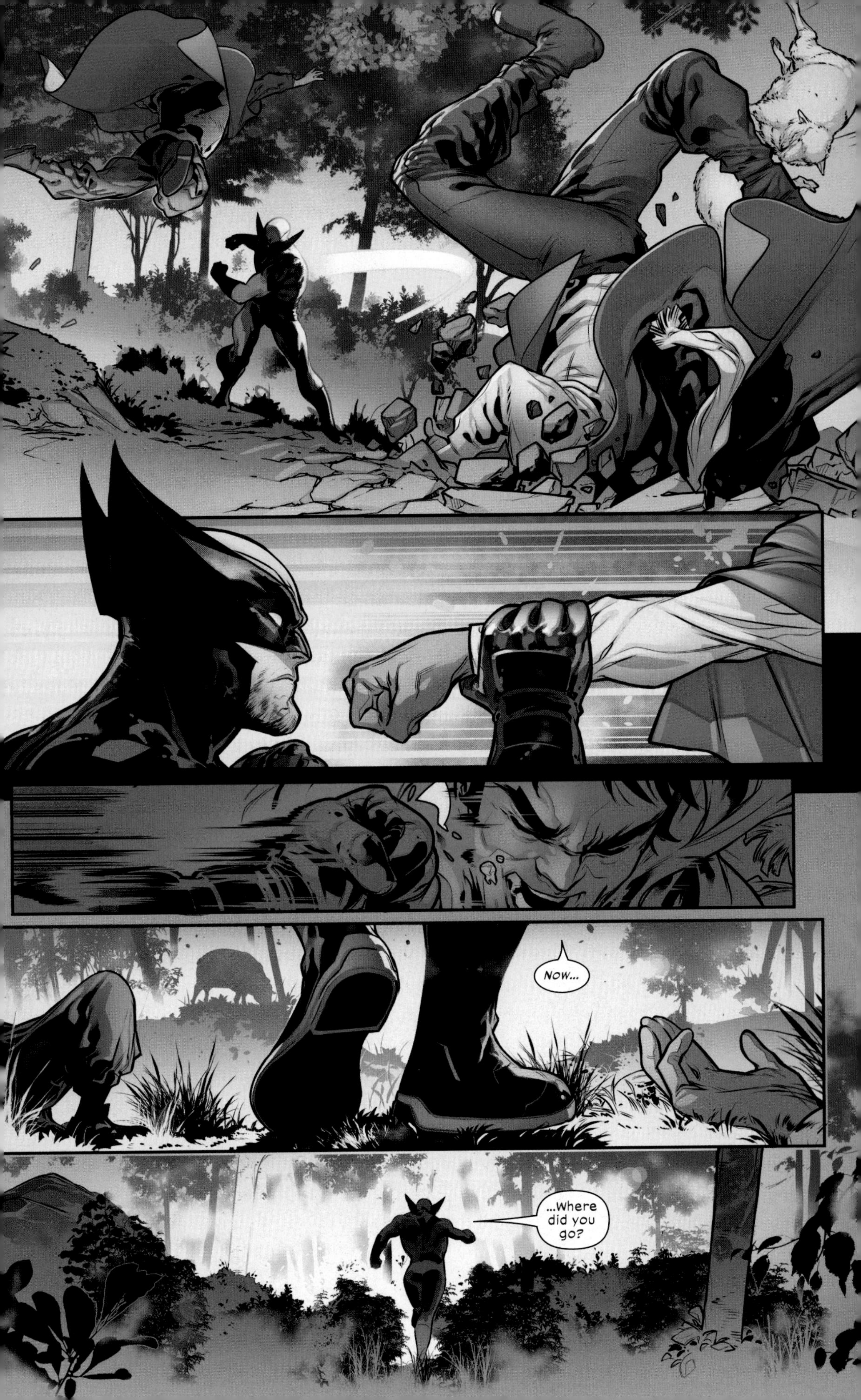
NOW...
...Where did you go?

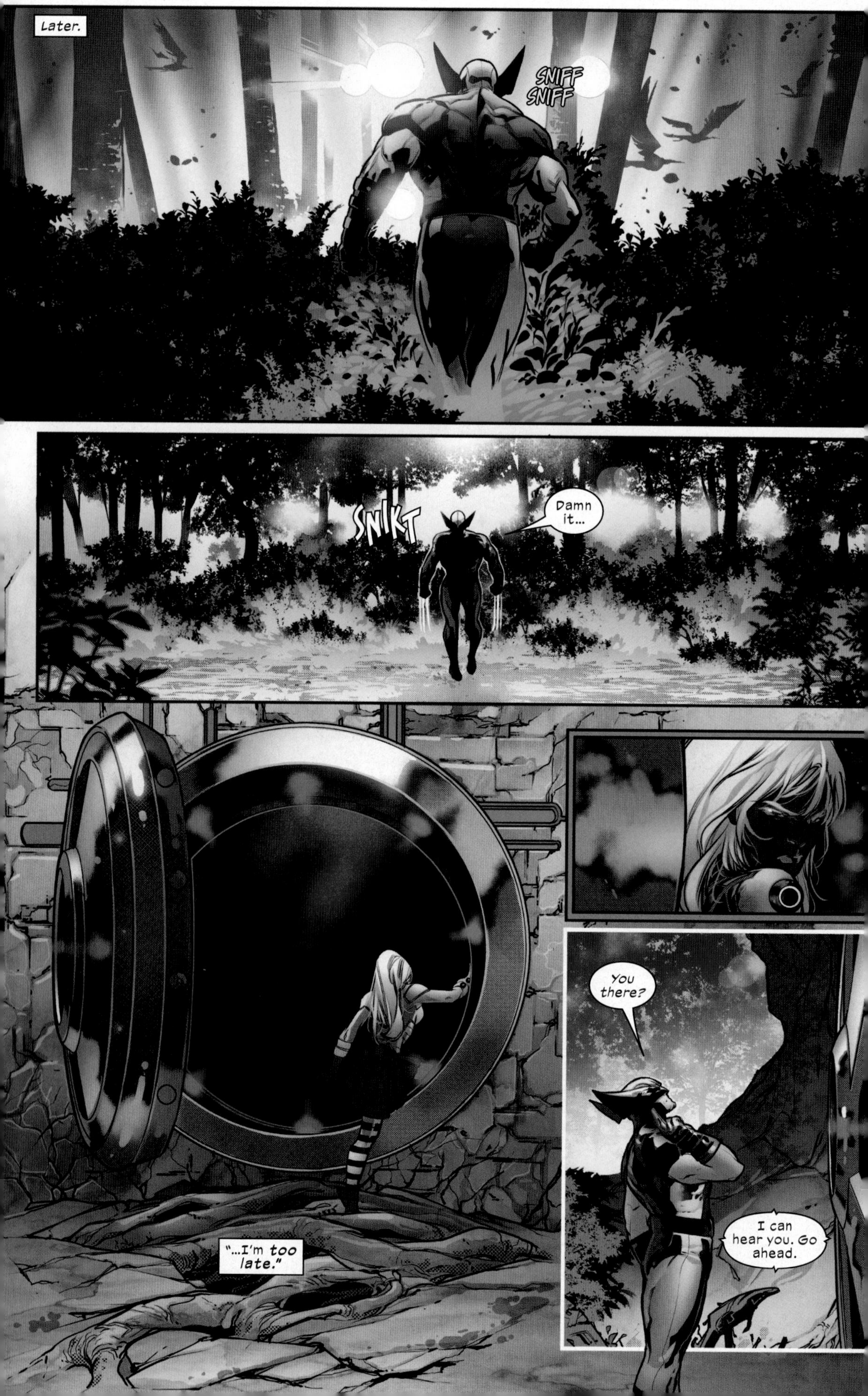
Later.
SNIFF
SNIFF
SNIKT
Damn it...
"...I'm too late."
You there?
I can hear you. Go ahead.

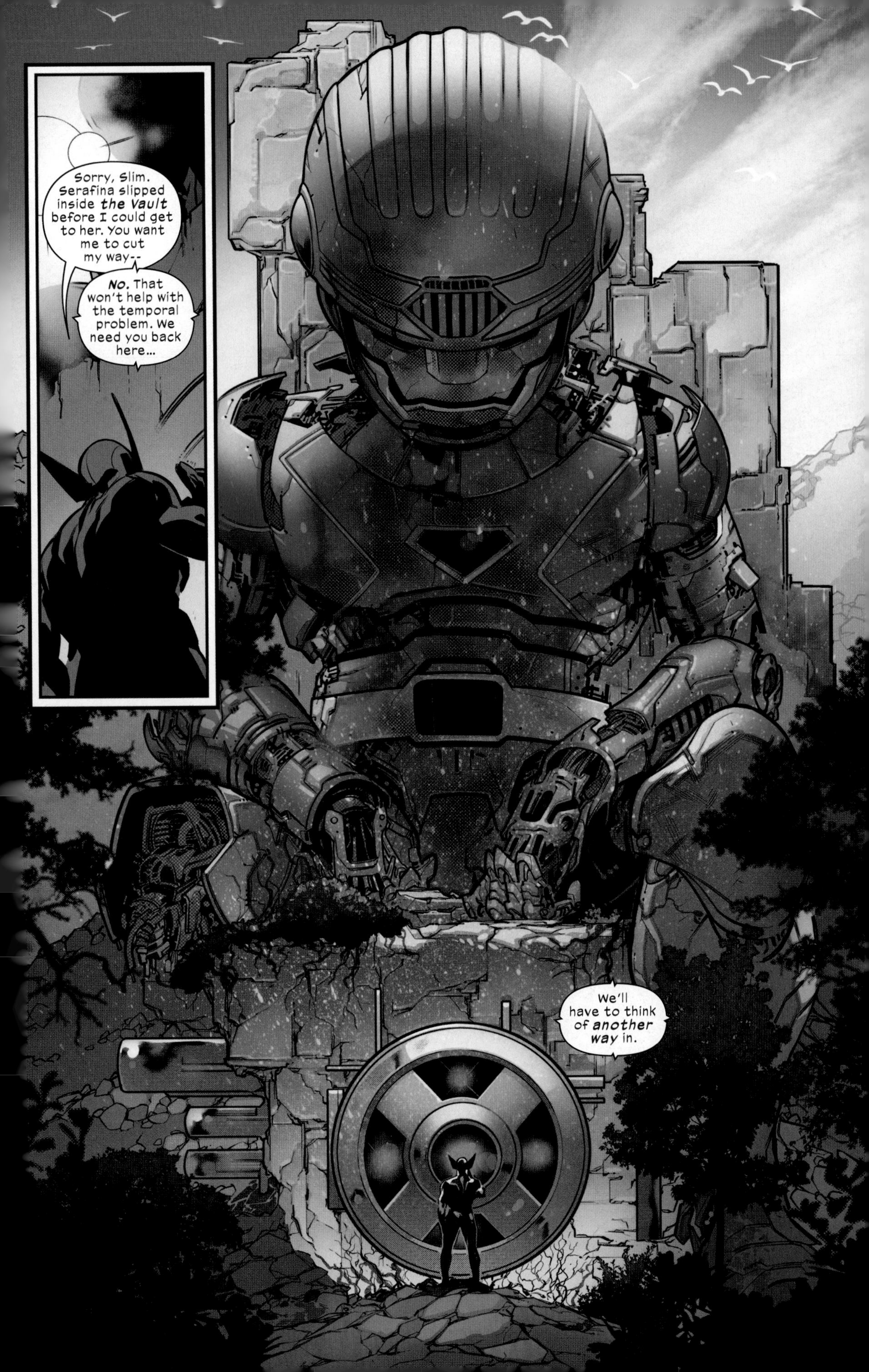
Sorry, Slim. Serafina slipped inside *the Vault* before I could get to her. You want me to cut my way--
No. That won't help with the temporal problem. We need you back here...
We'll have to think of *another way* in.

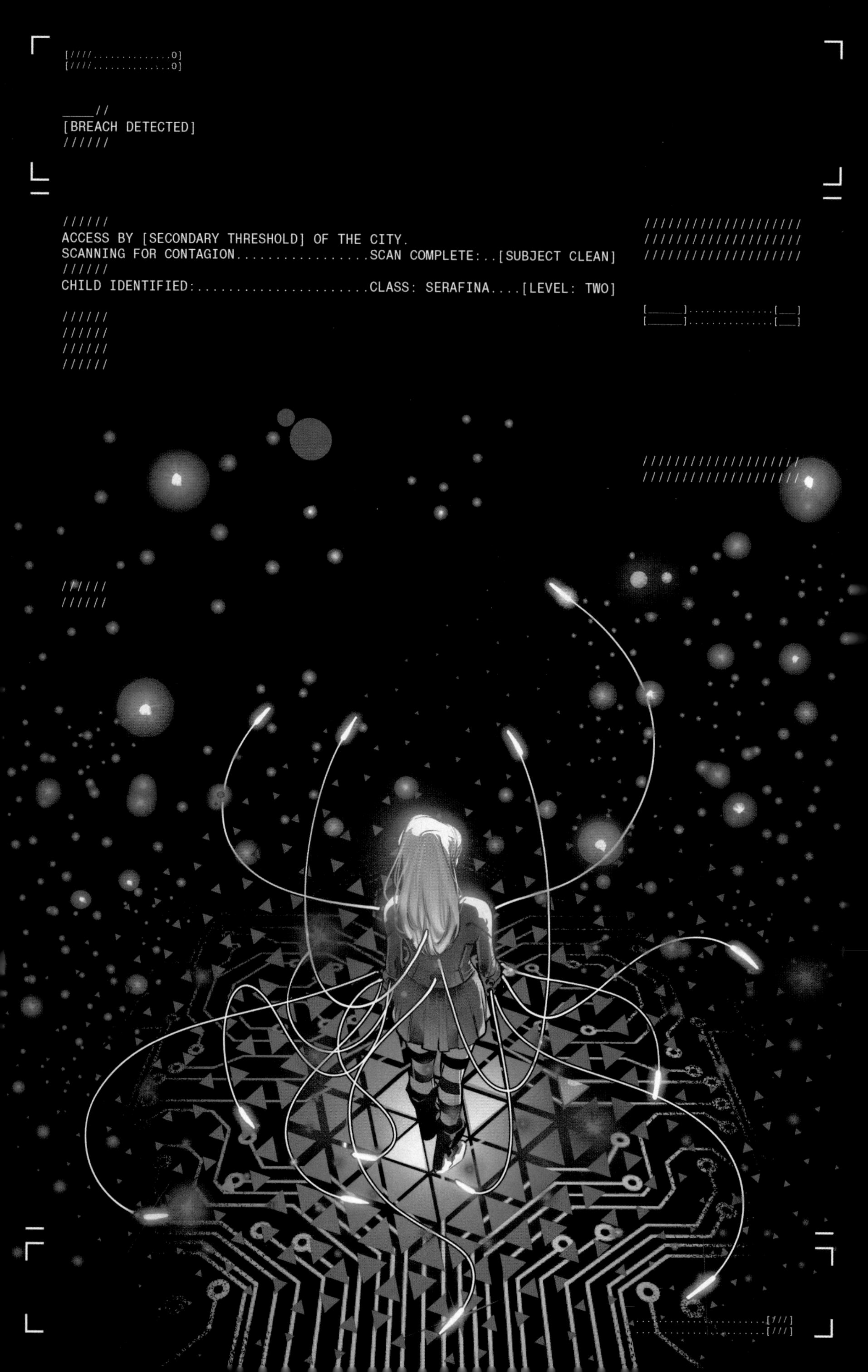

[BREACH DETECTED]
ACCESS BY [SECONDARY THRESHOLD] OF THE CITY.
SCANNING FOR CONTAGION..................SCAN COMPLETE:..[SUBJECT CLEAN]
CHILD IDENTIFIED:.......................CLASS: SERAFINA....[LEVEL: TWO]

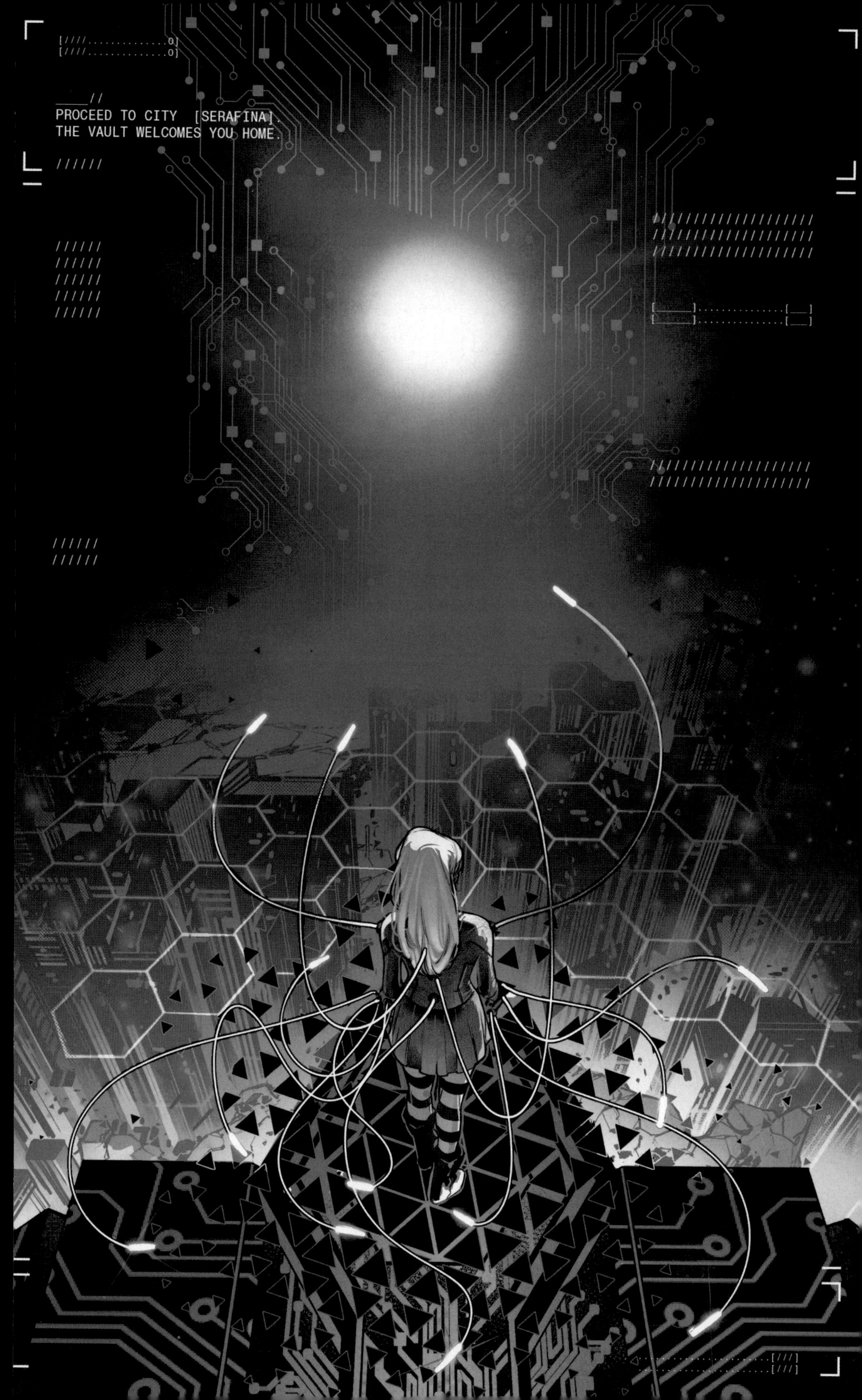
PROCEED TO CITY [SERAFINA].
THE VAULT WELCOMES YOU HOME.

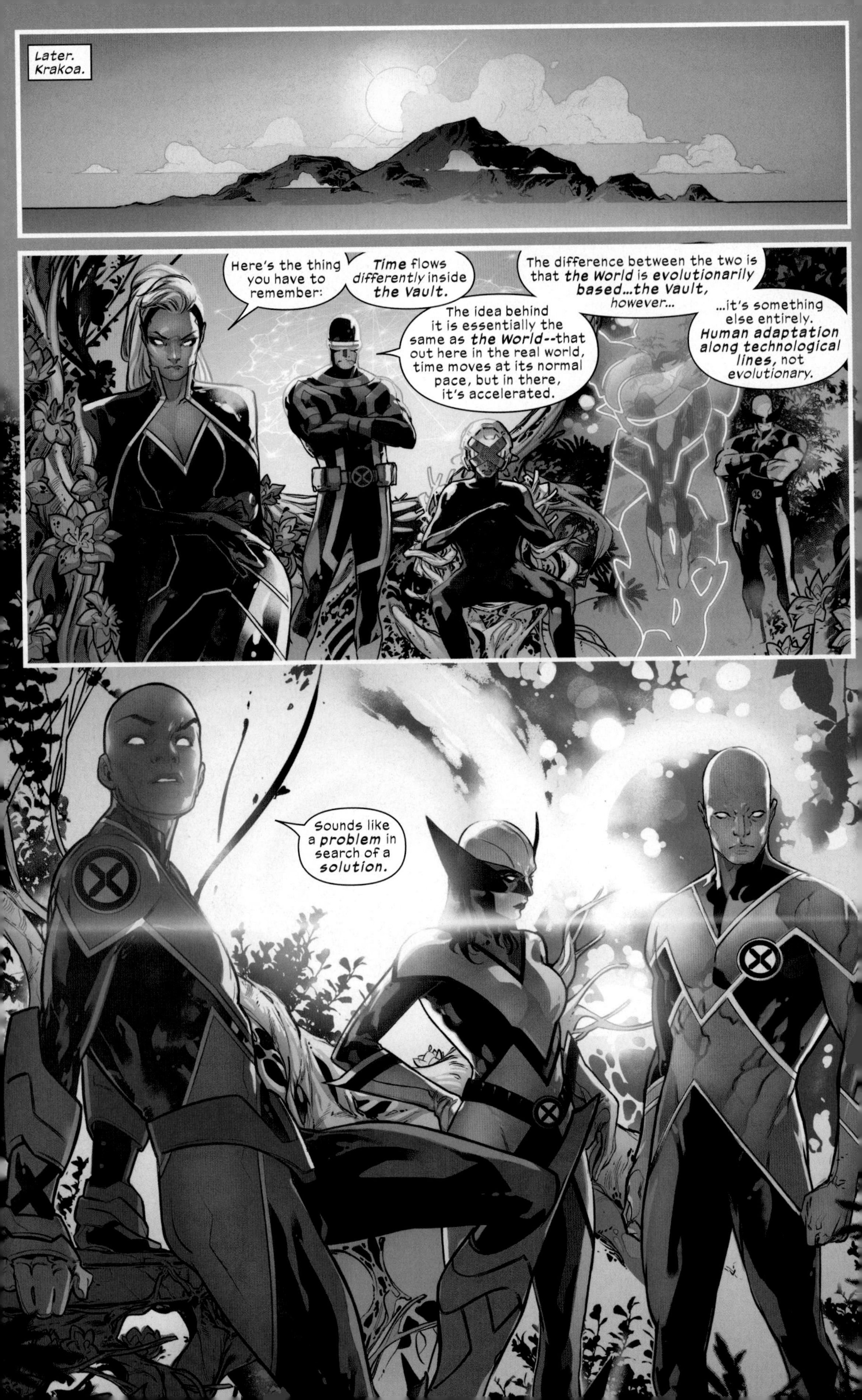
Later. Krakoa.
Here's the thing you have to remember:
Time flows differently inside the Vault.
The idea behind it is essentially the same as the World--that out here in the real world, time moves at its normal pace, but in there, it's accelerated.
The difference between the two is that the World is evolutionarily based...the Vault, however...
...it's something else entirely. Human adaptation along technological lines, not evolutionary.
Sounds like a problem in search of a solution.

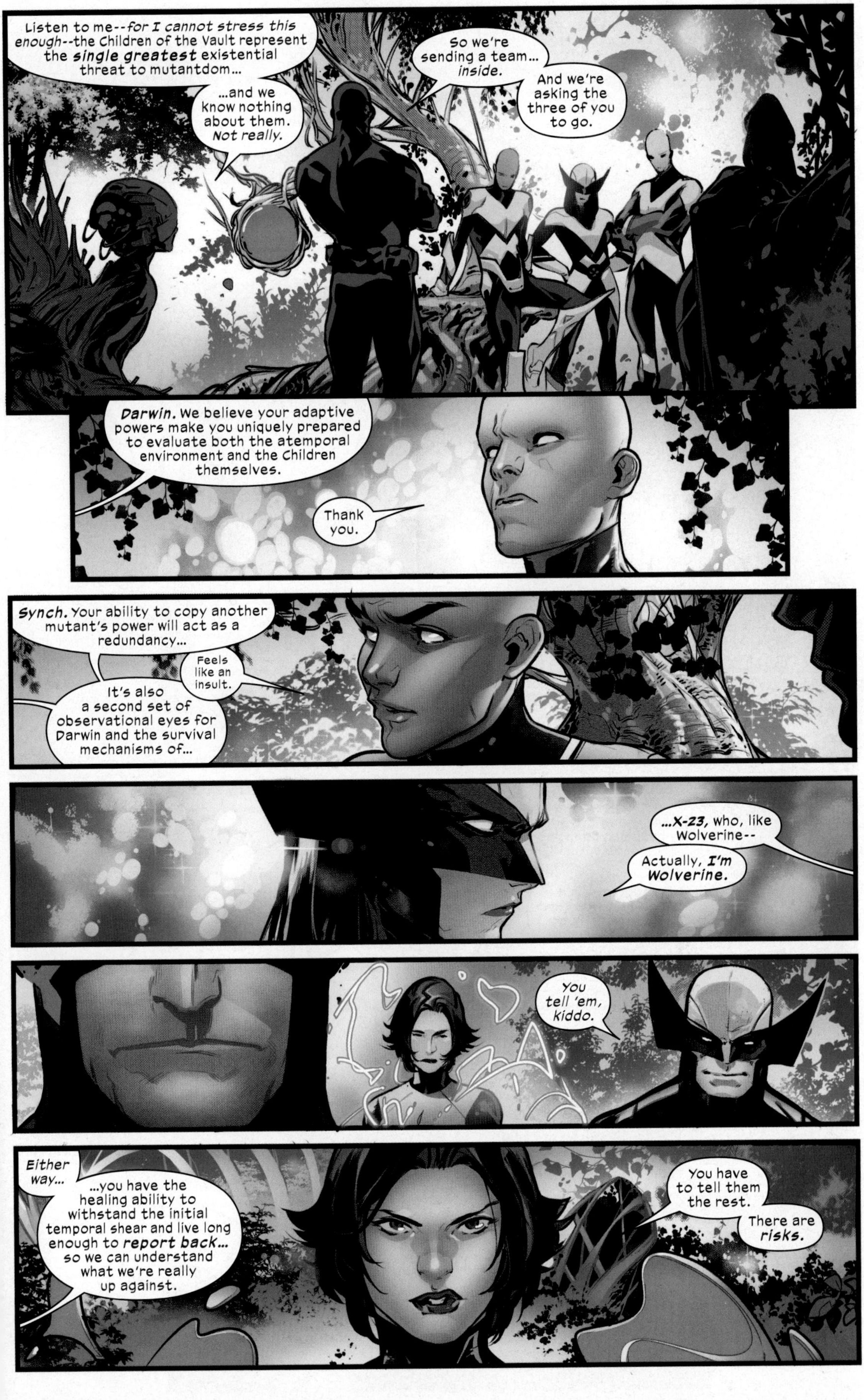
Listen to me--for I cannot stress this enough--the Children of the Vault represent the single greatest existential threat to mutantdom...
...and we know nothing about them. Not really.
So we're sending a team... inside.
And we're asking the three of you to go.
Darwin. We believe your adaptive powers make you uniquely prepared to evaluate both the atemporal environment and the Children themselves.
Thank you.
Synch. Your ability to copy another mutant's power will act as a redundancy...
Feels like an insult.
It's also a second set of observational eyes for Darwin and the survival mechanisms of...
...X-23, who, like Wolverine--
Actually, I'm Wolverine.
You tell 'em, kiddo.
Either way...
...you have the healing ability to withstand the initial temporal shear and live long enough to report back... so we can understand what we're really up against.
You have to tell them the rest.
There are risks.

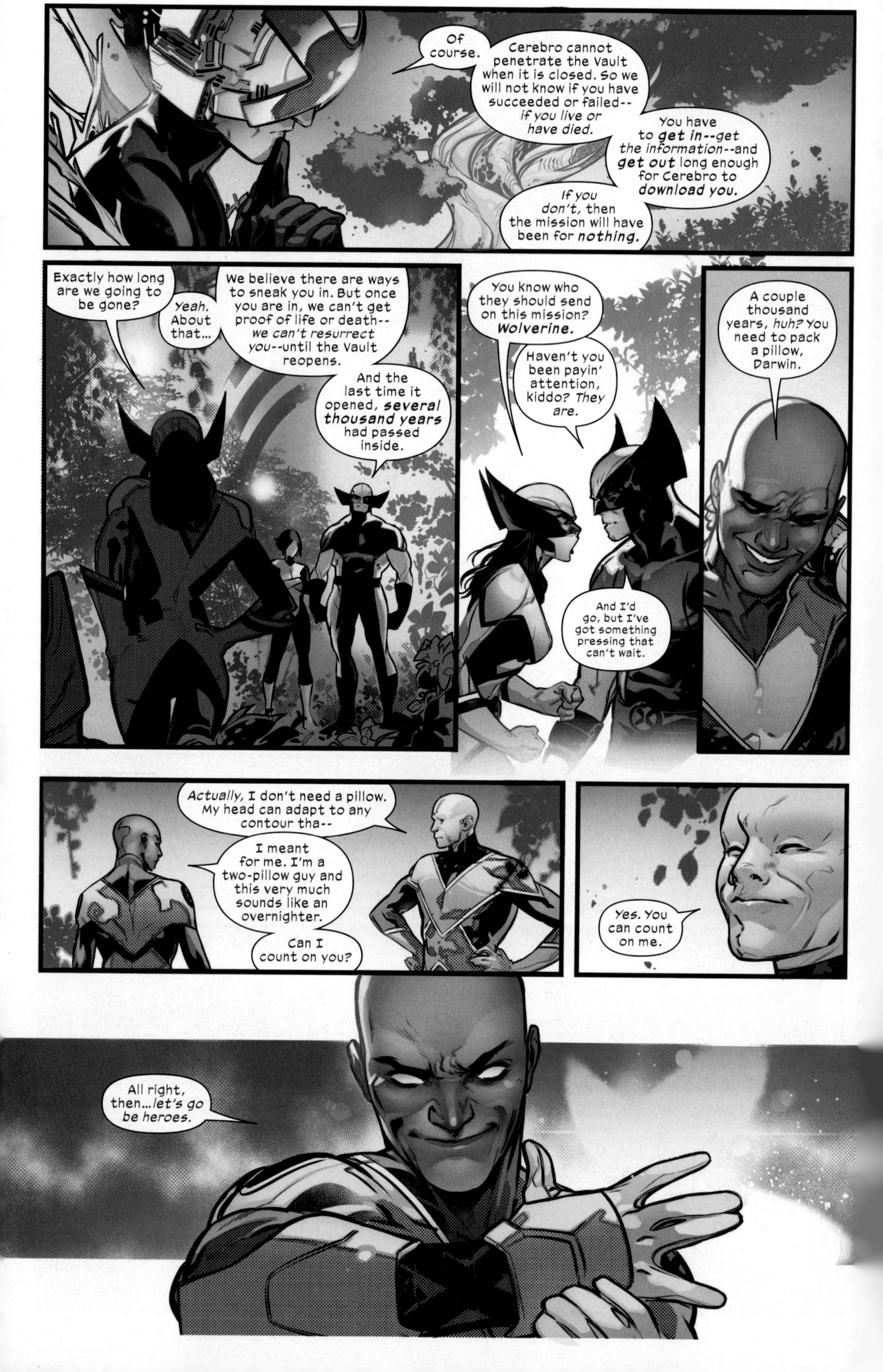
Of course.
Cerebro cannot penetrate the Vault when it is closed. So we will not know if you have succeeded or failed--if you live or have died.
You have to get in--get the information--and get out long enough for Cerebro to download you.
If you don't, then the mission will have been for nothing.
Exactly how long are we going to be gone?
Yeah. About that...
We believe there are ways to sneak you in. But once you are in, we can't get proof of life or death--we can't resurrect you--until the Vault reopens.
And the last time it opened, several thousand years had passed inside.
You know who they should send on this mission? Wolverine.
Haven't you been payin' attention, kiddo? They are.
And I'd go, but I've got something pressing that can't wait.
A couple thousand years, huh? You need to pack a pillow, Darwin.
Actually, I don't need a pillow. My head can adapt to any contour tha--
I meant for me. I'm a two-pillow guy and this very much sounds like an overnighter.
Can I count on you?
Yes. You can count on me.
All right, then...let's go be heroes.

MEDICAL REPORT

PATIENT FILE: #14
RE: Post-resurrection analysis of Synch [Everett Thomas]

—

PHYSIOLOGY

One week after rebirth, the patient appears to be in good health and excellent physical condition. Testing also indicates there doesn't appear to be a detrimental upper limit to what we are calling "peak physical form." A review of Synch's training sessions from his time at the Massachusetts Academy shows that he is now operating at a four percent increase in natural physical ability. The Five, it seems, are correcting [possibly unconsciously] the minor imperfections of each mutant they resurrect.

[NOTE: Synch was one of the earliest resurrected mutants because it was believed that his powers could enable him to act as a substitute for any of the Five who might need one. And while this proved to be the case, it was unknown at the time that resurrection isn't taxing for the Five but restorative.]

—

PSYCHOLOGY

Unfortunately, while the patient appears to be physically fine, the same cannot be said for his psychological condition. I would stop short of saying Everett is in denial, but he is clearly putting on a brave face regarding his current situation.

There is no escaping the fact that he looks around and sees a world that has changed in ways that he doesn't fully comprehend. And while this is burdensome enough, to see other mutants who were once fellow students of his having changed and in some ways passed him by has proven to be incredibly difficult for him.

So much so that I cannot currently recommend the further resurrection of similar mutants in Everett's situation unless a less harmful solution presents itself.*

- Dr. Cecilia Reyes

*[NOTE: Because of this experience, the idea of clustering mutants together from similar backgrounds and time periods was tested by resurrecting the mutant Skin [Angelo Espinosa] ahead of [his scheduled] time to serve as a companion for Synch. The success of this served to adapt our early resurrection protocols to better serve mutant society.]

—

[////..............0]
[////..............0]

____//
FIELD DOWNLOAD:
CLASS: SERAFINA [LEVEL: TWO]

//////
REPORT FOR CHILD POD 5/600 [RECONNAISSANCE]

//////////////////////
//////////////////////
//////////////////////

............................CHILD: SANGRE.........DECEASED [_]
............................CHILD: PERRO..........DECEASED [_]
............................CHILD: SERAFINA.......CAPTURED [/]
............................CHILD: AGUJA..........DECEASED [_]
............................CHILD: FUEGO..........DECEASED [_]

[______]...............[___]
[______]...............[___]

//////
//////

PRIMARY ANALYSIS:
Mission failure.

SECONDARY ANALYSIS:
Increased threat activity level of non-augmented, naturally occurring human population
[Non-posthuman resistance expected. Threat level: secondary.]

//////////////////////
//////////////////////

Increased threat activity level of *Homo superior*
[Mutant resistance expected. Threat level: primary.]

CONCLUSION:
Vault opening delayed. Child level: Three necessary for successful occupation/subjugation of external environment [World].

//////
//////
//////
//////

//////
//////

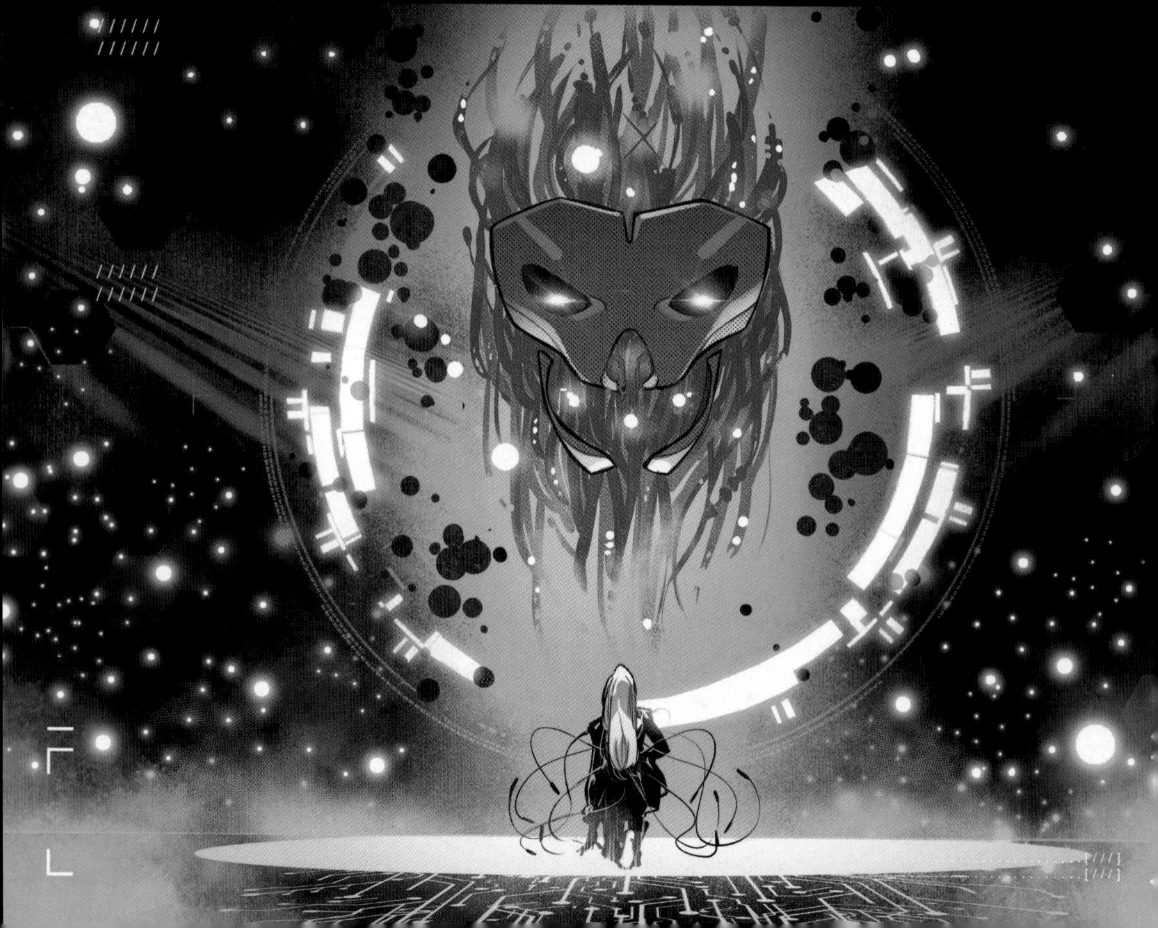

//////
//////

POD 1/600 [EMPIRE]............................LEVEL: TWO [UPGRADE]
POD 2/600 [JUDGE]............................LEVEL: TWO [UPGRADE]
POD 3/600 [BUILDER]..........................LEVEL: TWO [UPGRADE]
POD 4/600 [SWORD]............................LEVEL: TWO [UPGRADE]
POD 5/600 [RECONNAISSANCE]...................LEVEL: --- [RESTORE]
\\\\\\

.......RESTORE CHILD: CLASS: SANGRE.............LEVEL: ONE [RESTORE]
.......RESTORE CHILD: CLASS: PERRO..............LEVEL: ONE [RESTORE]
.......UPGRADE CHILD: CLASS: SERAFINA...........LEVEL: TWO [UPGRADE]
.......RESTORE CHILD: CLASS: AGUJA..............LEVEL: ONE [RESTORE]
.......RESTORE CHILD: CLASS: FUEGO..............LEVEL: ONE [RESTORE]

//////
POD 6/600 [KNIFE]............................LEVEL: TWO [UPGRADE]
POD 7/600 [FLIGHT]...........................LEVEL: TWO [UPGRADE]
POD 8/600 [COMMUNICATION]....................LEVEL: TWO [UPGRADE]
POD 9/600 [TEACHER]..........................LEVEL: TWO [UPGRADE]
POD 10/600 [SOLDIER].........................LEVEL: ONE [UPGRADE]
POD 11/600 [SOLDIER].........................LEVEL: TWO [UPGRADE]
POD 12/600 [SOLDIER].........................LEVEL: TWO [UPGRADE]
POD 13/600 [SOLDIER].........................LEVEL: ONE [UPGRADE]
POD 14/600 [SOLDIER].........................LEVEL: ONE [UPGRADE]
POD 15/600 [ENVOY]..........

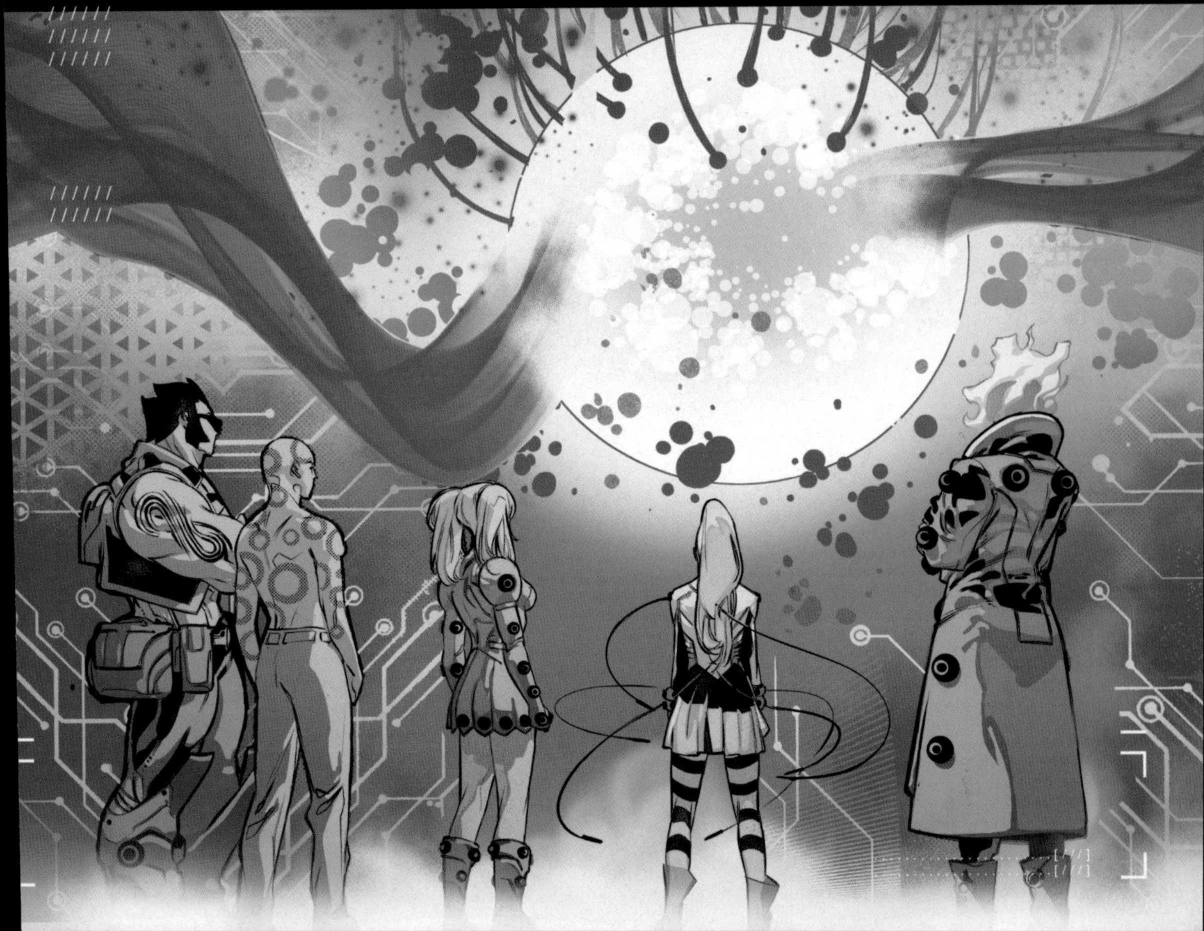

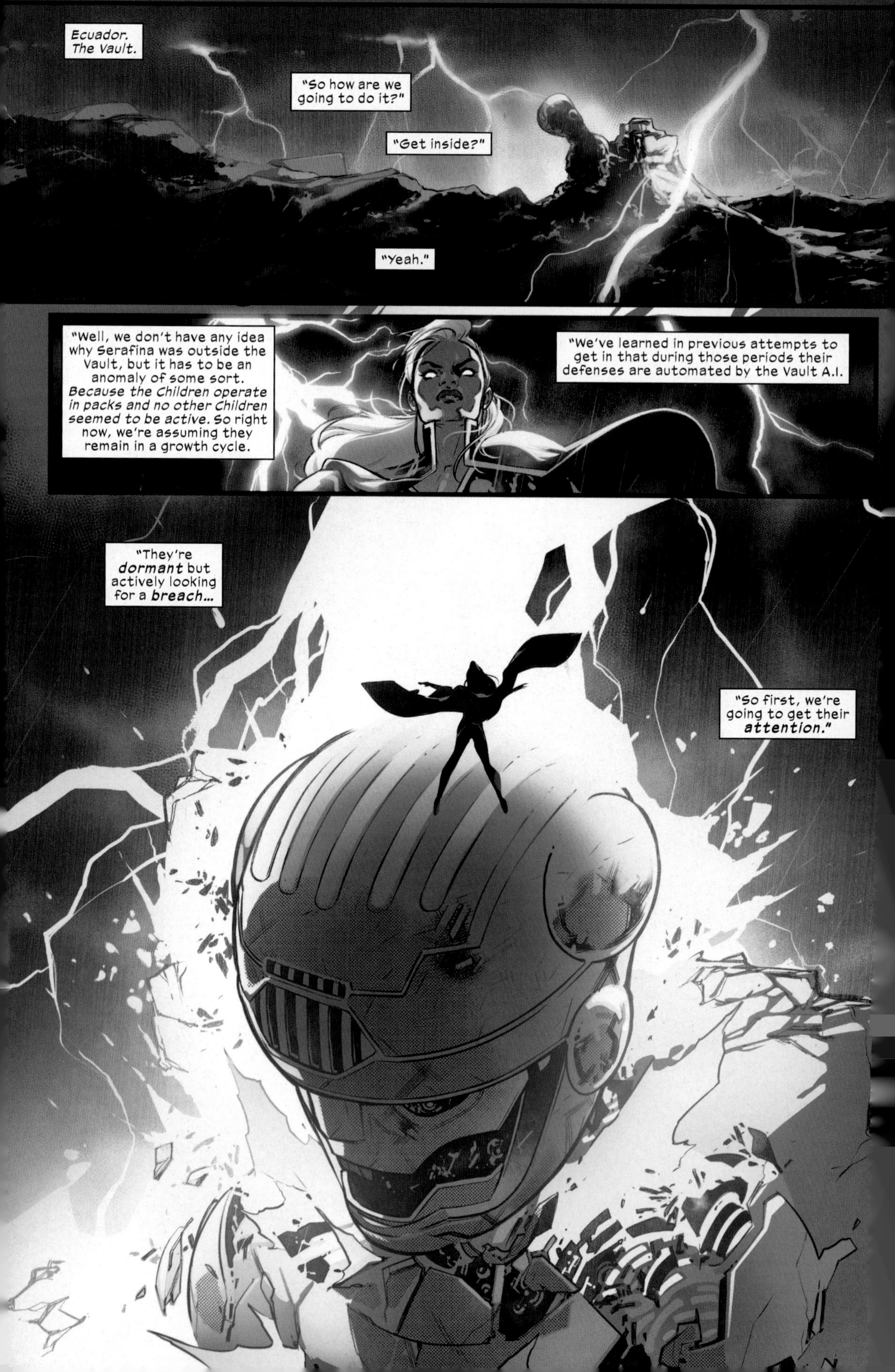
Ecuador. The Vault.
"So how are we going to do it?"
"Get inside?"
"Yeah."
"Well, we don't have any idea why Serafina was outside the Vault, but it has to be an anomaly of some sort. Because the Children operate in packs and no other Children seemed to be active. So right now, we're assuming they remain in a growth cycle.
"We've learned in previous attempts to get in that during those periods their defenses are automated by the Vault A.I.
"They're dormant but actively looking for a breach...
"So first, we're going to get their attention."

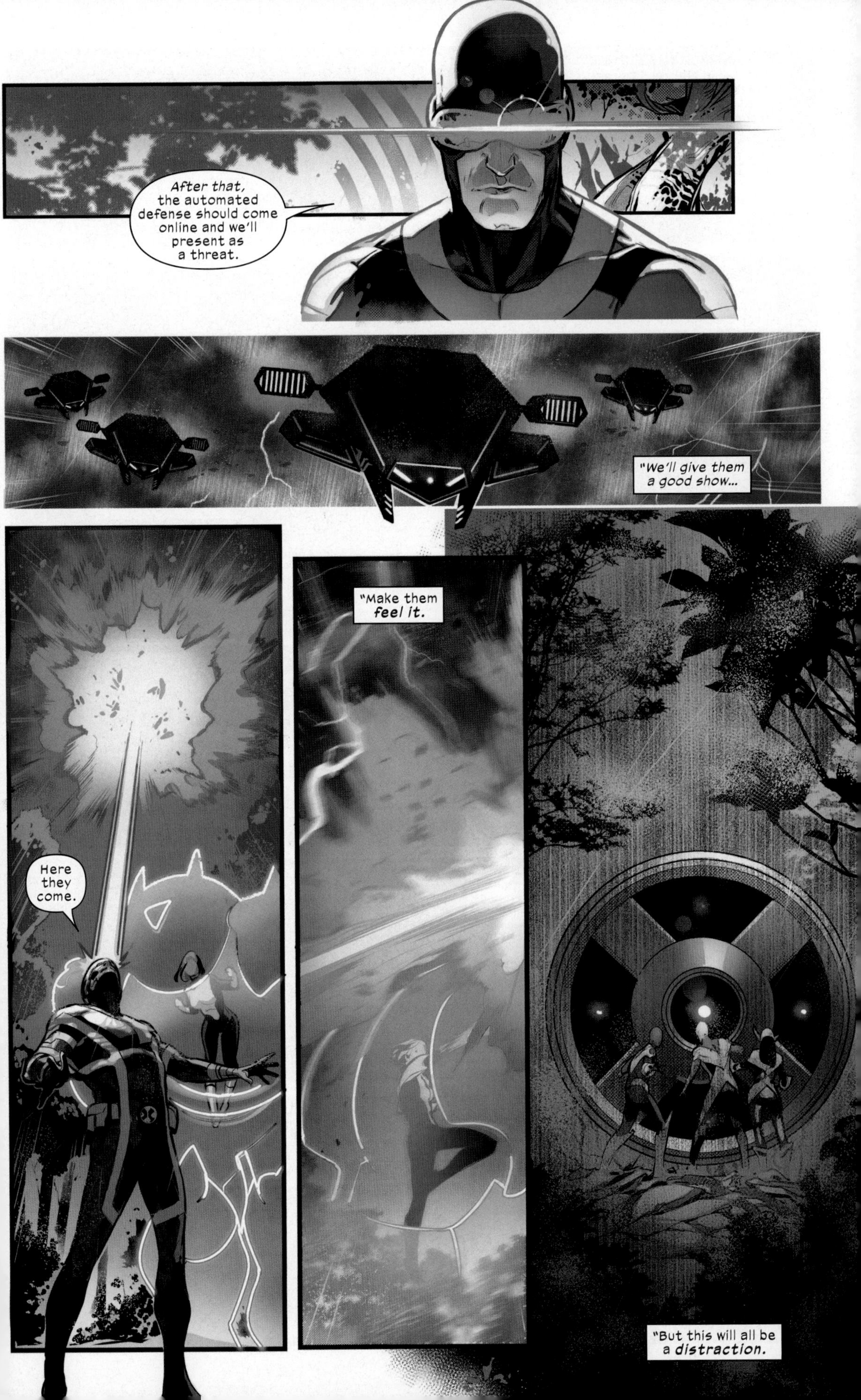
After that, the automated defense should come online and we'll present as a threat.
"We'll give them a good show...
Here they come.
"Make them feel it.
"But this will all be a distraction.

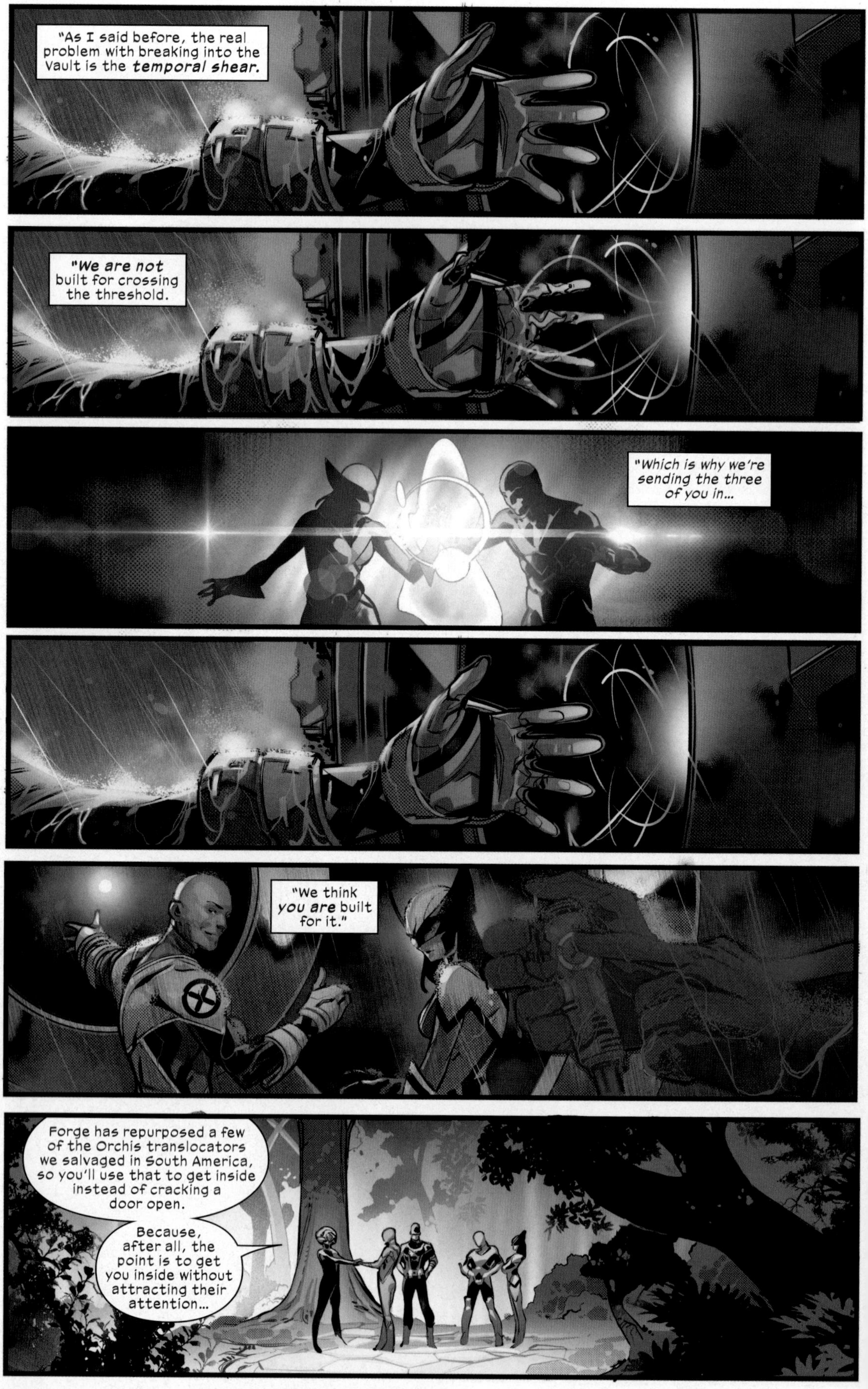
"As I said before, the real problem with breaking into the Vault is the *temporal shear.*
"*We are not* built for crossing the threshold.
"Which is why we're sending the three of you in...
"We think *you are* built for it."
Forge has repurposed a few of the Orchis translocators we salvaged in South America, so you'll use that to get inside instead of cracking a door open.
Because, after all, the point is to get you inside without attracting their attention...

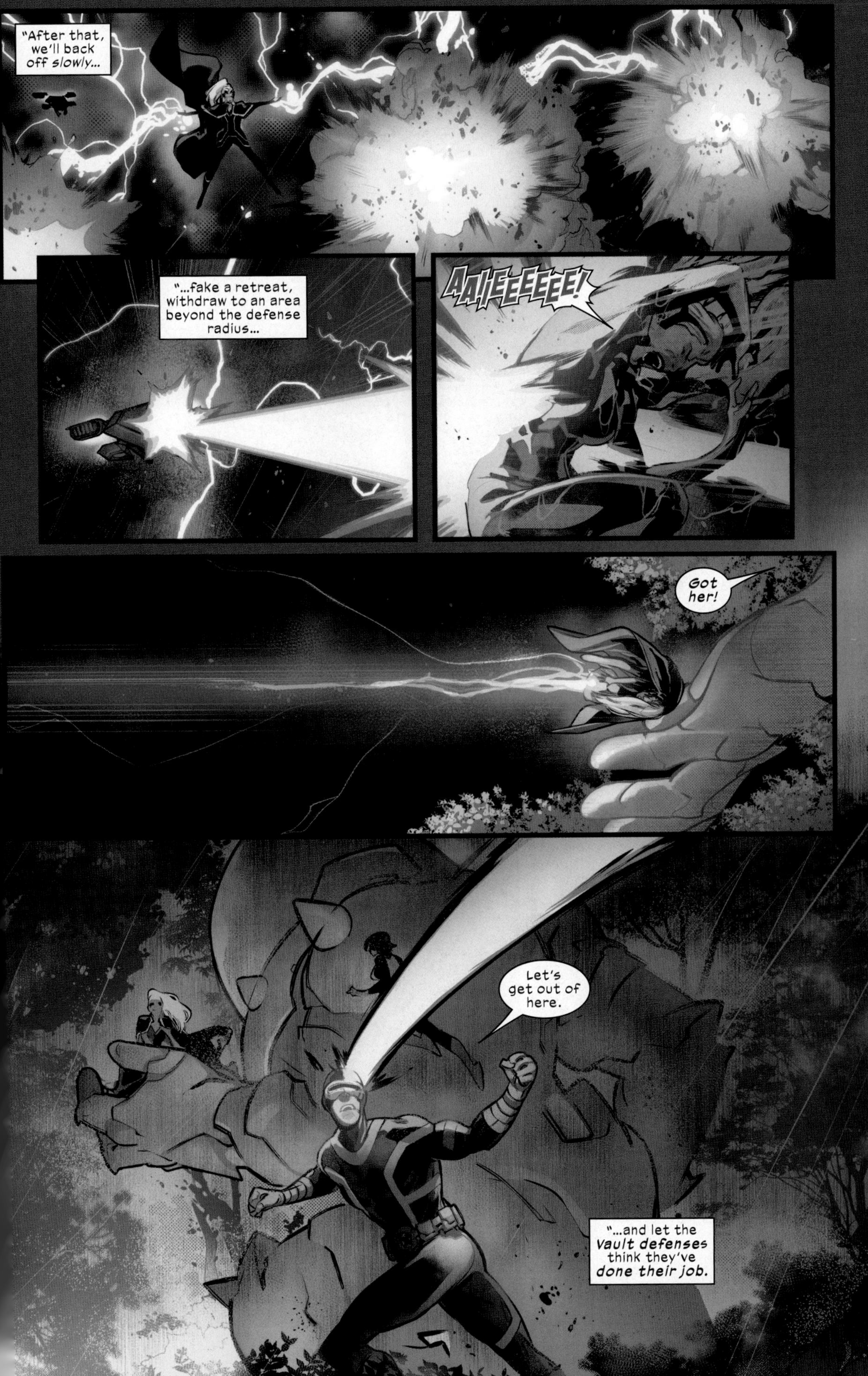
"After that, we'll back off slowly...
"...fake a retreat, withdraw to an area beyond the defense radius...
AAIIEEEEEE!
Got her!
Let's get out of here.
"...and let the Vault defenses think they've done their job.

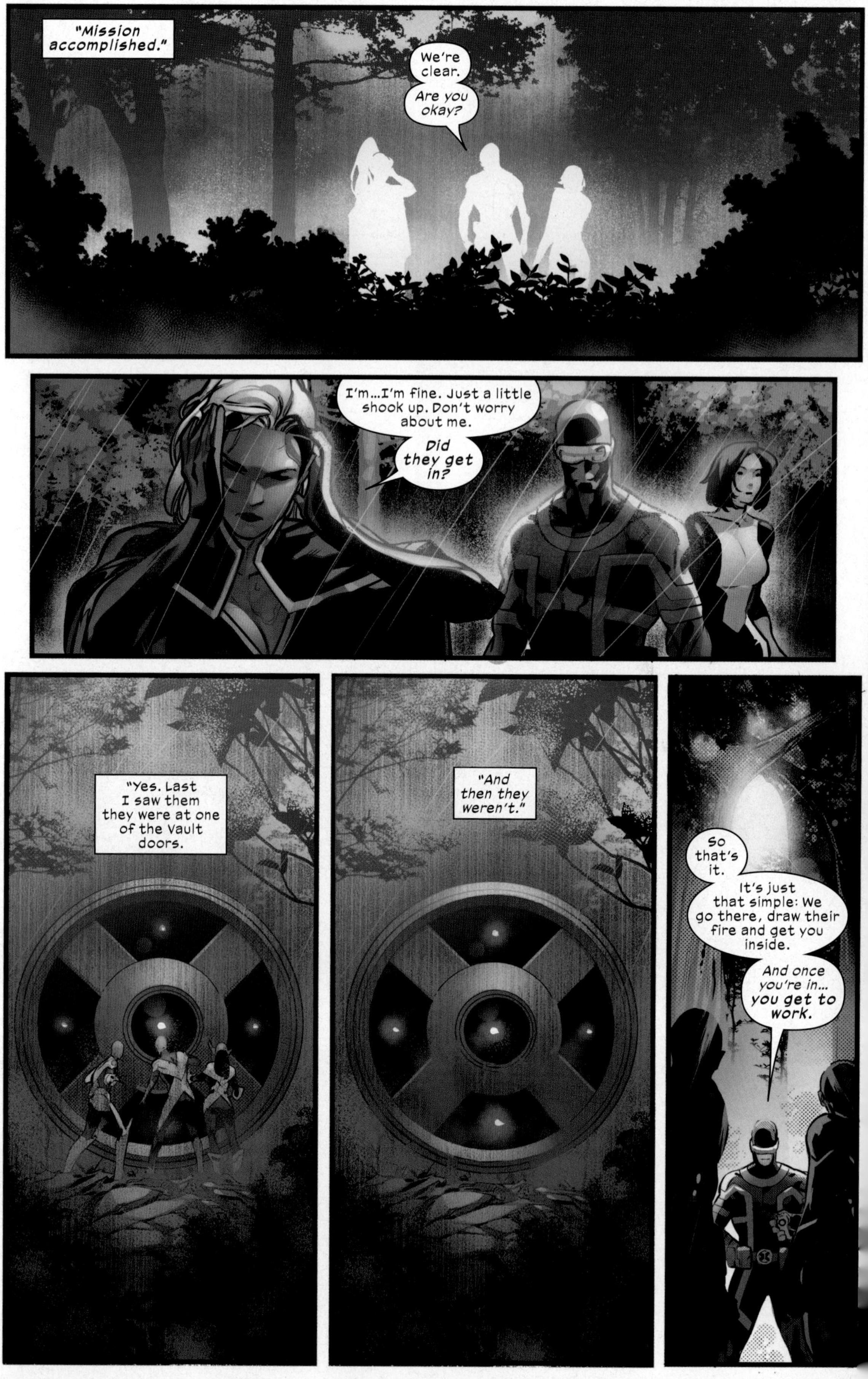
"Mission accomplished."
We're clear.
Are you okay?
I'm...I'm fine. Just a little shook up. Don't worry about me.
Did they get in?
"Yes. Last I saw them they were at one of the Vault doors.
"And then they weren't."
So that's it.
It's just that simple: We go there, draw their fire and get you inside.
And once you're in... you get to work.

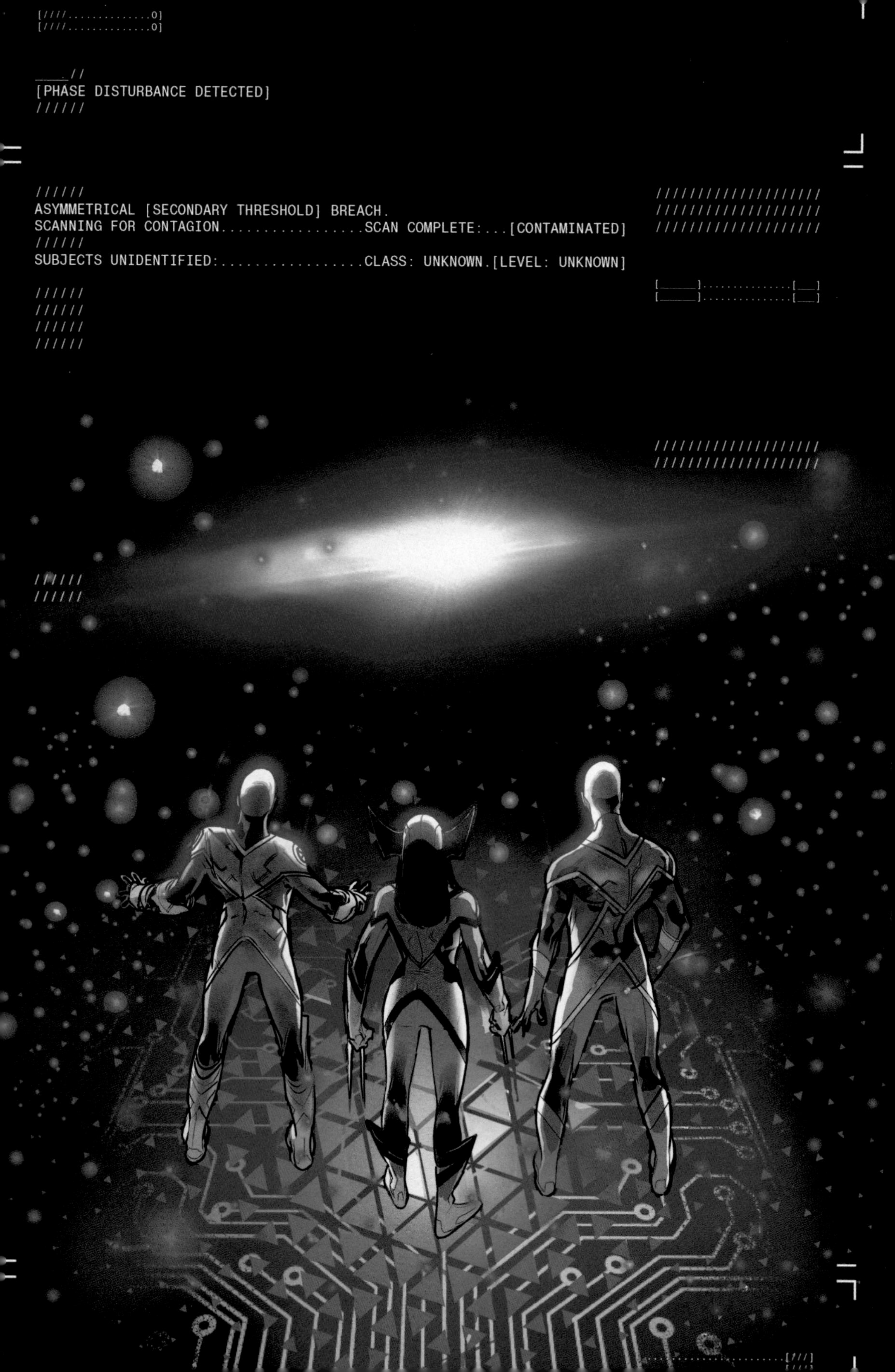
[PHASE DISTURBANCE DETECTED]
ASYMMETRICAL [SECONDARY THRESHOLD] BREACH.
SCANNING FOR CONTAGION..................SCAN COMPLETE:...[CONTAMINATED]
SUBJECTS UNIDENTIFIED:..................CLASS: UNKNOWN.[LEVEL: UNKNOWN]

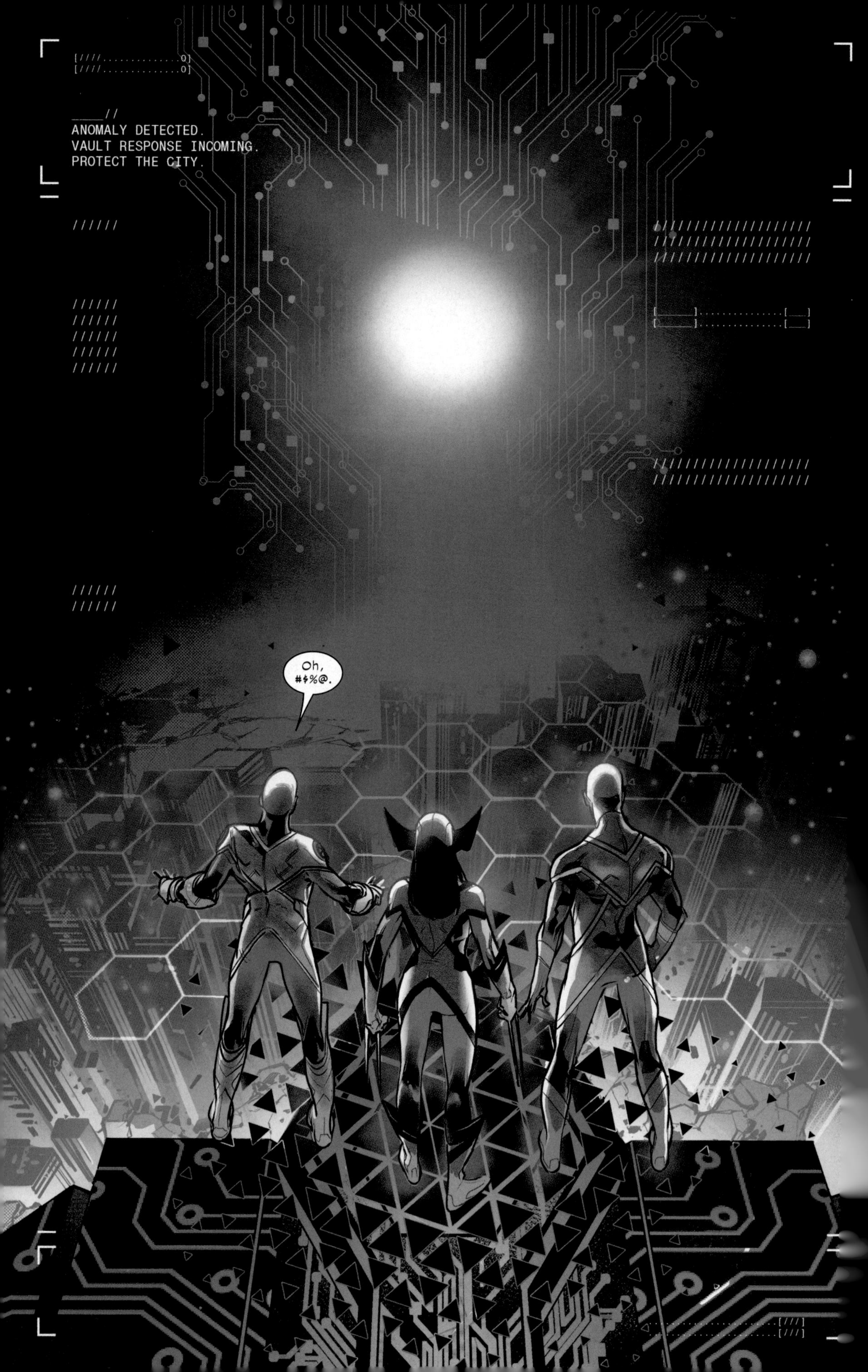
ANOMALY DETECTED.
VAULT RESPONSE INCOMING.
PROTECT THE CITY.
Oh, #$%@.

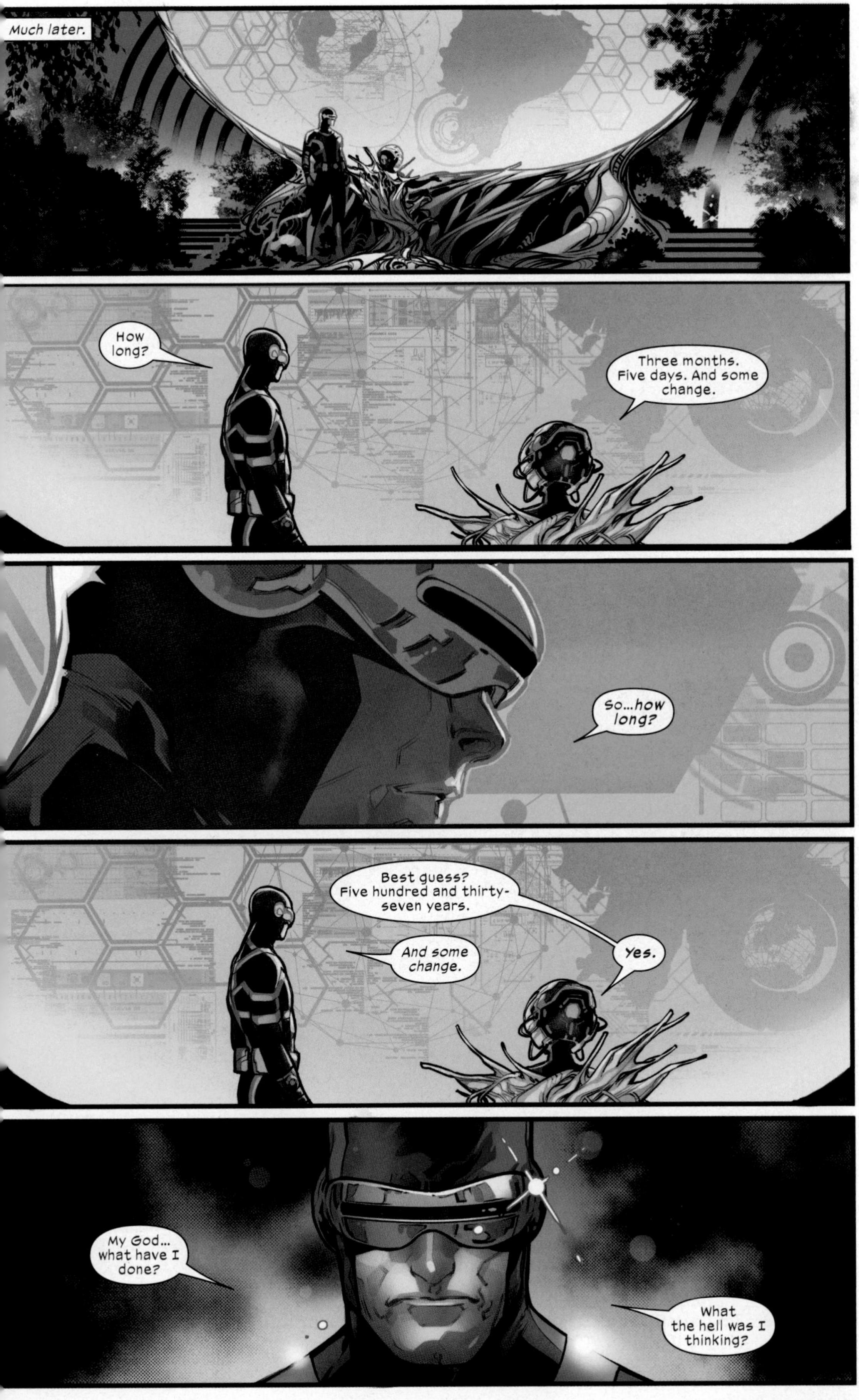
Much later.
How long?
Three months. Five days. And some change.
So...how long?
Best guess? Five hundred and thirty-seven years.
And some change.
Yes.
My God... what have I done?
What the hell was I thinking?

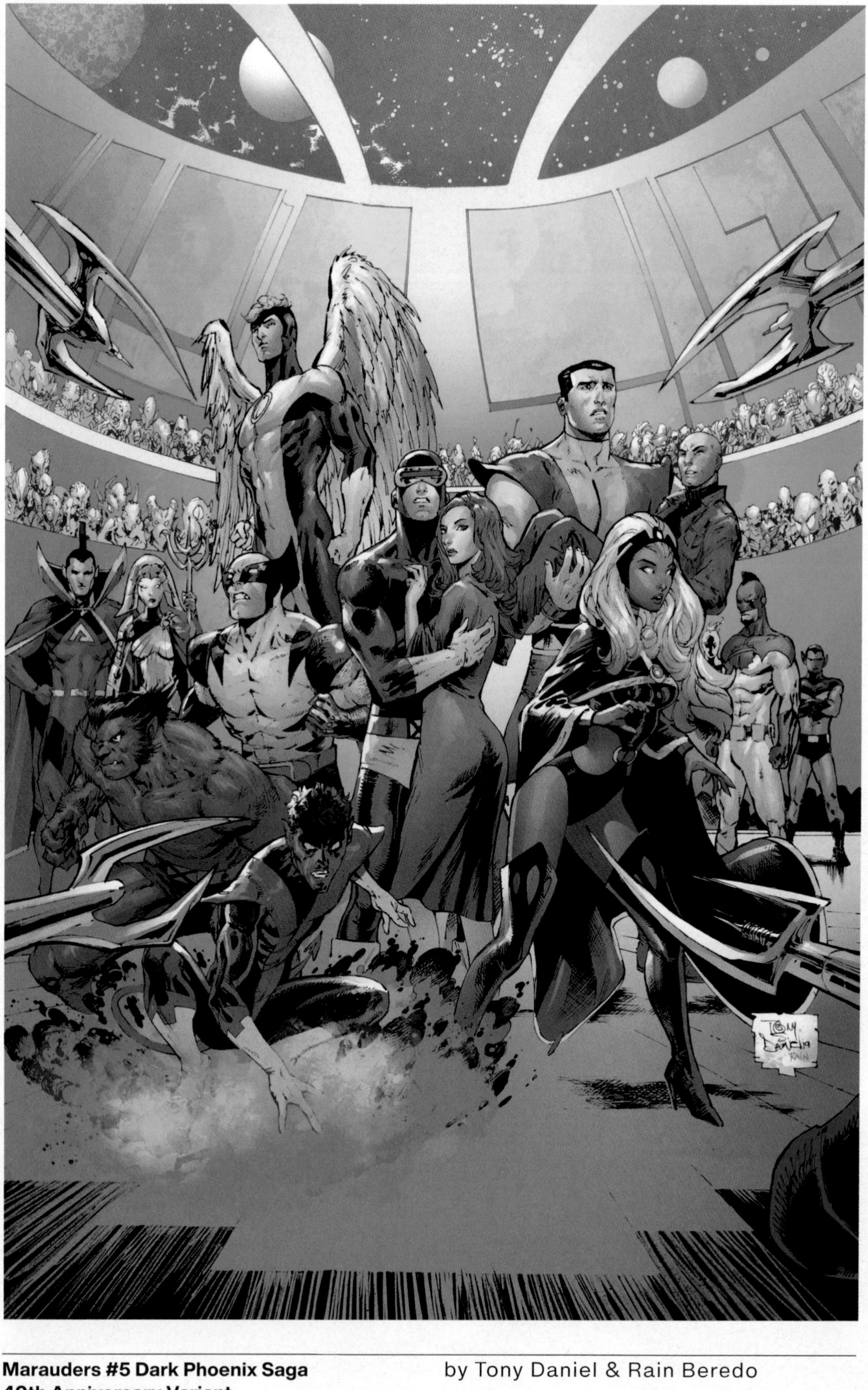

Marauders #5 Dark Phoenix Saga
40th Anniversary Variant
by Tony Daniel & Rain Beredo

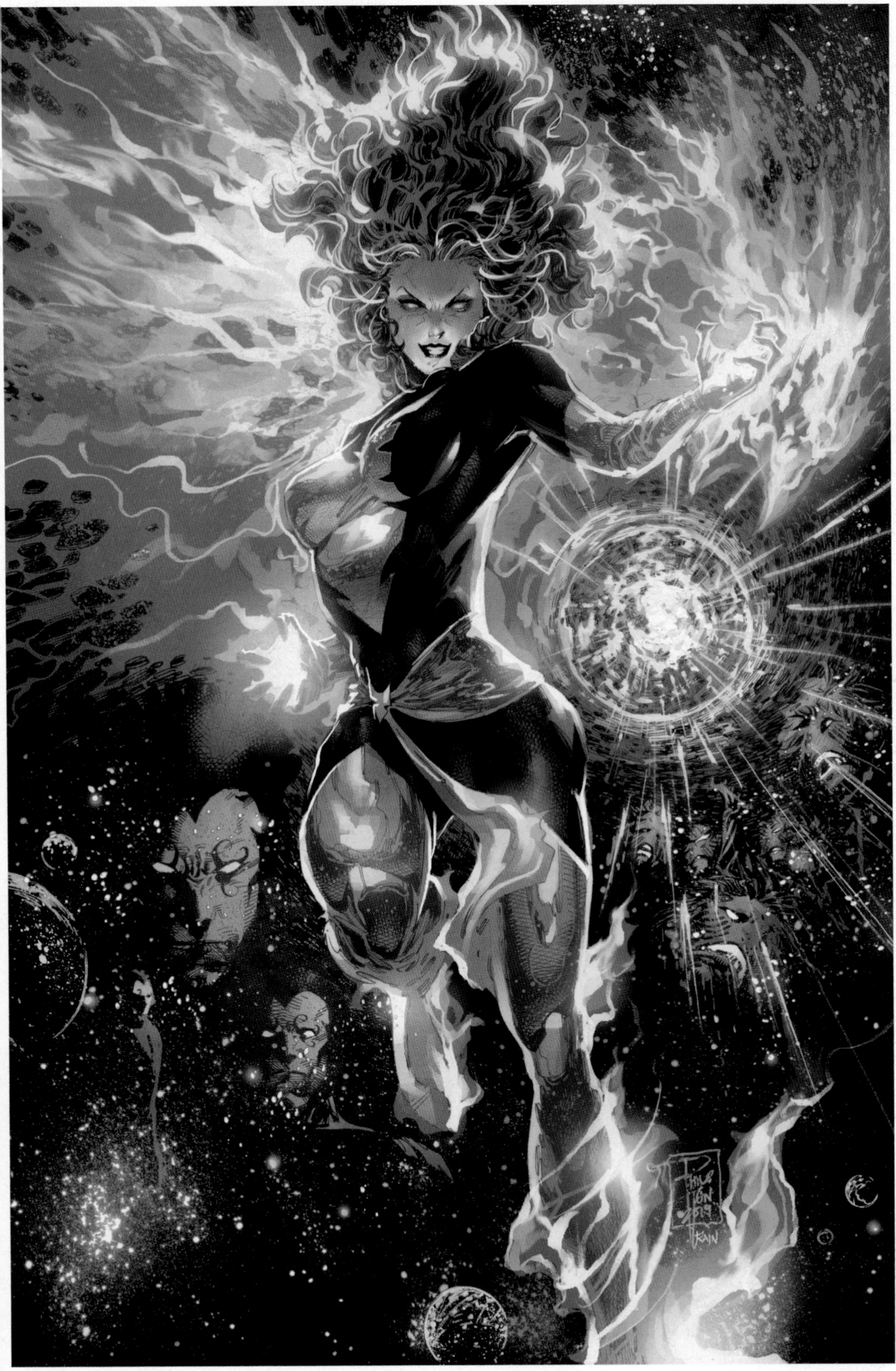

Excalibur #5 Dark Phoenix Saga
40th Anniversary Variant

by Philip Tan & Rain Beredo

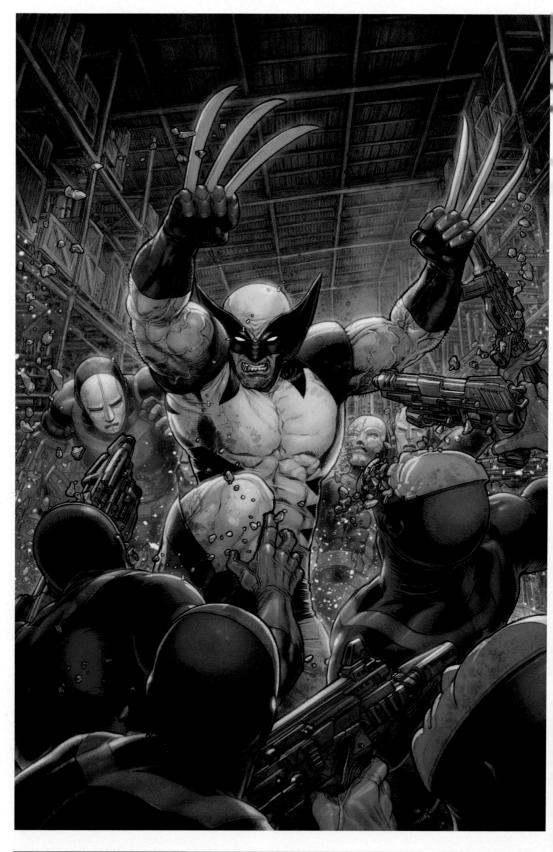

New Mutants #5 Dark Phoenix Saga
40th Anniversary Variant

by Juan José Ryp & Jesus Aburtov

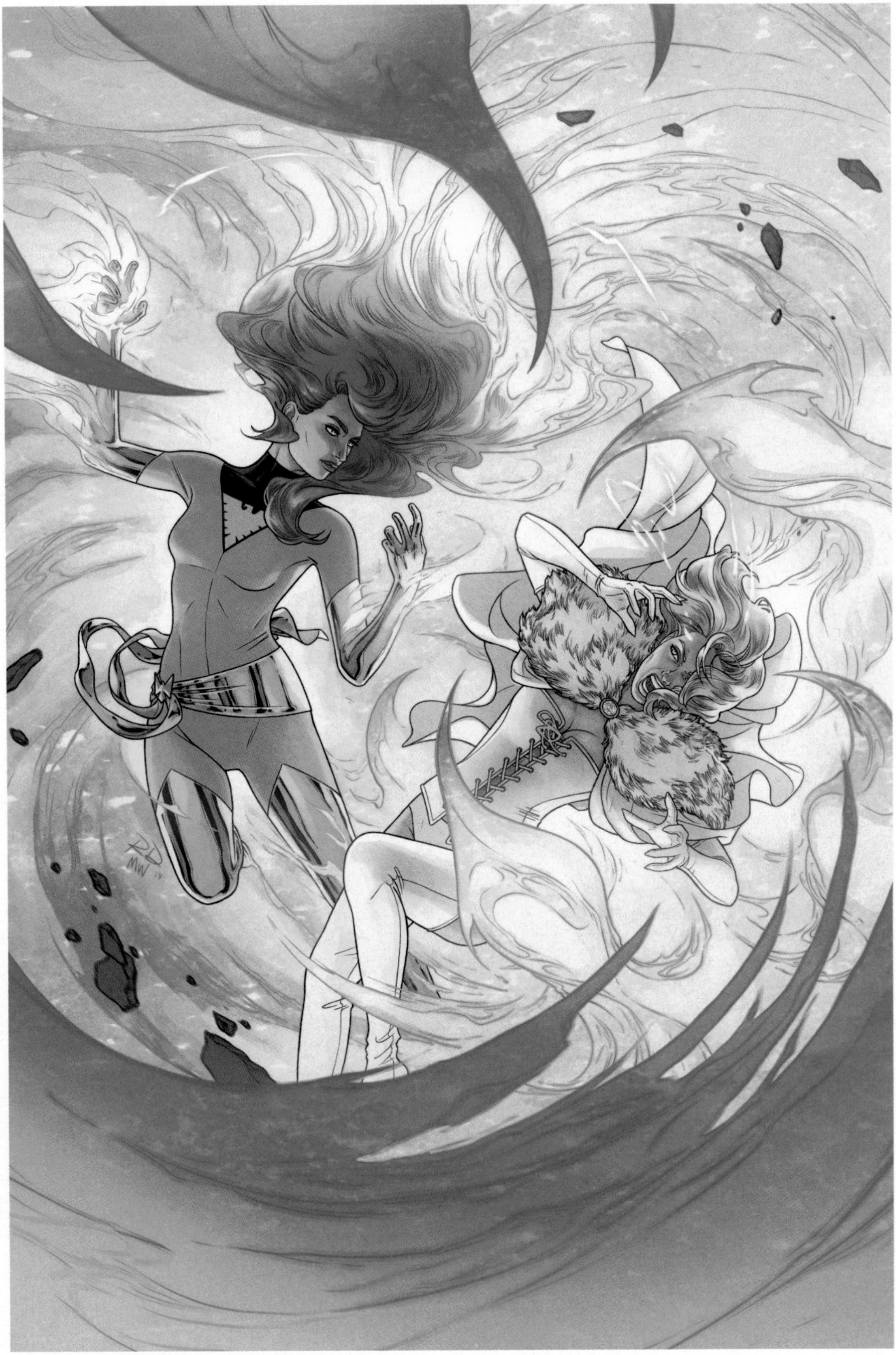

X-Force #5 Dark Phoenix Saga
40th Anniversary Variant

by Russell Dauterman
& Matthew Wilson

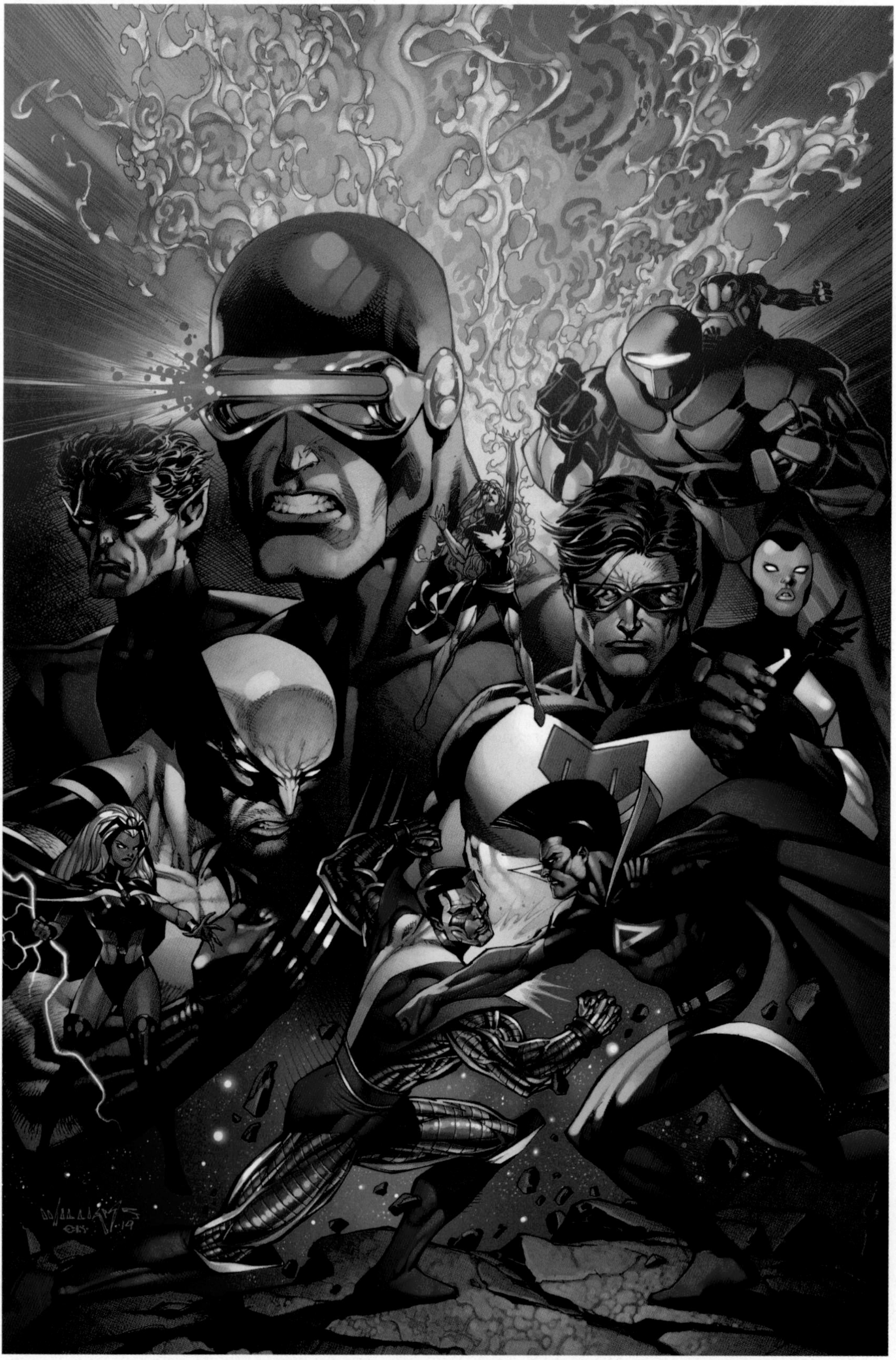

Fallen Angels #5 Dark Phoenix Saga 40th Anniversary Variant

by Scott Williams & Chris Stevens

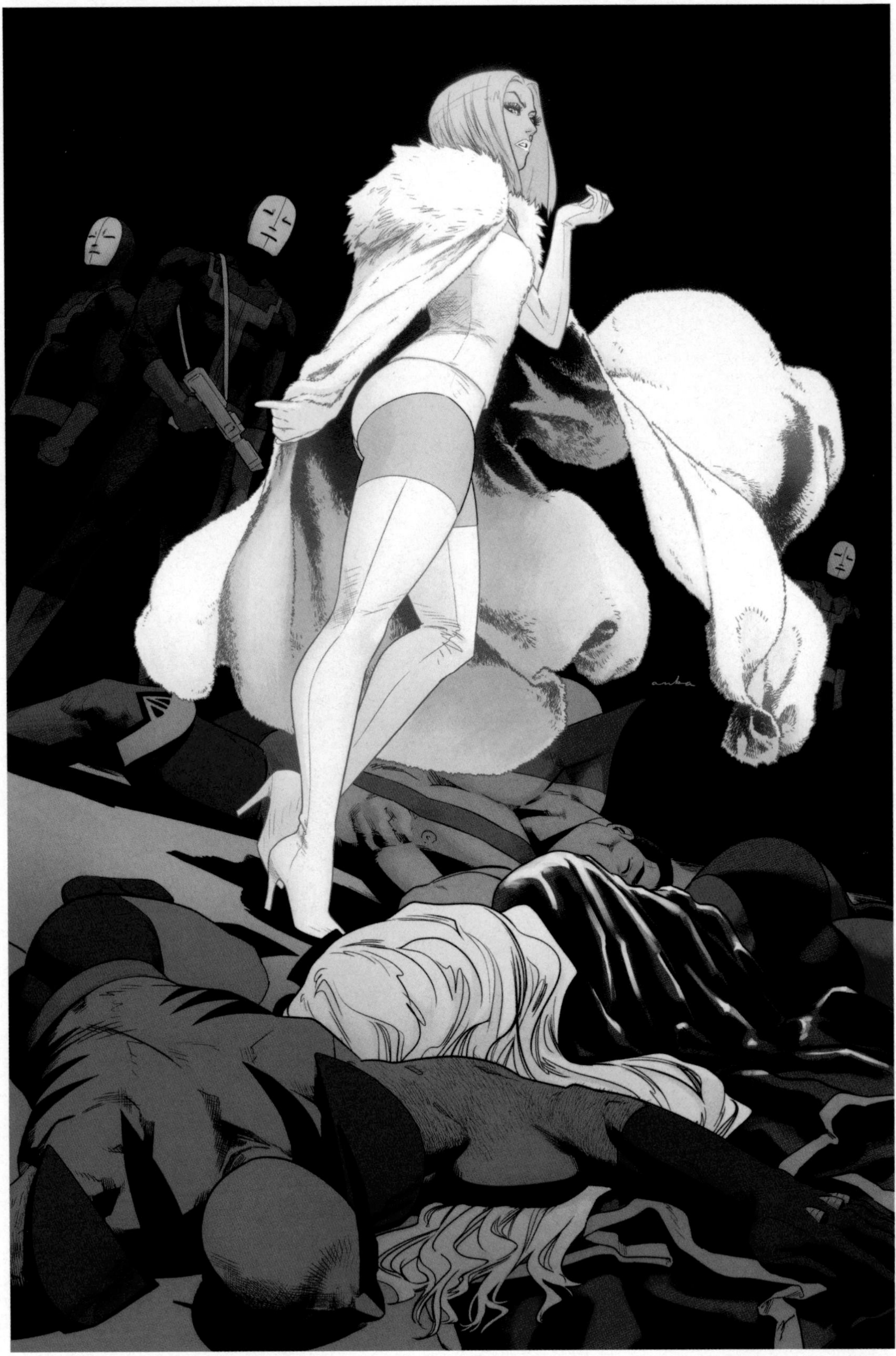
anka

X-Men #5 Dark Phoenix Saga
40th Anniversary Variant

by Kris Anka

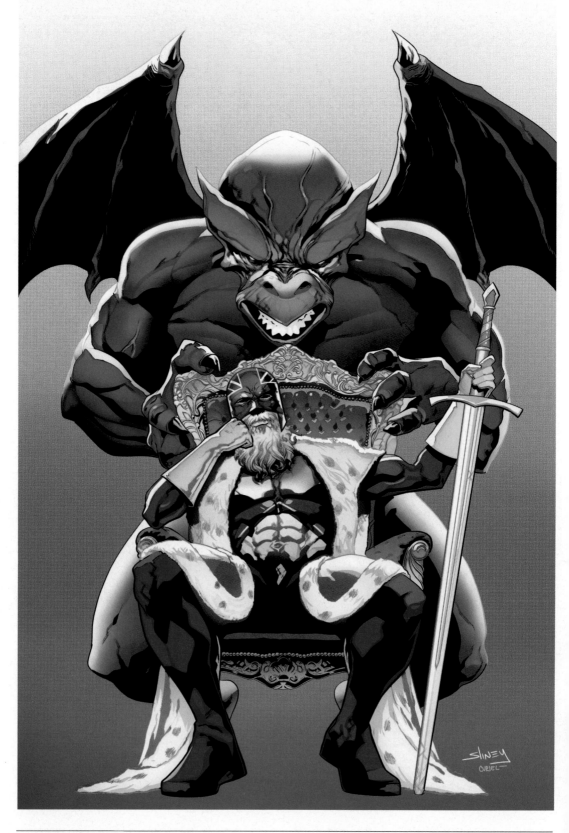

Excalibur #5 Marvels X Variant   by Will Sliney & David Curiel

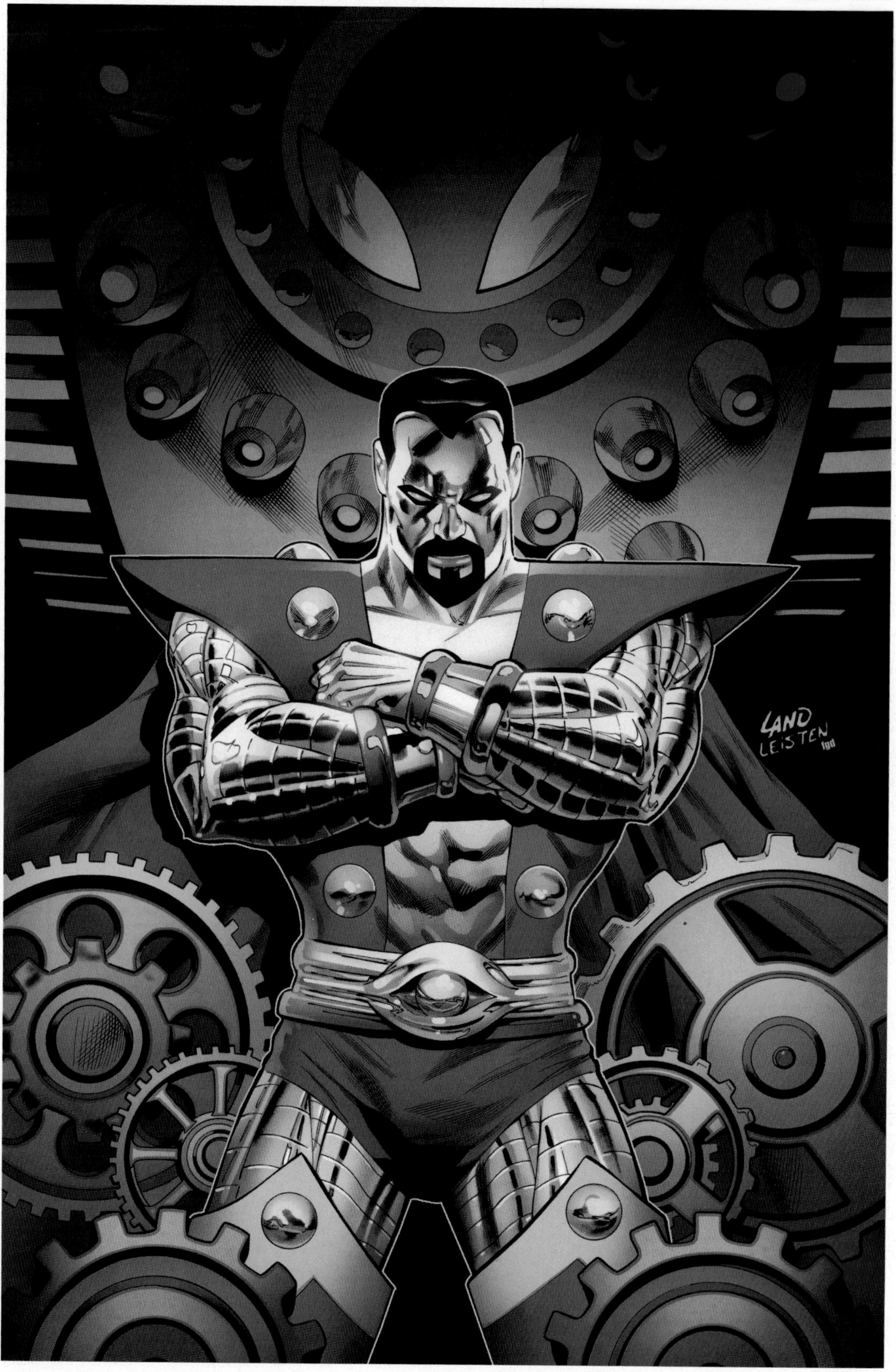
LAND
LEISTEN
fgd

X-Force #5 Marvels X Variant

by Greg Land, Jay Leisten
& Frank D'Armata

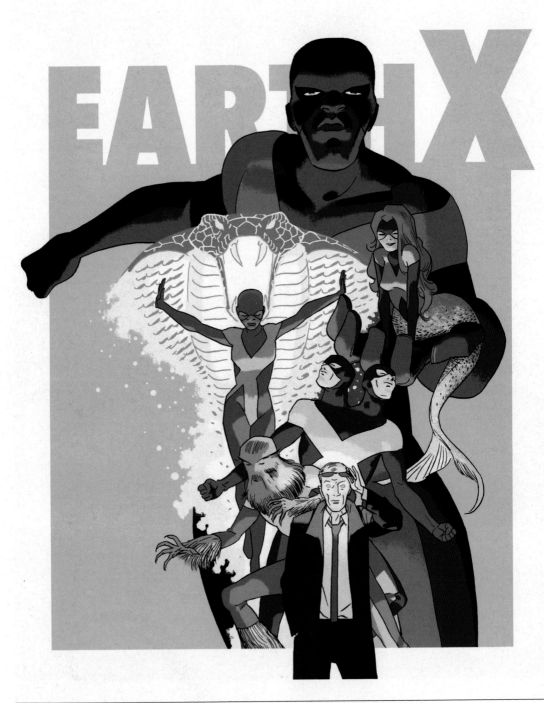

X-Men #5 Marvels X Variant   by Marcos Martin